Center for Basque Studies
Occasional Papers Series, No. 18

SABIN BIKANDI

Alejandro Aldekoa: Master of Pipe and Tabor Dance Music in the Basque Country

Center for Basque Studies
University of Nevada, Reno
Reno, Nevada

This book was published with generous financial support obtained by the Association of Friends of the Center for Basque Studies from the Provincial Government of Bizkaia.

Center for Basque Studies
Occasional Papers Series, No. 18
Series Editor: Joseba Zulaika

Center for Basque Studies
University of Nevada, Reno
Reno, Nevada 89557
http://basque.unr.edu

Library of Congress Cataloging-in-Publication Data

Bikandi, Sabin.
Alejandro Aldekoa : master of pipe and tabor dance music in the Basque country / Sabin Bikandi.
p. cm. -- (Occasional papers series ; no. 18)
Includes bibliographical references and index.
Summary: "An investigation into the life and music of Basque pipe and tabor dance music master Alejandro Aldekoa. Includes DVD of dance performances"--Provided by publisher.
ISBN 978-1-877802-89-8 (hardcover) -- ISBN 978-1-877802-93-5 (pbk.)
1. Aldekoa, Alejandro, 1920-1996. 2. Musicians--Spain--País Vasco--Biography. 3. Folk dance music--Spain--País Vasco--History and criticism. 4. Folk dancing--Spain--País Vasco. I. Title. II. Series.

ML419.A45B55 2009
781.62'99920092--dc22
[B]

2009042047

Irakatsitakoa baino ez dakienak, ez daki ezer ere ez.

The one who only knows what has been taught knows nothing.

Bizente Bikandi Bikandi
(Galdakao 1929–Dima 2009)

TABLE OF CONTENTS

Acknowledgments

The present work would have been impossible without the help and support of a number of individuals and institutions.

My thanks to the Provincial Government of Bizkaia for its support in helping me publish this revised version of my Ph.D. dissertation. Likewise, putting the DVD together would have been impossible without the help of the following: Eusko Ikaskunta (the Basque Studies Society) gave me permission to use the images of dancers in Berriz and Hipólito Amezua playing the *txistua* in the 1920s, recorded by Manuel Intxausti for the series "Eusko Gayak," and the Euskadiko Filmategia-Filmoteca Vasca (the Basque Film Library) facilitated these same images. The Bertsozale Elkartea (Friends of Bertsolaritza Society) and its Xenpelar Dokumentazio Zentroa (Xenpelar Archive) in Villabona (Gipuzkoa) facilitated images of the *bertsolariak*, Unai Iturriaga, Maialen Lujanbio, and Igor Elortza. Thanks to Juan Mari Beltran, director of the Herri Musikaren Txokoa (Folk Music Center) in Oiartzun (Gipuzkoa), for facilitating images of Basque musical instruments and the people who made and played them. And, finally, many thanks to Eresbil (the Basque Music Archive) in Errenteria (Gipuzkoa) for its speed and efficiency in providing Alejandro's image for the cover of the book.

Additionally, I would like to thank Cameron Watson for working on and overseeing this version of the work, and for steering the project toward a successful conclusion; Jose Luis Agote for giving a clear and helpful reflection of my words in his layout; and Bud Bynack for clarifying the text of the book for the readers.

I would also like to thank Joseba Zulaika for answering my first telephone call and Andoni Iturbe for generously supporting this project from the beginning. My heartfelt thanks also go to John Baily for teaching me everything I know about ethnomusicology, and for helping me with my research on Alejandro. And thanks, also, to Veronica Doubleday for her patient reading of the original manuscript and for all her encouragement, and to Julie Foster for all her help with my text in English. Furthermore, many thanks to Alexander Iribar from the Phonetic Laboratory of the Faculty of Philosophy and Arts at the University of Deusto for guiding me in the laboratory and for helping me with phonetic transcriptions and many other things.

Thanks to the people of Berriz for opening their doors to me, and especially to Roberto Maiztegi, Karmelo Angiozar, Jose Alberto Narbaiza, Rafael Albizuri "Otsue," and Rosa Mari Ostolaza, for their patience in my interviews with them. My thanks also to

Elena Amezua and Floren Berrojalbiz for opening up their home and their hearts to me, the second time I called round, and for letting me in on the secrets of the Patxikutarrak.

Furthermore, I would like to thank the Andra Mari dance group of Galdakao for giving me the opportunity to study dance and to dance. Thanks to the whole group (Koldito, Isa, Legarda, Igone, Garaiu, Alberto, Krutziaga, Larraitz, Soiartze, Ainara, Valencia, etc.) for all the great times: in rehearsals, in performances, on the bus, in the *txoko* . . . Thanks, also, to Mikel Zamalloa for providing me the initial means of becoming a member of the group. Thanks to Kepa Ajuria for teaching me the first steps of the *dantzari-dantza*. Thanks to Mikel Goitia for both dancing to my *txistua* melodies and his help in learning how to play music to dance to. Thanks to Jon Zamalloa for being a *txistua* master, colleague, and friend. Thanks to Kepa Artetxe for being everyone's master, as a Basque, a dancer and a friend, and to Mertxe Arrien for looking after everything.

My thanks go out to everyone from Atxanieta. Thanks to my cherished and beloved friend Maria Arriaga, for being Alejandro's wife, for running and looking after Atxanieta for so many years, and for always looking on me kindly when I called at the door or had a question. Thanks, also, to Germán, Amaia, and Jon Aldekoa for carrying on in their father's tracks.

I would also like to thank Jose Inazio Ansorena for teaching me the basics of being a *danbolinteroa*. Thanks, similarly, to Maximo Moreno for transmitting to me his love of music, and to Carmen Rodriguez Suso for pushing me to study.

Thanks, finally, to my family for always being there: Miren, Agus, Ibon, Eneko, Aintzane, Jabi . . . Thanks to Esteban Belandia for being so generous and because his reflections still bring a smile to our faces. Thanks to Kontxi Belandia and Bizente Bikandi, my mother and father, because I am who I am because of them, because everything I have done is because of them, and because they have always, always, been at my side.

Thanks, also, to my wife, Josune Ibarzabal, and our daughter, Ane Bikandi, for their smiles, their love and their warmth.

And thanks to the *Bikandi&Belandia Foundation* for giving me the *Sandrini* grant to undertake this research.

Introduction

The focus of this study is Alejandro Aldekoa Aranburu,[1] one of the last taborers and dance masters of the Basque Country. By following his life, I intend to show, on the one hand, how and in what way he defined himself in the face of an ever-changing environment and, on the other, the important changes that occurred in the music, culture, and society around him during his lifetime, from the 1920s to the 1990s. Through this exploration, I hope to show how he responded to a changing sociocultural environment and how he in turn affected those same surroundings.

Aldekoa was born in Berriz, a small town in the province of Bizkaia. He was Basque and had a marked nationalist ideology, like many of his counterparts. To have been born in a nation without a state—a nation in which, after centuries of Spanish and French domination, many people continue to struggle for the survival of Basque culture and identity—is a major determining factor that pervades almost everything that happens in this small country in the south of Europe, especially all things concerning culture in general and the expression of traditional root culture in particular. Aldekoa began his activity as a dancer and *txistularia* (pipe and tabor player)[2] during the Second Spanish Republic (1931–36), a time when the cultural expression of Basque nationalism thrived. He lived through the cruelties of the Spanish Civil War (1936–39), the bitterness of the postwar period, and the long dictatorship of General Francisco Franco (1939–75). Even after the death of Franco, with the arrival of the so-called Spanish democratic transition, a long-term solution to the question stemming from the nationalist aspirations of many Basques has still not been found. Throughout this time, Aldekoa found his space as a taborer and answered the demands of his sociocultural environment in this politically unstable society, a society also facing a drastic and rapid modernization. In Berriz, his hometown, the prosperous industrial growth of the 1960s provoked the creation of a new, concentrated urban nucleus, the disappearance of farming as the main way of life, and the arrival of Spanish immigrants, who changed the cultural outline of what had been until then a rural, agricultural, Basque population.

1. Although in the Basque Country two surnames are used in official documents, in a normal formal context, it is enough to mention the first surname; that will be the procedure followed in this work.

2. *Txistularia* is the present standard Basque name for a pipe and tabor player. In the plural, it would be *txistulariak*.

The complexity of the world in which Aldekoa lived and worked as a musician and dance master inevitably limits the possibilities of laying out a regular, defined, linear discourse in this work. To understand and explain what it means to be and to work as a taborer and dance master in a community such as Berriz requires me to deal with various issues, such as the history of the pipe and the tabor, the ideology of the Association of *Txistulariak* of the Basque Country, musical notation among Basque taborers, and the functions of dance at a community level. Consequently, I have opted for arranging the book in thematic sections that may, at times, appear compartmentalized, despite my efforts to place them within information structured around the central figure of Alejandro Aldekoa. The result is a kind of mosaic or impressionist picture that, I hope, will recreate a general image of the central "unit of analysis" in this work. Having said that, and despite attempting to be as brief and concise as possible, I have had to omit (or to mention only briefly) some aspects of this complex story that are less relevant to my central argument.

The *Txistua*

The *txistua* is a three-holed duct flute, played with one hand, leaving the other free to play the drum that hangs from the same arm that holds the flute.

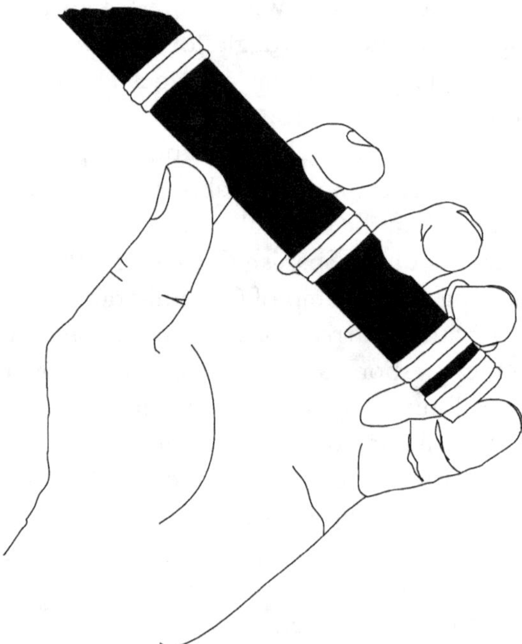

Figure 1. The *txistua* (plural, *txistuak*) is usually played with the left hand. The thumb covers the hole at the back and the first and second fingers the two holes at the front, the third finger is introduced into the ring used to hold the instrument, and the little finger covers the distal end. Illustration by the author.

In the past, the size of the *txistua* varied according to who the maker was or what materials were available. Previously, in all likelihood, the flutes were relatively small, due to the difficulty entailed in the making of long cylindrical tubes. At the beginning of the nineteenth century, Juan Ignacio de Iztueta commented that the old tabor pipes and tabors were much bigger, but he did not elaborate on the subject any further.[3] Whatever the case, with time, the *txistua* measuring approximately 42 to 43 centimeters (16.5 to 17 inches) in length came to be the standard model.

Figure 2. *Txistuak*. Photo by the author.

3. Juan Ignacio de Iztueta, *Gipuzkoako dantza gogoangarrien kondaira edo historia* (1824; Donostia: Euskal Editoreen Elkartea, 1990), 72. For a discussion of Iztueta in English, see Juan Madariaga Orbea, *Anthology of Apologists and Detractors of the Basque Language*, trans. Frederick H. Fornoff, María Cristina Saavedra, Amaia Gabantxo, and Cameron J. Watson (Reno: Center for Basque Studies, University of Nevada, Reno, 2006), 508–13.

The first three-holed flutes we know of in the Basque Country were made from cane or bird bones, but the first instruments we can really call *txistuak*, with a configuration similar to those today, were made from the wood of autochthonous trees such as cherry or walnut, and, for the best quality, boxwood. Later, tropical woods such as ebony or yellow sanders (*Bucherania capitata*) were introduced; their black or dark colors have ended up defining the appearance of the instrument today. For most people, the *txistua* now is a black-colored instrument and is represented as such in all contemporary iconography, so much so, in fact, that currently, many instruments made from other materials are later painted black to make them look "authentic."

Figure 3. The *txistua* of the Amezua family from Berriz. Photo by the author.

Figure 4. *Txistua* made in ABS plastic, with mobile mouthpiece and fipple, by Gancedo. Photo by the author.

In the second half of the twentieth century, *txistua* makers began to use synthetic materials because of their resistance and durability. Ebonite was widely used from the 1950s until the 1980s, a time when *txistua* makers began to experiment with different types of injected plastics. Today, for example, the Gancedos, father and son instrument makers, craft their *txistuak* both from various types of wood, especially yellow sanders, for its very high quality, and from ABS, a type of plastic that, apart from having excellent acoustic qualities, can also be turned on a lathe.[4]

4. Pepe Gancedo is the father of José Mari Gancedo, and they work together in their workshop in Amurrio (Araba) making *txistuak*, their trade for the last thirty years. These magnificent craftsmen should be considered, in my opinion, to be the best specialists in the construction of three-holed flutes, covering all types of demand, from cheap *txistuak* made from plastic for students to the best reproductions of old instruments and new prototype designs.

Apart from the type of wood or plastic used, the *txistua* also has a series of metallic components. We do not know when these components were first introduced.[5] There are the rings that, as well as serving as an adornment, strengthen the wooden instruments and prevent them from cracking.[6] There is also the mouthpiece and the fipple—the block that forms the floor of the windway. The fipple has proved to be an important technical advancement for stabilizing the emission of sound from this flute as it reaches the limits of its acoustic possibilities.[7]

An Instrument of Transposition

Much of the abundant literature on the *txistua* has followed the convention of writing as C what really sounds as F in the next octave, that is, an octave plus a fourth higher. For example, in music for *txistua*, what is written

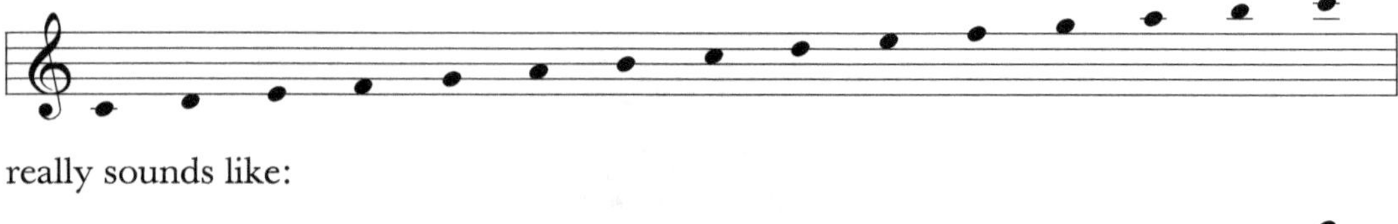

really sounds like:

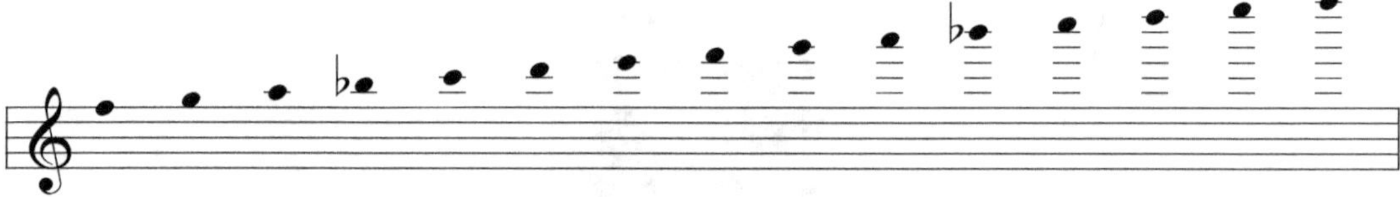

With the *txistua*, as with the rest of the three-holed flutes, the fundamental sounds that the tube emits within what we term the first level of harmonics are not used except in relatively modern pieces of music and nearly always as a sound effect, given the thin tone of this register. These first harmonics are not considered to be within the habitual range of the instrument and are normally written in F. With the same fingering as the harmonic notes of the octave above, but with a much gentler impulse of air, the following range of sounds can be obtained. They are written:

---

5. The Swiss professor Joseph Lauber (1864–1952), in his work "Los Chistularis" (unpublished ms., n.d.), mentions "the chistu [sic] (old, whistle flute of which the metallic fipple dates back to the XV century)." Quoted in Jose Luis Ansorena Miranda, *Txistua eta txisulariak: El txistu y los txistularis* (San Sebastián: Fundición Social y Cultural Kutxa, 1996), 31.

6. The latest research demonstrates, however, that these rings can constrain the wood to such an extent that, with time, the tube begins to narrow and bulge, having a detrimental effect on the sound. For some years now, the most modern instruments made from wood do not have rings. Of course, the quality of the wood (mainly ebony and yellow sanders) is very different from that of the old *txistua*, as is the process of drying and treating it. Prior to the institution of these improvements, the rings were almost certainly necessary.

7. Without leaving the style of execution and the traditional pitch range of the instrument, one can usually play up to the sixth harmonic.

However, its real sound is:

F/F-Sharp

During the nineteenth century, the general tendency toward a sharper or more "brilliant" tuning also affected music in the Basque Country. The numerous musical bands that emerged at this time adopted the new standard of tuning that was also eventually embraced by the pipe and tabor players. With time, the *txistuak* tuned in "brilliant" F came to be considered as in F-sharp a strange tonality that served to corroborate the theories of many folklorists about the uniqueness of the instrument, Basque music in general, the language, the culture, and so on. In fact, first *txistuak* to be tuned in F-sharp were made in 1980 as the result of research promoted by Jose Inazio Ansorena, professor of *txistua* at the Conservatory of Donostia (San Sebastián). At the same time, makers designed the first *txistuak* in F natural, thereby allowing the *txistua* to join other classical instruments. This was a response to the emerging role of the instrument in its then newly found academic degree course in conservatories. Since then, tuning in F-sharp has been considered more appropriate for traditional music, for playing outside or during public celebrations, and especially for accompanying dance, while tuning in natural F is considered more appropriate for classical and chamber music. Some *txistulariak*, mainly those who have not been able to keep up with the many innovations that flooded the world of the *txistua* in the final decades of the twentieth century, defended tuning in F-sharp as the traditional standard, making a big issue out of a relatively unimportant fact, that of a semitone more or a semitone less.

The *Danbolina*

Within the rural folkloric tradition, a *danbolina* (tabor) was just a drum that could be hung in such a way so as to allow it to be played with one hand, leaving the other one free to play the flute. The percussionist who accompanied the taborer, known as *atabaleroa*,[8] played the best drum he had at his disposal, whether it was an *atabala*, a side drum, or a *danbolina*. With time, measurements were standardized. The *danbolina* now measures approximately 25 centimeters (10 inches) in diameter, and the height of its shell, the body of the tabor, has to be approximately the same. The *atabala* is a little wider, between 28 and 30 centimeters (11 and 12 inches) in diameter, with a height of between 12.5 and 15 centimeters (5 or 6 inches).[9]

---

8. Player of the *atabala*, a snare drum wider and shorter than the tabor used with the pipe, played by one person with two sticks.

9. For more details about the measurements of the *danbolina*, *atabala*, and *bonbetea* ("bass tabor"), see the folded central sheet published in *Txistulari* 164, no. 4 (1995).

Figure 5. *Danbolina* and *atabala* of the Amezua family in Berriz. Photo by the author.

As for the length of the drumsticks, the majority of those used in the Basque Country are approximately 30 centimeters (12 inches) for the *danbolina* and 35 centimeters (14 inches) for the *atabala*.

The *txistularia* mostly performs outside. Given the high rainfall in the Basque Country, it is not strange to see the use of plastic drum heads (because of their resistance to damp), which became very popular among *txistulariak* in the 1970s. Since then, however, there has been a return to the use of skin heads, due, among other things, to a noticeable difference in the quality of the sound, aesthetic reasons, and a generalized tendency toward natural, traditional materials that are supposedly more environmentally friendly than plastic. Aldekoa and his sons alike, for practical reasons, normally used the tabor with plastic heads. In any case, synthetic heads greatly improved in the late twentieth century and with time it would not be surprising to see them used more often.

While much neglected, the snare is a fundamental element in the production of sound, although in the past it was not taken into account very much. By changing the tension of the snare, one changes the pitch and the color of the sound of the tabor. It is therefore interesting that the instrument makes this process easy without having to take the drum to pieces. To tighten the snare to its optimum point—what is known as "tuning" the tabor—the majority have a pin fixed into the drum around which the snare, usually made of cat gut, is wound. For some time now, a screw system to tighten the snare has also been common.

Changing Names

The standardized use of the word *txistua* to refer to the three-holed flute used by the taborers in some provinces of the Basque Country and the use of *txistularia* for the person who plays it appear to be very recent. According to José Luis Ansorena, "For us, the oldest written record dates from 1864, as can be read in the article 'El Tamborilero,' by Miguel Ostolaza, published in *La joven Guipúzcoa*," a newspaper.[10] Possibly by 1864, *txistularia* was already a common term, but everything seems to indicate that the name became standard during the twentieth century.

In Spanish, the word *juglar* was one of the most common terms used to denominate musicians of the pipe and tabor in old documents. Although originally a *juglar* was any performer who entertained people with his games and abilities (a musician, dancer, romancer or storyteller, or joker), in the Basque Country, it was almost exclusively used to refer to the pipe and tabor player. It was also common to use the name of the percussion instrument to denominate the group or the person who played it: *tamborer*, *tamborino*, *tambolín*, *tamborín*, *tamboril*, *músico tamboril*, *tamborilero*, *tamboriltero*, *tambolintero*, *tuntunero*, or *chunchunero*. When the name of the flute was used, as well as "flute" or "flautist," other names such as *pífano*, *silbato*, *silbo*, *silbo vizcaíno*, and *chilibistero* also appeared. Documentation in Euskara is more scarce and recent, and the known terms are *txilibitua*, *txirula*, *txirola*, *txürula*, *txulula*, *txilibitularia*, and *txilibistaria*.[11]

Whatever the case may be, in popular oral tradition and in a fashion similar to other areas where the pipe and tabor survived, it was the tabor that gave its name to the set, marking it as the principal instrument.[12] The tabor was most likely considered the main instrument because it is responsible for beating the rhythm and its importance in marking out dance steps.

The Importance of Berriz and Alejandro Aldekoa

The most famous scholars of music and traditional dance in the Basque Country concur in considering the town of Berriz as a place of special folkloric interest, a kind of Basque folklore reserve, or, as Gaizka Barandiaran describes it, "Berriz, nest of Basque folklore." Barandiaran continues: "Thanks to Iztueta," the aforementioned author of definitive descriptions of Basque dances and transcriptions of Basque music in the early nineteenth century, "we possess and conserve on paper the precious written testimony of our choreographic folklore; that same testimony, with various slight differences, as is to be expected, we have by word of mouth in Berriz."[13] Similarly, in an article about the dances

10. Ansorena Miranda, *Txistua eta txisulariak*, 27.

11. Ibid., 28.

12. This is the case for the English terms "tabor" and "taborer."

13. Gaizka Barandiaran, "Berriz, nido del folklore vasco," *Programa de fiestas* (Berriz: Berrizko Udala, 1964).

of Bizkaia, Iñaki Irigoien describes the special interest that the dances of the County of Durango (in which Berriz is located) have for folklorists:

> One of the most representative dances of Euskal Herria [the Basque Country], for its rhythm, for the strength and beauty of its figures, is the *Dantzari dantza* [sic]. Represented in it is the personality of the area, which, throughout centuries of practice, has given it shape, carrying out the ritual and traditions that we will never know or understand in their true dimension today. Choreographic changes and even new dance numbers have been made, but we do believe that the rhythm, the mobility, the simplicity and the natural manner of the dance, transmitted by the dancers who have performed these dances from generation to generation, have been maintained.[14]

It must have been the rhythm, mobility, simplicity, and natural manner of the dance, "transmitted by the dancers who have performed these dances from generation to generation" that impressed Sabino Arana, the founder of the Basque Nationalist Party in the 1890s, so much when, in 1886, he attended an exhibition of local dancers in the Euskal Jaiak (Basque Festivals) of Durango with his brother Luis. Such was the impact that those millennial dances passed down by "word of mouth" from one generation to the next had on Arana that in 1902, he composed the national anthem of Euskadi (the Basque Country) based on the theme of the first number of the *dantzari-dantza*, called the *agintariena* (literally, of the authorities). The apologetic defense of the singular and differential characteristics of the dances of the County of Durango by the founder of Basque nationalism, the use of its music for the national anthem, and a whole series of historical and social determining factors converted the *ezpata-dantza* or *dantzari-dantza* into the Basque dance par excellence, the Basque national dance.[15] From then on, the diffusion and expansion of the dance was incredible, and consequently the dance began to undergo inevitable choreographic, musical, and contextual changes.

One might deduce from all this that the "success" and importance of the dances of the County of Durango, and especially those of Berriz as "the nest of Basque folklore," are based on two fundamental characteristics: first, their antiquity, and second, the way the dances and their music have been conserved within the tradition of oral transmission.

The Antiquity of the Dances

The first documented information about the dances of Berriz dates back to the beginning of the seventeenth century, although this does not mean that they did not exist before that time. The following references appear in the account books of the town's

14. Iñaki Irigoien, "Bizkaiko Dantzak," *Dantzariak* 1 (1978): 22. The *dantzari dantza* or *dantzari-dantza* ("dancer's dance"), is a ritual dance suite from the County of Durango consisting of nine dances: *agintariena, zortzinangoa, ezpata joko txikia, banangoa, binangoa, ezpata joko nagusia, launangoa, makil jokoa,* and *txontxongilloa.*

15. *Ezpata-dantza* means "dance of swords." The use of the name *ezpata-dantza* (which basically refers to any kind of sword dance) was extended to refer to the *dantzari-dantza* or any of its subsequent versions in the whole of the Basque Country. In many areas, the term is still used today as synonymous with the *dantzari-dantza.*

municipal archives (here I use the interrogative marker "?" to refer to illegible or unreadable words):

> Year of 1605. Also, two hundred reales paid to those who did the fiestas.
>
> Year of 1615. Also, a hundred and thirty-two reales paid to Felipe de (?) Geryaga (?) who provided the dancers for the fiesta of San Pedro (?).
>
> Year of 1662. Also, the payment to the dancers of this municipality the sum of two hundred and forty-two reales for the fiesta celebrated on the Day of San Pedro last year, 1661, for which I present receipt.
>
> Year 1668. Also, two hundred reales I pay to Joan Bautista de Mugueitio y Asategui for the cost of the fiestas of San Pedro and his dancers.

Aside from the documents found in the municipal archive, many other references to the dances of Berriz and the County of Durango can be found in different works written by authors of all eras. One of the most outstanding, due to its detailed choreographic descriptions and the importance it has had among folklorists of the Basque Country, is the work of a German philologist, philosopher, and diplomat Wilhelm von Humboldt (1767–1835), who visited the Basque Country in 1799.[16]

Putting to one side the documented antiquity of the dances, their fame and popularity is above all due to the myth created around their origin. For the majority of the Basque people, they are the war dances of their ancestors, the dances of the first people to inhabit the land—the dances of the very first Basques.

Oral Transmission

Until the beginning of the twentieth century, it was quite common for one person to be the pipe and tabor player and the master of dances at the same time. While the dancers were replaced mainly for reasons of age (in the Basque Country, dancers are usually young people, although there are many exceptions),[17] the *txistularia* continued playing and teaching, acting as a transmitter of dances through different generations.

Along these lines, the main person responsible for the transmission of the dances in Berriz, at least since the eighteenth century, has been the taborer of the town, who also has served as dance master. What makes Berriz different is not so much the fact that it has had a municipal taborer, something quite common throughout the Basque Country, but the fact that the trade of taborer, the knowledge of the dance and its music, was transmitted by word of mouth within the same family until well into the twentieth century. The English folklorist Rodney Gallop even made a point of mentioning this Berriz family

16. See Wilhelm von Humboldt, *Reiseskizzen aus Biscaya* (Berlin: G. Reimer, 1841). In the present work, I use a Spanish translation, *Los Vascos* (San Sebastián: Roger, 1999). For a discussion of Humboldt's research in the Basque Country in English, see Madariaga Orbea, *Anthology of Apologists and Detractors of the Basque Language*, 492–508.

17. I mean dancers of ritual dances such as the *dantzari-dantza* and *soka dantza*. In Berriz, it was said that only unmarried dancers could dance in the official group.

in *A Book of the Basques* (1930): "Sometimes, even, there are regular dynasties of *chistularis*, like the Amezuas of Berriz, who have been musicians for two centuries."[18] The Amezua family, known as the Patxiku, Patxiko, or Patxikutarrak,[19] worked as taborers in Berriz for at least five generations. Their last member, Serafín Amezua, was the immediate predecessor of Alejandro Aldekoa in the post of municipal taborer. Therefore, some knowledge of the professional trajectory of the Patxiku is essential to understanding Aldekoa's later career and "the old tradition" that he referred to so many times.

Vicente de Urquiza claims that the first documented information about the performance of a *txistularia* in Berriz dates back to 1676. According to the archives, from this date on, and for the next few years, the taborers hired for the town's fiestas came from other places, such as Eibar, Elorrio, and Durango. "It seems that around the year 1770," states Urquiza, "there was already a *txistularia* and *atabaleroa* in the town, because, from that date, his salary for the next decade was fixed, not subject to alteration, at: *txistularia*, 36 reales, and *atabaleroa*, 34 reales, playing on the customary days."[20]

But it was in 1814 when the name *músico tamborilero* (taborer musician) was first mentioned in the account books. He was Juan Bautista de Amezua y Basaguchia Gañecoa, and although he was only twelve years old in 1770, it is possible that he was the first official taborer of the municipality. From then on, the trade of taborer was handed down from father to son within the Amezua family, nicknamed Patxiku, forming the following chain:

	Date of birth	Name and Surname
1	04-09-1758	Juan Bautista de Amezua y Basaguchia Gañecoa y Lasuen de Suso
2	07-14-1805	Juan Domingo de Amezua de Basaguchi Ganecoa y Gallasategui
3	10-12-1846	Francisco de Amezua y Mallabibarrena
4	08-22-1870	Hipólito de Amezua y Aguirre
5	10-12-1899	Serafín de Amezua y Usaola

Aldekoa knew both Hipólito Amezua and his son, Serafín Amezua, in active service. When Hipólito Amezua played, his sons, Serafín and sometimes Jesús, would accompany him on the *atabala* (drum).[21] Serafín, who had no male heirs, was accompanied by his brother, Jesús, who did not know how to play the *txistua.* Serafín's only daughter, Elena,[22] could not continue the family tradition, because in those days, it was unthinkable for a woman to become a *txistularia.* After the death of Jesús in an accident, Serafín's

18. Rodney Gallop, *A Book of the Basques* (1930; Reno: University of Nevada Press, 1970), 182.

19. Fermin Barceló explains in detail the possible origin of the nickname Patxiku as used by the Amezua family, contending that it derives from the proper name Francisco or Bautista. See "Aproximación a las fuentes para el estudio de la música popular en una comunidad local: Berriz," Ph.D. diss., University of Deusto (1993), 22–26.

20. Vicente de Urquiza, *Antigüedades de Berriz* (Bilbao: Caja de Ahorros Vizcaína, 1988), 75.

21. According to Elena Amezua, he must also have played before with his brothers, Sebastián and Ezequiel.

22. Elena Amezua Arancibia, born in Berriz on August 13, 1925.

son-in-law, Florencio Berrojalbiz, from the neighboring town of Abadiño (County of Durango), who, in his time, had been a good dancer and *aurreskularia*,[23] started to accompany Serafín on the drum. The last two Patxiku did not retire from active service until their deaths, Hipólito at the age of eighty-four in 1954 and Serafín at the age of seventy-four in 1973. Hipólito was officially a civil servant employed by the town hall, whereas Serafín worked on contracts for services rendered as a taborer.[24] For many years, father and son worked together, sharing the town posts and performances in the surrounding area. Each had their own obligations, although on many occasions they would play together, even in different regions.[25]

Figure 6. Hipólito Amezua (*txistua* and *danbolina*) and Serafín Amezua (*atabala*) with the selected dancers and the bailiff in front of the house of the Marquise of Berriz (ca. 1920). Photo courtesy of the Amezua family.

---

23. Dancer of *aurreskua*, literally meaning "the hand in front" or "the first hand." The *aurreskua* is the first dance of the dance suite *erregelak* or *soka dantza* ("rope dance").

24. According to his daughter Elena, when he reached retirement age, his family discovered that he was not registered as an employee of the town hall, but that he worked on contracts for services rendered.

25. As Serafín Amezua's daughter told me: "They used to go to Nabarniz [a village near Gernika in Bizkaia] for two days, walking over the mountains with the drum on his shoulders" (personal communication). Angel Berguices confirms the presence of Serafín Amezua at the fiestas in the majority of the towns and villages on the right-hand side of the Gernika estuary. "Trikitrixa (farrea) y acordeón en Busturialdea: Historia y hombres," unpublished ms. (1990), 9.

As was usual, the trade of taborer did not pay enough money to live from music alone. Hipólito and Serafín Amezua, as well as working on the family farm, were also cattle traders. They supplemented their income by working in the Durango slaughterhouse, slaughtering the cattle they had sold to the butchers of the town.

The Importance of Alejandro Aldekoa

Alejandro Aldekoa was born in Berriz in 1920 and learned to dance as a child. By the age of ten, he could dance the whole repertoire of the ritual dances of Berriz, something very unusual for a boy of his age. At the age of twelve, he started to play the pipe and tabor. One year later, he performed in public for the first time, accompanying a group of dancers. In 1952, he made his debut as dance master with what was to be his own dance group, named San Lorenzo, through which several generations of dancers subsequently passed. At the end of the 1960s, he took over from Serafín Amezua as municipal taborer and dance master, in charge of the main fiestas. Aldekoa remained in active service practically until the day of his death on June 20, 1996.

From his position of taborer and dance master, Aldekoa played an important and decisive role in the maintenance of the traditional dances of Berriz for the last forty years of the twentieth century. Indeed, thanks to Aldekoa, we know how the dances were danced and how the pipe and tabor were played, not only as something that forms part of Basque historical memory, but also part of a reality that is still alive today, with its logical transformations, in his hometown of Berriz. The most emblematic dance groups of the Basque Country (Andra Mari, Argia, Elai-Alai, Beti Jai Alai) and every scholar of Basque dances met with Aldekoa at some time or another to learn from his mastery. It was he who transmitted Berriz's dances and unique style of dancing to the new generations while carrying out the duty of the old trade of municipal taborer, which would have otherwise been lost.

Many folklorists and researchers consulted Aldekoa about choreography, dance steps, and customs, but none of them ever wrote a detailed study about him, his work, his surroundings, or his conception of music and dance. I hope to fill this void, if only partially, with this work.

The Research

I need to start an account of the research approaches that inform this book by giving a brief account of my own personal and professional career as both a native-born Basque *txistularia* and a university-trained ethnomusicologist, because this background formed the basis of my investigation and undoubtedly contributed in one way or another to the development of what follows. I began to play the *txistua* at the age of eight with Máximo Moreno, conductor of the Municipal Band of Galdakao (Bizkaia), parish organist, and music teacher. At the age of fifteen, after Máximo Moreno's death, I was appointed teacher of *txistua* in the Galdakao Academy of Music. That same year, I began my formal study of the *txistua,* which had been recently incorporated into the Bilbao Conservatory. In 1988, I gained a "superior level degree" in the Donostia Conservatory under the supervision of Jose Inazio Ansorena. In 1989, I earned the position of *txistularia* in the Municipal Band of Bilbao, a position I still hold today.

During this time, I have combined my work as a teacher in various schools and conservatories throughout the Basque Country with playing in assorted groups. I have also collaborated in the production of the journal *Txistulari,* published by the Association of *Txistulariak* of the Basque Country, writing several articles, pieces of music, and arrangements. Furthermore, I was editor of the journal from 1992 to 1995. As a result of this experience, I have accumulated a great amount of information about the pipe and tabor in the Basque Country, ranging from its performance technique, pedagogy, and repertoire to its history and players. I have used this information directly in the writing of this work and as a starting point for new inquiries.

In 1991, the journal *Txistulari* asked me to write an article on Alejandro Aldekoa, and that was the reason for my first visit to the *txistularia* of Berriz. In the spring of 1996, while I was completing a master's degree in ethnomusicology at Goldsmiths College, University of London, I went back to Berriz to interview the local dance master and taborer because he was now the central character in my dissertation. Even though I knew that a few weeks before my visit he had been in the hospital, it was a real shock when his daughter Amaia told me that Alejandro Aldekoa had cancer. She also told me that he did not know about the disease and that he thought it was just a "spot on the lung," something not surprising for a heavy smoker like him.

This news was a heavy blow for all of us, but the family agreed that my visits could serve (among other things) as a kind of occupational therapy, for Alejandro enjoyed everything related to dance and music, and he also enjoyed my company. As a result, in April 1996—always with his daughter Amaia helping me, keeping me informed about the development of the disease, and only when it was convenient for Alejandro—I began visiting Alejandro at house in Aretxandieta in the evenings after his siesta, where, in the kitchen, we would talk about so many things. In the following months, we recorded about sixteen hours of videotapes, and I think that my interview planning at that time was covered successfully. I have to confess that I thought Alejandro was going to be there to continue working together at least for some time, and I did not think (or rather, I did not want to think) he was going to leave us so soon. On June 2, days before his death, the Association of *Txistulariak* of the Basque Country awarded him their gold medal in a memorable event. However, I was preparing my general theory exam at Goldsmiths College at the time and could not be there. When I came home after the exams, Alejandro was critically ill in the hospital, and his relatives asked me not to visit him, because the emotion of a meeting would have been dangerous for him. I was in the corridor of the hospital, yet could not say goodbye to the person who, by that time, was, among other things, a good friend. Alejandro Aldekoa died on June 20, 1996.

Seeing Oneself as a Stranger

It is often said that doing ethnography is all about "being there," about experiencing the subjects encountered in fieldwork firsthand, but also about placing that experience in the perspective the professional and putatively objective discourses of the social sciences. As such, the concept of "being there" is inherently problematic.[26] As Clifford Geertz has noted, "confinement to 'experience-near' concepts leaves an ethnographer awash in immediacies, as well as entangled in vernacular. Confinement to 'experience-distant' leaves him stranded in abstractions and smothered in jargon."[27] For many years, ethnomusicological research was focused mainly on the study of other people's music. The study of "the other" was considered the only way to obtain a certain degree of objectivity and cross-cultural perspective. As a researcher native to the culture that I study, I am supposed to confess and justify my personal ideological framework here in order to safeguard the "objectivity" of the research. I am supposed to maintain the distance necessary to be able to understand and explain as critically and rigorously as possible an important part of my own culture. To do this research well, I am supposed to see myself as a stranger in order to acquire an experience-distant formulation of concepts. But this is not a simple process. For example, the anthropologist Joseba Zulaika also chose to study his native Basque culture, thereby becoming "the fieldworker returning to his natal village with newly acquired perceptive powers and academic detachment" and coming to terms with the fact that "writing about one's own culture more effectively precludes the anthropologist from imposing on his informants sets of values that are deemed radically incompatible with his own."[28]

I am a native Basque musician who, thanks to my education, especially during my postgraduate studies at Goldsmiths College in the University of London, learned about theories and methods in ethnomusicology that opened up new perspectives and approaches to the study of my own music. It could be said that at the university, I learned what is relevant for ethnomusicology and how to research and write about music. I learned to "translate" my experience and knowledge about music, making it accessible to others—a kind of "translation" from "emic" concepts, analyses, and points of view, that is, from how a participant in Basque culture thinks, feels, and sees things, to the etic, nonparticipant perspective, from "experience-near" to "experience-distant."

However, from the point of view of the community studied here, the Basque people of Berriz, unlike the case of Zulaika's research of his own village, I am considered something of an outsider. Indeed, in this regard, I am not a native. That is, although I am Basque, I am not from Berriz. The same applies to the dance and music repertoire: It is

---

26. See, for example, John Borneman and Abdellah Hammoudi, eds., *Being There: The Fieldwork Encounter and the Making of Truth* (Berkeley: University of California Press, 2009).

27. Clifford Geertz, *Local Knowledge: Further Essays in Interpretive Anthropology* (1983; London: Fontana, 1993), 57.

28. Joseba Zulaika, *Basque Violence: Metaphor and Sacrament* (Reno: University of Nevada Press, 1988), xviii and xix.

"their" music, "their" dances, and "their" ritual. For them, I am an outsider learning to perform and researching their culture.

It is nevertheless very difficult for me to establish the limits between the two roles or stances, and to divide myself into a native on the one hand and a researcher on the other. I do not know if there is a successful method to enable anyone to "see oneself as a stranger," or if the task is at all possible or even convenient when we are trying to understand a culture in depth and "to grasp the native's point of view, his relation to life, to realize his vision of his world."[29] I think that my approach is just as personal and subjective as any other, in that it is shaped by my culture, beliefs, education, and background.

It is true that quite often during my fieldwork, I had to make an effort to be seen as a stranger—as "foreign"—by the people from Berriz and especially by Aldekoa. Time and again, during our interviews, when I asked about something he thought I knew beforehand, stupid questions coming from a Basque *txistularia* like me, I had to remind him that I was a foreigner ("Imagine that I am a martian who has never seen a *txistua*," I said on one of those occasions) or remind him that we were working for a group of foreign people from the University of London. I had to use similar arguments when I was interviewing other people to make sensible my questions about local matters, which for them involved well-known or irrelevant issues.

The Conservatory and Tradition

The *txistua* received official recognition in the 1980s. When the *txistua* entered Basque conservatories, upon seeing the study program, some of my fellow *txistulariak* thought that we would be able to pass the advanced level exams with no problem whatsoever. Instead, we found a whole new world, a world we did not know: our *txistua* was of no use, and they spoke of tuning, articulation, and breathing, a series of concepts unknown to us. Some of us humbly enrolled in the conservatory not only to study *txistua*, but to study all the rest of the subjects on the program.[30] In this new context, we thought that all our problems would be solved, thanks to new techniques, new repertoires, new accompanying instruments, études, sonatas, mechanism exercises, and official degrees. Others (indeed, the majority), either due to age, laziness, or arrogance, or maybe because the conservatories and their teachers did not know how to transmit a more open and conciliatory message to the *txistulariak*, were left behind when the "conservatory train" began to accelerate. This process thus led, albeit unintentionally, to a split within the world of Basque taborers, forming two very different and ever more distant groups: the

---

29. Bronislaw Malinowski, *Argonauts of the Western Pacific* (1922; New York: E. P. Dutton, 1961), 25.

30. The conservatory study program, very similar to that of the other wind instruments, was made up of eight years of *txistua* (fourth grade elementary, sixth grade intermediate, and eighth grade advanced) as well as the following subjects: six courses of music theory (reading music), two of choir, two of harmony, one of musical content, two of chamber music, two of orchestra, one of musical dictation and transposition, two of the history of music, two of the history of art, two of aesthetics, one of acoustic elements, one of pedagogy, and two of teacher training, after which one received the qualification of Profesor Superior de Música (advanced music professor).

"conservatory" *txistulariak* and the rest. In general, the first group is made up of people who enter a professional educational system, gaining degrees and later a full-time music-related job. The second group is made up of people who are amateurs and play the *txistua* in fiestas, in the street, at weddings, and in dance groups. There are, of course, many exceptions, and this division oversimplifies the complex reality of the Basque *txistulariak.*

When I was conducting my interviews, Aldekoa was considered a consummate and veteran *txistularia.* He was seventy-six years old, and the heir and guardian of the traditional dances of Berriz. I was a young, thirty-year-old *txistua* teacher, educated basically in a conservatory. I had been the director of the journal *Txistulari,* and I was studying in London. I thought that being a "conservatory" *txistularia* would somehow create a barrier in my relationship with Aldekoa. I therefore took care not to show my technical and theoretical knowledge, so that he would not think I was arrogant, and I always treated him with respect and admiration for the master I knew him to be. Little by little I realized that Aldekoa was not against a conservatory education, and he himself was proud of his own academic education in music, as well as of the fact that some of his own students were attending the conservatory. When our conversations dealt with issues related to the teaching of the *txistua* and *danbolina,* somehow or other, a charming relationship of complicity flowed between us. We felt like two colleagues talking about our job.

Politics

In the Basque Country, political conflict invades every aspect of life. Even among Basque people, one must take care to not show openly one's political ideas, because it is worse to be suspected of treason (in this context, "treason" usually means just an ideological or political discrepancy) than to be openly declared an enemy (Spanish or French). Moreover, because of their significance in the construction of Basque identity and ethnicity, culture and especially folklore are intimately related to the political situation of the Basque Country. For this reason, tension, discord, and conflicts are quite frequent among local musicians, dancers, dance groups, choreographers, researchers, and fans of traditional music and dance.

Faced with this situation regarding my relationship with Aldekoa, I tried to combine sincerity with discretion when something related to politics arose. I tried to match Alejandro's own sincerity in front of the camera, where he confessed various personal and intimate details about his life, work, family, and his conduct in other relationships in his social world. I tried to be discreet in terms of suppressing my natural tendency to be critical of local politics and politicians, because I did not want to offend his sensitivities and sensibilities on these issues.

In a few days, I established a fluid relationship with Aldekoa. Our political thoughts about the Basque conflict were clearly defined, and we trusted each other. Knowing a little of his political ideology, although something personal and confidential, was important insofar as it helped me to understand his career and his position in the social and political milieu of Berriz. This in turn helped me to locate and explain some of the conflicts and tensions inside the community.

Rivalries in Berriz

Apart from the tension derived from the Basque political problem during my fieldwork, I also had to be aware of another important conflict, this time at a local level: the rivalry between Aldekoa's dance group and the other Berriz dance group, Iremiñe. Iremiñe was created in 1969 from within the ranks of Aldekoa's group, San Lorenzo (see below for more detail about this group), and from that moment on, the rivalry between San Lorenzo and Iremiñe formed one of the most important social conflicts in Berriz. I realized quite soon that if I was going to interview and work with people from both groups, I had to behave carefully. I decided that the best option was to show clearly that I was aware of their problems and conflicts, to explain the aims of my research, and to show that I wanted to know both sides of the story.

The help of Berriz's mayor, Rosa Mari Ostolaza, was important. She introduced me to some of the local people, most of them dancers. Rosa Mari Ostolaza was a dancer herself in the Iremiñe Dance Group when she was young, but she always showed respect toward Aldekoa and his authority in everything related to dance. Perhaps because of that and her efforts to solve the problem between the dance groups, she was very much respected by everyone. Thanks to her advice and support, my role as a researcher acquired a greater relevance. In short, it became more "official."

The fact that I was doing the research as a student at the University of London was important as well, because from the local point of view, it gave a certain international projection to the research. Aldekoa was proud of that, and when he introduced me to his neighbors, he would say: "He is writing a book on our music and dances for the University of London."

I do not know if it was due to the help of the mayor, the prestige of the University of London, or a combination of other, different reasons, but I managed to move between dancers from both groups fairly well. That said, there were some occasions when it was especially difficult to do this, such as during the celebration of the fiestas of San Pedro (Saint Peter) and Santa Isabel (Saint Isabel), when the dancers kept an eye on me to see whom I greeted, whom I talked to, and what kind of relationship I had with the "enemy." However, I think that today, I have a fluent communication with both groups, even though they know I am working and have a good relationship with the "enemy" as well. Possibly things changed after Aldekoa's death. Perhaps people from one group tried to convince me that they were better than people from the other group.

In the course of my research, I came across another kind of rivalry—between Alejandro Aldekoa and his predecessor, Serafín Amezua, the last *txistularia* of the Amezua family and the heir of a long family tradition going back to the eighteenth century. Aldekoa, through a long and not particularly clear process, gradually took over Serafín Amezua's duties and, in the end, his post. I tried to find out more about the conflict between these two musicians and their families, but it was not easy. Part of the problem is explained below, but even now, many years later (Serafín died in 1973), most people are still reticent to talk openly about this old problem. Elena Amezua (Serafín's daughter) and Florencio Berrojalbiz (his son-in-law) claim that there was no problem between Aldekoa and their father, that the transition was smooth, and that they were good friends and colleagues. Regardless, unlike the conflict between the local dance groups, this one did not affect my relationship with local people as a researcher in the community of Berriz.

Sources of Information

The basic method I used for collecting information was the personal interview. During the spring of 1996, while I was collecting information for my dissertation, Alejandro Aldekoa and I would frequently meet at his home in Berriz. The basic material for this work comes from those discussions, conversations, and interviews, which were usually recorded on video. From the very first moment we met, we got on together very well, like colleagues, as I've said, but I have always preferred to consider him and treat him as my teacher, my master. We were both pipe and tabor players, and we were both Basque. Maybe that is why we felt comfortable with one another from the first moment, even in front of the video camera, which came to be a part of his kitchen furniture every afternoon when we met after his siesta. For this reason, the video material shows, on occasions, very personal opinions and points of view and even includes confessions of an intimate nature. For the sake of brevity, I will refer to them as "interviews," despite the implication this word has in terms of a formally structured and impersonal verbal exchange.

Apart from Aldekoa, I interviewed everyone who, in my opinion, had at some time or another enjoyed an important relationship with him, whether personal, strictly musical, or both. Many of the interviews, such as informal meetings in bars, at rehearsals, and at performances, were conducted "off the record" and outside the context of a formal, investigative discussion. As was to be expected, the most interesting revelations and confessions arose from these interviews, but the information received has, at times, been of a limited use due to the wish for confidentiality of some of the informants.

From among the rest of the people in Berriz I interviewed and consulted, I would highlight the following:

- Alejandro Aldekoa's family: María Arriaga, his wife; Germán and Jon, his sons; and Amaia, his daughter.
- Elena Amezua, the daughter of Serafín Amezua and Florencio Berrojalbiz, a former dancer who married Elena and became Serafín's son-in-law. Florencio Berrojalbiz played the drum with Serafín Amezua in the latter part of his career.
- Roberto Maiztegi, who danced with Aldekoa and in 1969 founded the group Iremiñe.

- Rafael Albizuri (nicknamed Otsue, "The Wolf"), one of the best dancers to dance with Aldekoa.
- Iñaki Uribe, Ismael Aldekoa, and Jabier Urkijo, dancers from Alejandro's first group, formed in 1952.
- Rosa Mari Ostolaza, mayor of Berriz.
- Eduardo Urzelai, organizer and promoter of the Basque *Jota* Dance Championship of Bizkaia, held in Berriz every year from 1954 to 1974.

With regard to the choreography of the dances from Berriz, the organization of the ritual, and the style of dancing in Berriz, the information given by Aldekoa in the interviews had to be complemented. In order to describe the ideal dances and ritual as Aldekoa thought it should be, apart from the people mentioned above, I have used the following sources of information:

- Videotapes given me by Aldekoa's family, especially a recording of the San Pedro's Day ritual in 1990 made by an unknown couple who kindly gave a copy of it to the dance master.
- Videos and recordings of Aldekoa playing and teaching that I found in the archives of the dance group Andra Mari of Galdakao.
- The work of José Luis Etxebarria (1969), who wrote a detailed description of the dances from Berriz in collaboration with or under the supervision of Aldekoa.
- Kepa Artetxe, dance master of the group Andra Mari of Galdakao, disciple of Alejandro Aldekoa and a kind of living encyclopedia of the dances from Berriz.

Learning to Perform as a Research Technique

When I began my work on Alejandro Aldekoa, I considered myself a competent musician, even a brilliant pipe and tabor player, but I suddenly realized that I had no idea of how to play for the dance, no idea of the repertoire, the repetitions, or the meaning of "following the dancers." If I was going to write about Aldekoa, a pipe and tabor player and a dance master, I felt I had to learn the job, and the only way was to do just that—to learn to perform.[31]

I thought that the best way to learn Aldekoa's dance repertoire was by going to Berriz and learning directly from those who danced with the master, especially his son Germán, who was himself a dance master. But I found that the dance group San Lorenzo did not arrange any kind of classes or lessons, and worse still, that they did not have any regular rehearsals where I could observe and learn, so learning to dance in Berriz would instead depend on my personal contacts with the dancers. After several attempts, I found

31. See John Baily, "Learning to Perform as a Research Technique in Ethnomusicology," in *"Lux Oriente" Begegnungen der Kulturen in der Musikforschung*, ed. Klaus Wolfgang Niemöller, Uwe Pätzold, and Chung Kyo-chui (Kassel: Gustav Bosse/ Cologne: Gustav Bosse Verlag Kassel, 1995), 331–47.

this approach to be almost impossible, and in the end, I chose to learn the dances of Berriz with the group Andra Mari of Galdakao, for several reasons.

For one thing, the dancers from Andra Mari are considered the heirs of the choreographic tradition of Berriz transmitted to them by Aldekoa, with whom they learned to dance. The group's dance master, Kepa Artetxe, also was considered the best master of the old style of *solture* dance,[32] another important part of Aldekoa's repertoire. The group's activities (rehearsals, performances, classes) allowed me to come into direct contact with the repertoire and offered me a better chance to learn. In addition, the group had an interesting audio and video archive, and finally, I was living in Galdakao at that time, making it all the more convenient.

Andra Mari, like many other groups, was not exactly open to outsiders, and it took time to convince its members about the sincerity of my purposes and to be accepted. In the beginning (1996–97), they needed someone to play the *alboka*,[33] and that was my chance to help the group and become a member of the team of musicians. I needed to learn the repertoire of Berriz and the *solture* dances, and they needed me to play the *alboka*. Although I was the *alboka* player of the group, in rehearsals, when there was no other *txistua* player, I was allowed to play for the dancers, especially during the dances of Berriz. From the outset, the dancers understood that I was there to learn how to play for the dance by "following the dancers." Fortunately enough, they made many comments on and criticisms of my performances, giving me instructions and advice, something uncommon in the group because for the rest of the musicians, any kind of criticism from the dancers was taken as an offense. On the contrary, for me, these comments were (and are) extremely helpful. Anyhow, learning Aldekoa's repertoire, especially the *aurreskua* and *atzeskua*, took time and considerable effort. Once I knew the music—"the notes"—however, I realized that to be able to "follow the dancers," I also had to learn to dance: "A good *txistularia* must be a dancer," everyone insisted.

Jon Zamalloa was the leader of the musicians in the group. I took care not to interfere with his leadership, always making clear his position as master and mine as apprentice. He is a good *txistularia*, an expert at playing for dance, and someone who, like Aldekoa, was first a dancer. He could have been very helpful in my research, teaching me the dances and how to play the repertoire, but because he was an engineer in a big company, his limited availability forced me to change my plans.

Someone who was always ready to help was Kepa Artetxe, the old dance master, from whom I learned many things about the ritual dances of Berriz and the *solture* dances, their choreography, the different styles, and the changes during the last decades. But what I actually needed was to learn to dance, to perform, and it was not easy to convince the dancers to teach me, a known musician in his thirties. It is true that the working timetable of this amateur group was very demanding, and the extra effort of teaching an

32. *Solture* means "free" or "untied," swift dance. See the Glossary.

33. A kind of hornpipe played in the Basque Country. See the Glossary.

individual like me was a kind of luxury. It was Kepa Ajuria, the president of the group, now retired from active dancing due to an injury to his knees, who, on seeing my interest and the lack of response from the dancers to my demands, eventually taught me the first steps of the *dantzari-dantza*. Later, I managed to secure a teaching session with Kepa Artetxe and his son-in-law, Mikel Goitia, that I recorded on video. Later still, Mikel Goitia began to teach me and two other young *txistulariak* the dances of Berriz. At the same time, I learned the *solture* dances (*jota* and *arin-arina*) by rehearsing with the senior dancers (I was at the back of the room to avoid disturbing them) and used the video at home as a learning tool. I found a better disposition to teach the *solture* dances especially from Larraitz Artetxe, Kepa's daughter, with whom I have collaborated in some dance courses by playing the *txistua*.

In spite of all this help, the learning process was slow and complicated, and my knowledge is still a long way behind that of the great master, Aldekoa. However, the little that I learned helped me to reinterpret and understand the relationship between choreography and music, and in the end, how music and dance form a single entity. As I have observed, at present, dance and music are taught as separate subjects. Musicians do not learn anything but music, and dancers do basically the same as regards dance. Many dancers are not able to sing what they dance or the rhythm they mark while dancing. This has been a problem during my own learning process, for my musical-analytical approach found no response from the dance teachers.[34] On the other hand, I found that many dancers are afraid of musicians' knowledge about rhythm analysis and their knowledge of the science of music.

In the end, dancers and musicians speak different languages, and there are few who are able to teach dance and music as a whole. The same problem applies to dance research, where even today, only a few specialists are trained in the analysis of both music and dance, and this has been one of the main challenges of this research. Perhaps this is the reason why most dance masters in the past were musicians.

The analysis and rhythmic transcription of the dances from Berriz was one of the most difficult and time-consuming tasks during the research. In the beginning, I tried to transcribe the rhythmic value of the steps using the video, but I discovered that I was not able to distinguish the basic patterns from the personal variations of each dancer. I had to learn to dance, and so I did.

Once I knew the dances, the next problem was to analyze and transcribe them. If the discourse on music is a dilemma,[35] akin to the difficulties involved in describing a piece of visual art or a photograph in words, the problem gets worse when the movement of the body is added to the music. Regarding the notation of the dances for analytical purposes, in the end, I thought that the video images included in the DVD accompanying this work, plus a standard rhythmic transcription of the steps, might serve the purposes of

34. I call them "dance teachers" because I think they are far from being masters in a proper sense.

35. Charles Seeger, *Studies in Musicology 1935–1975* (Berkeley: University of California Press, 1977), 16–30.

the study, and that is how the dances are shown. By contrast, learning Labanotation (or another dance notation system) would take too long, and it seems to be a very complex notation system, not very well known among ethnomusicologists, and one with many limitations.

A Note on Editing the Verbatim Texts

All the interviews with Alejandro Aldekoa were carried out in his native tongue, Euskara. I used his dialect, which made things easier. We were both Basque, and we understood each other not only through the things we said, but also by the things we did not say.

The transcription and translation of the discourse used by Aldekoa was difficult. The transcription was made literally, trying to write what Aldekoa actually said and therefore consciously forgetting the rules for writing standardized Basque in an attempt to reflect the richness of his speech. From a purely linguistic point of view, it is interesting material for the study of local dialectal variants of Basque in Berriz.

For the translation of certain words, I opted for leaving or introducing some terms in Euskara, written in italics, that are explained the first time they are used in the text, either in parentheses or in the footnotes. As a rule, these are also included in the glossary. For example, instead of using the English term "farm" or "country house," I opted for the local term *baserria.* While the first two terms are too general, the last specifically refers to the Basque farm. I have followed similar criteria with other words that have proved difficult to translate. The translation of Spanish and Basque quotations is also mine.

For Aldekoa and most of the Basque people, the term *solfeggio* or *solfège* (*solfeoa* in Basque) refers not only to "the singing of scales, intervals, and melodic exercises to solmization syllables" as defined in the *New Grove Dictionary of Music and Musicians*, but to the whole theory of music and especially the ability to read and perform music from scores.

In Aldekoa's quotations, I tried to preserve the structure of the original speech, the style of Alejandro Aldekoa. I added only a few editing changes to make the text comprehensible, such as the name of the speaker in certain dialogues to know who says what. In chapter 1, although almost all the discourse, the content of the text, is Aldekoa's, I have used a more narrative style in the third person. This is a chapter that deals with Aldekoa's life and experiences as a taborer and dance master. Except for a few notes to help explain or put things into context, they are about parts of his life in which he himself, through our interviews together, was the main source of information.

The DVD

The illustrative DVD accompanying this work shows the ritual dances of Berriz as they were performed by Alejandro Aldekoa and his group of dancers on June 29, 1990, San Pedro's Day. The video was recorded by an unknown couple from Begoña (a neighborhood in Bilbao), who gave a copy to Aldekoa a week later. I am aware of the limitations of these video images (the image and sound quality is poor in places, and some parts of the ritual dances and context are missing). Although there must be other videos of Aldekoa playing during the local festivals, this is the best version I could obtain.

In order to illustrate Aldekoa's point of view about who is a musician and what music is, as discussed at the beginning of chapter 5, a brief video example of the mentioned activities (*bertsolaritza*, *trikitrixa*, *panderoa*, *alboka*, *txalaparta*, and *dultzaina*) is shown on the DVD.

Furthermore, the DVD also includes examples of the *zortzikoa* and *ezpata-dantza* rhythms analyzed in chapter 5, where I address specifically the different ways that Serafín Amezua and Alejandro Aldekoa played the *eskasak* and the *banangoa.*

The images of the dancers from Berriz dancing the *dantzari-dantza* before the outbreak of the Spanish Civil War in 1936, mentioned in chapter 3 when dealing with the *txontxongilloa* dance, are included in the DVD as well.

CHAPTER ONE

Alejandro Aldekoa: The Life and Working Practices of a *Txistularia* in the Basque Country

To situate the life and work of Alejandro Aldekoa, we need to begin with the Basque Country itself, then gradually narrow it down to the locality of Berriz and to Aldekoa's activities as a *txistularia* there. We need to begin with a wide focus, because to understand a Basque, one has first to understand the Basque Country.

Euskadi, Euskal Herria, the Basque Country, or the Country of the Basques, is situated in the south of Europe between France and Spain, in the western part of the Pyrenees, opening onto the Atlantic Ocean through the Gulf of Biscay and the Bay of Biscay. It is made up of seven provinces: Araba (Álava), Bizkaia (Vizcaya), Gipuzkoa (Guipúzcoa), and Navarre (Nafarroa in Basque, Navarra in Spanish) in Hegoalde, or the southern Basque Country, and Lapurdi (Labourd), Behe Nafarroa (Basse Navarre), and Zuberoa (Soule) in Iparralde, or the northern Basque Country. Its 20,644 square kilometers of territory (7,974 square miles) is located between latitudes 42 degrees and 44 degrees in the temperate region of the Northern Hemisphere. Its mountains, running parallel to the coastline, create a natural barrier, which as well as dividing the flow of its rivers, modifies the north-south climatic currents, creating

Figure 7. The Basque Country in Europe.

several different microclimates: temperate and humid maritime on the coast, arid Mediterranean in the south, and mountain alpine in the valleys of northern Navarre and the highest areas of the country. The variety of climate and landscape is considerable for such a relatively small territory. One can enjoy a mild winter in Donostia-San Sebastián on the coast or a cold one in Iruñea-Pamplona, inland in Navarre. Likewise, a warm, humid summer can be found in coastal Bilbao (also known as Bilbo), or a hot, dry one inland in Tafalla. In a two-hour drive by car, a visitor to the Basque Country can contemplate the coastal beaches, the leafy beech forests of the mountains, and the irrigated land of the Basque part of Errioxa (La Rioja), until finally arriving at the desert area of the Bardenas in the south of Navarre. Annual rainfall in the coastal areas exceeds 1,000 millimeters (just under 40 inches), whereas in the south, it is less than 60 millimeters (just over 2 inches). The average temperature difference between Bilbao and Vitoria-Gasteiz, cities less than 60 kilometers (37 miles) apart, is more than 5 degrees Centigrade—41 degrees Fahrenheit.

Most of the mountains, except for those in the Navarrese Pyrenees and a few others, namely Gorbea (1,475 meters, 4,839 feet), Anboto (1,268 meters, 4,160 feet), Txindoki (1,341 meters, 4,400 feet), and Aitzgorri (1,544 meters, 5,066 feet) do not exceed a height of 1,200 meters—just under 4,000 feet. The coastal provinces of Gipuzkoa and Bizkaia are boxed in between the sea and the mountains, causing considerable geographic unevenness with short, fast-flowing rivers forming an irregular and steep coastline.

Figure 8. The Basque Country and its present division into seven provinces.

The origins of the Basque people and Euskara, their language of pre-Indo–European origin, are unknown. Basques are considered "the mystery people of Europe," and because of that, many scholars have studied the Basque Country. It has been established that human beings have lived in the present Basque territory for at least two hundred thousand years. Important remains of human occupation, dating back to Paleolithic times, have been found in archaeological sites such as Santimamiñe, Axlor, Lezetxiki, and Izturitze.

The complex history of the Basque Country reflects the many changes that have taken place in its territorial and political demarcation. The north of the country, more mountainous, of difficult access, and of lesser economic and strategic interest, maintained a greater level of isolation in the face of foreign influences than the south, which was more exposed to the penetration of other cultures and the establishment of socioeconomic formations alien to the characteristic development of Basques in the north. Thus, the influence of Celtic, Roman, and Arab invasions were more noticeable in the south than in the north. (According to some authors, Bizkaia and Gipuzkoa were the least Romanized provinces in the whole of southwest Europe.) This was also the case with the process of Christianization. Initiated in the fourth century, it was not homogeneous in the Basque Country and for centuries coexisted with paganism.

During the Middle Ages, the Old Kingdom of Pamplona (Iruñea, Navarre) constituted what has been termed the first Basque "state." Until the twelfth century, a political nation, Nafarroa (Navarre), and a cultural nation, Euskal Herria (the Basque Country), coincided in this area. Since that time, however, the Old Kingdom of Pamplona, the Country of the Basques, Nafarroa, or Euskal Herria, has been divided progressively according to the existing correlation of forces at a given time. At present, Euskal Herria is divided between two states: the Spanish kingdom and the French republic.[1] In France, the three Basque provinces of Lapurdi, Nafarroa Beherea, and Zuberoa do not have any special administrative status, being included in the French *département* of the Atlantic Pyrenees with the non-Basque province of Bearn. For its part, the Spanish administration divides the Basque Country into two autonomous entities, the Basque Autonomous Community and the Foral Community of Navarre.

For centuries, political life in the Basque Country was governed by local laws or *fueros* (charters), the written rules of habits and customs practiced since former times—common law committed to paper. The *fueros* constituted the legal regime that, in one way or another, regulated the local self-government of the Basque Country and relations between the central power of the monarchy and the local authorities: the General Assemblies of Bizkaia, Araba, and Gipuzkoa and the Legislative Assembly of Navarre. The *fueros* established the law of *hidalguía universal* (universal nobility), which, in addition to making the status of noblemen universal and establishing legal equality for all the Basque

1. The present border line in the Pyrenees between the Spanish and French states was finally established in 1856.

Country's inhabitants, also implied considerable economic fiscal autonomy, exemption from military service, and its own code of civil law, which still survives today.[2]

The two nineteenth-century Carlist Wars (1833–39 and 1872–76) pitted Carlos María Isidro de Borbón and Isabel II, brother and daughter of the late King Fernando VII, against one another over succession to the Spanish throne. The Carlists defended tradition under the motto "Dios-Patria-Rey," "God-Country-King," whereas those in favor of Isabel II defended the liberal revolution that had taken some effect in the Spanish state. In the Basque Country, Carlism spread through rural areas, whereas the bourgeoisie of the *villas* (cities or towns) generally supported liberalism. As a result of the liberals' victory, a process of abolishing the *fueros* began in 1839, at the end of the First Carlist War, with the promulgation of the law of October 25, 1839. This law confirmed that the *fueros* were not above and could not interfere with the constitutional unity of the monarchy—"sin perjuicio de la unidad constitutional de la monarquía," "without prejudice for the constitutional unity of the monarchy." The Second Carlist War ended on February 26, 1876, with the flight of Carlos VII and without any peace treaty having been signed. With the passing of the Law of July 21, 1876, the Basque *fueros* were finally abolished, initiating a long period of constraints on the status of Basque autonomy.

These constraints also produced a reaction. The abolition of the *fueros*, industrialization, which threatened traditional ways of life, and a great influx of Spanish immigrants, which weakened the presence and use of Euskara, together with a growing Romantic, nationalist ideology, led Sabino Arana to found the Basque Nationalist Party in 1895.[3] Arana believed the Spanish "invasion" to be the origin of all the problems in the Basque Country and that independence was the only solution. Basque nationalism at the time was essentially traditionalist and Catholic, as expressed in its slogan, "Jaungoikoa ta lagizarra," "God and the Old Law," "God" underlining the weight of religion and "the Old Law" clearly referring to the old *fueros* and traditional habits and customs. This was what distanced Arana from the Carlist ideology, which, he claimed, made the mistake of linking the cause of the Basque *fueros* to a Spanish dynastic question.

During the first third of the twentieth century, as a result of widespread industrialization, a modern, plural, and complex society developed in the Basque Country. Capitalist development created a proletarian mass out of which emerged socialism, both of a Basque and a non-Basque variety. After a coup d'état in September 1923, the dictatorship of General Primo de Rivera was installed in Spain with the blessing of the Spanish monarchy. Political activity was prohibited (only one governmental party was legalized, Union Patriótica, the Patriotic Union), but trade union and cultural activity were still allowed. Consequently, Basque nationalism now centered on cultural activities, including, for

---

2. For an appreciation in English of the extent of self-government implied by the *fueros*, see Gregorio Monreal Zia, *The Old Law of Bizkaia (1452): Introductory Study and Critical Edition*, trans. William A. Douglass and Linda White, preface by William A. Douglass (Reno: Center for Basque Studies, University of Nevada, Reno, 2005).

3. The EAJ-PNV, Eusko Alderdi Jeltzalea-Partido Nacionalista Vasco (Basque Nationalist Party), that is now a Christian Democratic Party.

example, the celebration of the Day of the Basque language (*Euskararen Eguna*), which occurred for the first time in Arrasate (Mondragón), Gipuzkoa, in 1927. Many cultural associations were founded at this time, such as the Basque Mountain Federation (Euskal Herriko Mendigozale Elkartea) in 1924, the first choreographic group of the country, Elai-Alai, in 1927, and the Association of *Txistulariak* of the Basque Country (Euskal Herriko Txistularien Elkartea), also in 1927. Concomitantly, the church distanced itself from the fundamentalist Carlist ideology and began to support the Basque nationalist movement, which helped to extend and find popular support for nationalist principles.

Yet Primo de Rivera's rule gradually imploded, together with the role of the disgraced monarchy that supported it. A contemporary account illustrates vividly these last days of the dictatorship in the Basque Country, as well as the close connection between cultural expression and Basque nationalist feeling. Traveling in the Basque Country at the time, Violet Alford was witness to a large pro-Basque cultural gathering:

> I think a still more wonderful site was the Aurresku [a dance, discussed later] at the Conferencia de Estudios Vascos (Conference of Basque Studies) at Vergara [Bergara, Gipuzkoa] in July, 1930, when top-hatted and béreted delegates from all the provinces, and from the Basque Country across the seas, took part. They seemed to feel their coming emancipation from the monarchy which had suppressed their liberties, withdrawn their ancient privileges, and even then was working for the gradual extinction of their greatest possession, the age-old Basque speech. A misguided Royal Infante had come to the meeting. The thousands of Basques leaped "con ardor" the traditional dances, and caring nothing for the Royal presence, rose bareheaded *en masse* to sing their song of national aspiration, Guernikako Arbola, the Tree of Guernika. The band, as misguided as the visitor, immediately afterwards struck up the Royal March of Spain and the vast assembly, to a man, sat down. The incident showed the way the wind blew in the Basque Provinces.[4]

After the proclamation of the Second Spanish Republic in April 1931, political events led the PNV (the Basque Nationalist Party) to a progressive rapprochement with Spanish left-wing political parties in an attempt to try to obtain autonomy for the Basque Country. However, the Spanish right, supported by the bourgeoisie and alarmed by the rise of the left-wing parties, especially following the triumph of the Popular Front in the elections of February 12, 1936,[5] organized a coup d'état on July 18, 1936. Led by General Francisco Franco, the coup failed as such, and instead escalated into a civil war that lasted for three years. In the Basque Country, local capitalist forces sided with the rebellion, while the PNV defended the democratic republican regime. The bishops of Iruñea and Gasteiz condemned the Second Republic and encouraged Basque Catholics to fight against "Communism,"[6] a terrible contradiction for Catholic Basque nationalists, who

---

4. Violet Alford, "Ceremonial Dances of the Spanish Basques," *The Musical Quarterly* 18, no. 3 (July 1932): 474.

5. The Popular Front (Frente Popular) included republicans, socialists, and Communists.

6. The term "Communism" has been widely used by the right for propagandistic purposes. All the republican parties, Communist or not, were included within the term.

found themselves forced to fight alongside Communists and anarchists in defense of the Republic. At the height of the Civil War, the Republican government passed the Statute of Autonomy for the Basque Country, and on October 7, 1936, José Antonio Agirre was named *lehendakaria* (president) of the Basque government.

During his term in office, a Basque army was established, freedom of religion was maintained, confiscation of personal property was limited to those who had supported the rebellion, and even a Basque currency was issued, so that the Basque Country functioned as practically an independent state. General Franco, after his failed attack on Madrid in March 1937, concentrated all his military potential on the northern front, with the objective of advancing systematically. On June 19, 1937, Bilbao was conquered, and after a long military conflict, the last pocket of Republican resistance, Madrid, fell into pro-Franco hands in April 1939.

The forty years of Franco's regime saw the repression of everything Basque rise to unthinkable limits: Euskara and any Basque cultural activity were persecuted. Basque nationalism (termed "separatism") was considered a crime. Increased industrialization, consolidating the power of the financial bourgeoisie, brought with it massive immigration that did nothing but aggravate even more the perception among many sectors of the Basque population that their land was being invaded by the Spanish state.[7] Spanish repression encouraged Basque resistance. State violence (states of emergency, arrests, military-style court-martials of civilians, and executions) increased the numbers of Basque nationalist supporters, and in the 1950s, a revolutionary, nationalist group, using armed force as a means to combat what it saw as the imperialist enemy, was born: ETA, Euskadi ta Askatasuna (the Basque Country and Freedom).

After the death of Franco, the Spanish Constitution of 1978 was promulgated. In the referendum to ratify the new constitution, most inhabitants of the Basque Country abstained, considering that the historical rights of the Basque people had not been respected. Despite this, a statute of autonomy was passed by majority vote in a referendum of October 1979, a statute that, under the name of the Basque Autonomous Community, included only three of the seven Basque provinces: Araba, Bizkaia, and Gipuzkoa.

At present, the Basque political problem remains unsolved for most of the Basque people, many of whom still claim the right of the Basque Country to self-determination and seek the territorial unity of the whole of Euskal Herria.

Berriz: Home of Ajejandro Aldekoa

Berriz is located on the high course of the Ibaizabal River, in the eastern part of the province of Bizkaia, on the south slope of Mount Oiz (1,020 meters, or just over 3,345 feet) and its valley. It has an area of almost 30 square kilometers (11.5 square miles) and forms

---

7. At present, less than 50 percent of the inhabitants of the Basque Country descend from the Basque people living there in 1880.

an important communications crossroad, being on the main route between Bizkaia and Gipuzkoa by road and rail. In the past, it was also one of the main communication routes with the provinces of Araba and Castile through the High Deba region in Gipuzkoa and a point of access to the pilgrims' road to Santiago de Compostela.

Berriz is one of the rural municipalities of the old *merindad* (county) of Durango that belonged to the Kingdom of Navarre until approximately 1200, whereas the rest of Bizkaia had belonged to the Kingdom of Castile for quite some time. It was for this reason that when the County of Durango joined Bizkaia, it had a different legal status and held its own general assemblies in nearby Gerediaga (today, a neighborhood of Abadiño). The County of Durango was made up of fifteen municipalities: Abadiño (Abadiano), Berriz, Mallabia (Mallavia), Mañaria, Iurreta, Garai (Garay), Zaldibar (Zaldívar), Arrazola, Axpe, Apatamonasterio, Izurtza (Izurza), Durango, Ermua, Otxandio (Ochandiano), and Elorrio. Although the last assembly of the County of Durango was held on December 27, 1875, it continues to enjoy its own social, political, and cultural identity today, and it was Alejandro Aldekoa's "area of influence," the area where he developed his career as pipe and tabor player and dance master.

Figure 9. The Province of Bizkaia, the County of Durango, and its fifteen town councils today.

In 1957, 92 percent of the population of Berriz made their living from farming. In the following twenty years, the town's population doubled, and the industrial sector came to employ 67 percent of the working population, with only 8.4 percent still dedicated exclusively to the farming sector. In the 1960s, industrial growth and its consequent immigration changed the profile of Berriz to the extent that in 1971, only 38 percent of its inhabitants had been born in the town. In 1920 (the year that Aldekoa was born), Berriz had 2,048 inhabitants, and in 1950 (a year before Aldekoa married), the population was 2,138. Yet in 1977, the population had grown to 4,279. Aldekoa therefore witnessed tremendous changes in his surroundings during his lifetime. His hometown, Berriz, changed from a rural, dispersed town to a concentrated urban one, and from an economy and society primarily based on agriculture to an industrial economy with a large number of newly arrived Spanish immigrants.

Aldekoa: The Early Life of a *Txistularia*

Alejandro Aldekoa was a man with a very precise memory and good communication skills, a man who had a story to tell and who knew how to tell that story. As a result, I have organized this account of his hometown and his beloved Basque Country, how he learned music and dance, his chance to become a fully employed professional *txistularia*, the effects of the Spanish Civil War, his Basque nationalist ideology, his understanding of the trade of *txistularia*, and the importance of the ritual dances for the people of Berriz in the Basque Country during the second half of the twentieth century according to information given me by Aldekoa himself. Except for a handful of additional comments, contextual information, and a few editing changes, what follows is basically Aldekoa telling the story of his life and career.

Aldekoa's biography is not a unique, isolated, or extreme case. Instead, it reflects the ups and downs in the life of most Basques who experienced the Second Republic, the Spanish Civil War, and Franco's dictatorship. In that sense, his testimony reflects a part of the history of a country through a highly personal, but culturally and socially embedded point of view—that of a local pipe and tabor player.

Childhood

Alejandro Aldekoa was born on March 27, 1920, in the Aretxandieta *baserria* (farmhouse), situated in the Mendibil (also known as San Lorenzo, after the chapel there) *auzoa* (neighborhood) in Berriz, where his family lived as tenant farmers.[8] The *baserria* was at the Bidebarrieta crossroads. Its proprietor later sold the farm, and the buildings were demolished. In its place today is a driving-school track. Aldekoa built his own house in 1960 on land he bought on the other side of the road from the Aretxandieta *baserria*. His father, Ambrosio Aldekoa Mardaras, had been born in the same *baserria*. His mother, Marina Aranburu Garitazelaia, originally from Mallabia, went to live there after her marriage

8. "Aretxandieta," "Aritz-andieta," "Atxanieta," or "Atxañeta" means "Place of Large Oak Trees," or oak grove. The name of the *baserria* was often given as a nickname to its inhabitants. Therefore, Aldekoa was also known as Atxanieta or Atxañeta.

to Ambrosio. Alejandro was the youngest of three brothers. The eldest, Vitoriano, was five years his senior, and the middle brother, Jorge, three years older. Like most of the population in Berriz, the family lived off the land and especially by cattle farming. As in the case of his two brothers, as a child, Aldekoa helped with the work in the vegetable garden and looked after the cows. The economic situation of tenant farmers was quite precarious. To try to help improve the situation, his brothers were forced to look for outside work. One became a barber and the other a butcher. Until he was fourteen years old, Aldekoa attended the normal public primary/junior school, leaving without obtaining any qualifications.

Learning to Dance

In those days, as was usual, there was an official, town hall–appointed *txistularia* in Berriz. One of his most important duties was to organize the dances for the celebrations of the days of the patron saints of Berriz, San Pedro on June 29 and Santa Isabel on July 2. Two months beforehand, the *txistularia* had to begin the selection process and prepare the dancers who were going to participate in these celebrations. He selected and prepared the group for the celebrations, but the enthusiasm for folk dancing among the young was so great that they did not miss an opportunity to dance or to learn and practice the dances. According to Aldekoa, everybody was always excited about the celebrations and the dances, almost certainly because they were their only source of entertainment. There was no television or local soccer team, and Berriz did not have a movie theater, so the young people sought their entertainment in singing and dancing. On seeing this enthusiasm, parents who had been dancers themselves began to teach their children at least the basic dances such as the *banangoa* (literally, one-by-one dance, where dancers perform one by one). This was the case with the Aldekoa family. It is said that Ambrosio, as well as being a great enthusiast of dance and Basque culture in general, was a good dancer who ensured that his passion for dance was passed down to his children. From him, Aldekoa learned the basic parts of the *dantzari-dantza* (dancers' dance) and the *erregelak* (the rules), as well as many other things referring to the customs and rituals surrounding the dance. While his father taught the *erregelak* to his older brothers, Alejandro, paying attention to everything that had anything to do with dance, watched, practiced by himself, and learned the complicated steps of the *aurreskua* (literally, the hand in front, or the first hand) and the *atzeskua* (the hand in the rear, or the last hand) before his brothers.

Although there was an officially selected group of dancers for the town celebrations, young people used to meet together informally to learn and practice the dances by themselves. Aldekoa's brothers, along with their group of friends (all of them some four years older than Aldekoa), used to meet in the evenings in a clearing on Mount Toston, above the small chapel of San Lorenzo, to practice. They already knew the melodies, the tunes for the dances, so they sang the music themselves. Everybody participated in the learning process, commenting on and criticizing the performance of the group as a whole or of particular individuals: "Like this, not like that." Group contributions to the learning process were very important. When any doubts or arguments arose, they usually went in search of the advice from Alejandro's father, who was always willing to help. Thus, little by little, between friends, they formed their own dance group.

Aldekoa went along to those dance sessions as "the little brother." He would watch what the older ones did while harboring one hope: that someone would be missing, and they would call on him to complete the group (for the *dantzari-dantza*, eight dancers are required). When they were all there, he would sit patiently, watching and waiting to substitute for somebody if the occasion arose. Aldekoa rarely missed any of those dance sessions. By watching the practice sessions and following the advice and instructions of his father, Aldekoa, his brothers, and the rest of their friends learned to dance by themselves.

Because he was so young, Aldekoa was the center of attention every time he danced. On more than one occasion, during the patron saints' day celebrations and after the official dancing had finished, he was invited to dance the *aurreskua* in front of the spectators. Very few ten year olds had learned to dance the *erregelak* at all, due to the difficulty and complexity of the dance.

After the Dancer, Txistularia

In 1931, the Second Spanish Republic was proclaimed, and in the summer 1932, the *batzokia* (the PNV social center or club) of Berriz was inaugurated very near to where Aldekoa lived. Indeed, his father was one of the founding members of the *batzokia.* Aldekoa remembered attending the opening celebrations, where, down in the street, he listened to a speech by José Antonio Agirre, the first *lehendakaria* or president of the Basque government, from the balcony of the *batzokia.* In order to enhance the occasion even more, a famous *txistularia* from Eibar, León Laspiur,[9] was invited to Berriz. After the celebration, a lunch was given at which the doctor of Berriz, Jose Luis Ugarte, a friend of Ambrosio's who shared his enthusiasm for local dance and folklore, and who was also one of the founders of the *batzokia,*[10] approached Aldekoa's father, pointing out Laspiur's skills:

> "He can certainly play the *txistua*—he can at that! You've got a lad, the young one, the one that can dance the *dantzari-dantza* so well and has a good ear for music. Why don't you teach him to play the *txistua*? To play like he can over there, well, that would be really something!"
>
> "Maybe you're right, yes, why not?"[11]

---

9. In 1931, Laspiur took charge of the Municipal Band of *Txistulariak* in Eibar, replacing Policarpo Iriondo. After the war, he was not allowed to return to his position as a punishment for his links with Basque nationalism.

10. A photograph of that time exists in which José Luis Ugarte appears as a taborer, together with the dancers from Berriz and the town flag in the center. Hipólito Amezua (then then taborer of Berriz) lent the *txistua* and tabor to him for the occasion.

11. Alejandro Aldekoa, interview by the author, March 1, 1991.

And with no more said, they went up to the virtuoso *txistularia* and asked him if he would be willing to teach Aldekoa. León Laspiur answered:

> "Has he done *solfeggio*?"[12]
>
> "No, he has no idea!"
>
> "Well, to be able to learn, he needs *solfeggio*; without *solfeggio*, I can't teach him. If he learns *solfeggio*, I'll teach him; if he doesn't, I won't."[13]

Near Aretxandieta, Aldekoa's house, was the convent of the Mercedarias de La Vera Cruz.[14] The town's young priest, Don Modesto Arana, lived there with his mother.[15] A native of Berriz, from the same neighborhood of San Lorenzo, Don Modesto Arana was, above all, a piano and organ teacher. Ambrosio, Alejandro's father, was a close friend of Don Modesto's family, so close, in fact, that when Modesto Arana was born, it was Ambrosio who went to call the doctor. As soon as he found out about the conversation at the inaugural lunch and of Ambrosio's intention to let Aldekoa learn to play the *txistua*, the musical priest offered to teach Aldekoa to read music whenever he wanted. Aldekoa began to go to daily music classes with Don Modesto. With the enthusiasm and ability of the student, on the one hand, and the pedagogical capabilities of Don Modesto, on the other (Aldekoa remembered Don Modesto as being an exceptional teacher), Aldekoa was sufficiently prepared to begin his first *txistua* lessons after only two months. His first *txistua*, made by Guillermo Lizaso in Errenteria (Rentería), Gipuzkoa, cost seventy-five pesetas and the *danbolina* sixty pesetas.

Continuing his daily music lessons in Berriz, Aldekoa also began to go to nearby Eibar once a week, on Saturdays, to learn to play the *txistua* with León Laspiur. Aldekoa remembered his first *txistua* lessons, the positions of the notes, re-me-fa-soh, the scale, and so on. At that time, the method used was one written by Father Hilario Olazaran,[16] but Laspiur made up the majority of the exercises and pieces that he used in his lessons

---

12. *Solfeggio* or *solfège* is a technique for teaching sight singing in which each note of the score is sung to a special syllable, a "sol-fa syllable."

13. Alejandro Aldekoa, interview by the author, March 1, 1991.

14. Founded in 1550 by Martín de Aguirresacona, parish priest of the rural area, the convent itself did not have a priest until 1725. The church was built in 1783. Felipe Andrés García, *Berriz: Estudio histórico-artístico* (Bilbao: Diputación Foral de Bizkaia, 1997), 208.

15. "Don" in Spanish means "esquire." It is used similarly for "mister" or "sir," as a mark of respect. In towns, it could be said that "don" becomes part of the name of certain people, especially the priest and the doctor. Modesto Arana Fuldain was sentenced to thirty years in prison after the Civil War for having been chaplain to the Basque Army. However, the sentence was reduced, and in 1944, he was named organist of the Jesuit residence in Bilbao. In 1949, he was named director of the choral society, giving important concerts alongside the Symphony Orchestra of Bilbao and the Spanish National Orchestra. He was also named corresponding member of the Academy of Fine Art of San Fernando. A director, teacher, composer, and improviser on the organ, he is remembered in Berriz for his concerts playing the parish organ. Angel Berguices, "Dos siglos de música culta y tradicional en el Duranguesado (1800–1986)," unpublished ms., 1986, 56.

16. In 1927, the journal *Euskalerriaren alde* presented a competition to find a method for playing the *txistua*, no longer than fifteen pages long, that would then be published in the journal. *El Txistu, lo que es y cómo se toca* (1927; Donostia: Txistulari, 1994), by Father Hilario Olazaran, won. It was the first method for playing the *txistua* ever published. As noted here, the work was republished in 1994 for the journal *Txistulari* to celebrate its author's one hundredth birthday. Later, Father

himself, so that his student could tackle the difficulties that arose progressively. Aldekoa spoke of Laspiur having his own method. Some of the exercises and pieces he used were originals,[17] while others were copies of classical pieces from the repertoire of the *txistua.* Photocopiers did not exist in those days, so the whole repertoire had to be copied, compiled, and distributed by hand.

Laspiur worked for the Eibar city hall in the mornings, having the afternoons free to dedicate himself to music and to the writing, copying, and preparation of material he used in his lessons. With these scores, Aldekoa began to practice pieces such as *Artzai Kantak* without realizing the complex nature of the work he was playing.[18] Only later, when he had access to the journal *Txistulari*, did he discover the importance of the pieces he had studied. The journal *Txistulari* arose from the intention to publish the *txistularia* repertoire, making access to it easier. Aldekoa registered in the association at the age of thirteen, in 1933. He also managed to obtain a copy of the method by Olazaran, from which he learned to play *fandangoak* (triple-time dances) and dance music by himself, apart from the method he followed with León Laspiur. In time, he began to study pieces of music with an ever-increasing technical difficulty, and when he finally managed to master the *txistua* sufficiently, after approximately two years, he began to study the tabor. Aldekoa was of the opinion that if one could not achieve competence on the *txistua*, albeit to a minimum level, one could not even begin to try to play the tabor, because coordination is very difficult, and the result would be chaotic.

Aldekoa's greatest difficulty when learning the tabor was in learning the beats of minuets and fandangos, due to their rhythmic structure and the necessary use of the drumroll. Nevertheless, he eventually mastered them, and soon after, Laspiur began to initiate his student in the use of glottal articulation, using a "t" and "k" sound alternately to achieve greater speed in the emission of notes on the *txistua.* Many traditional *txistulariak* only used the "t" sound, using the tip of the tongue when articulating as if to whisper the word "too." Aldekoa used the term "perform" to refer to the use of the glottal articulation. For him, it was an important concept for classifying taborers. When he said that somebody was "a good performer," "not a performer," or "performed something," he was talking about the person's ability to use glottal articulation. In his opinion, this was what differentiates an ordinary or even a good *txistularia* from a very good one or a virtuoso. For Aldekoa, "a performer" was synonymous with musical and interpretative quality.

Apart from the exercises and pieces of music given to him by his teacher, Aldekoa did, of course, learn to play the dances of Berriz. Lacking the musical scores for the *erregelak* or the *soka dantza* (rope dance) from which to play, Ambrosio, his father, sang

---

Hilario also published *Txistu, método y repertorio de flauta baska* (Bilbao: Ordorika, 1933), one of the most widely used and popular methods of playing the *txistua* ever written.

17. Forty-six musical pieces written by León Laspiur have been published in the journal *Txistulari.*

18. *Artzain Kantak* (Shepherd Songs), by Eusebio Basurko Zabaleta, is one of the emblematic pieces of music in the *txistularia* repertoire, and a theme whose variations demand a high level of skill for the player to be able to dominate all the registers and difficulties the piece presents. For many taborers, *Artzain Kantak* is synonymous with difficulty and virtuosity.

them to Don Modesto Arana, who transcribed them. This is the first known transcript of the *aurreskua* and the *atzeskua* of the *soka dantza* of Berriz and the one from which Aldekoa learned to play.[19] According to his own account, Aldekoa already knew how to sing the *erregelak*, but did not know the notes. These he learned from the score Don Modesto transcribed. The rest of the dances he learned by ear from the local taborers (Hipólito and Serafín Amezua) and from his father. At that time in Berriz, it was not usual for children to dance in public. The minimum age traditionally required to take part in the ritual, to be *plaza mutilla* (literally, town-square boy, meaning a young man eligible to perform the Berriz dances in public), and to be selected by the *txistularia* to dance was seventeen. However, most certainly influenced by the feeling prevalent at the time of the need to recuperate and boost Basque culture, and by the fashion for creating dance groups imitating the Euzko Gaztedi (Basque Youth Movement) group of Bilbao, a children's dance group was created in Berriz at around the time of the inauguration of the *batzokia*. This group could be regarded as the first folk dance group in the town. Aldekoa, his brothers, and their friends, who had all learned to dance by themselves, together made up the *batzokia* dance group. In 1933, at the fiestas of Zengotita,[20] a year after having started to study music and the *txistua*, Aldekoa played the *dantzari-dantza*, the *soka dantza*, the *fandangoa*, the *arin-arina* (literally, fast-fast), and the *biribilketa* (march) for the local *batzokia* dance group. This was an exceptional achievement for a young boy with only a year's study of music behind him. With that same group, he performed in Ibaiondo (Bilbao) during the important celebrations for San Ignacio's Day on July 31, 1934.

Later that year, owing to the lack of local *txistulariak*, Aldekoa was called to Eibar to accompany the dance group of the Eibar *batzokia*. He used to go to Eibar for the practice sessions, sleep there, and return home on the following day. It was a large group of about eighty dancers, in which girls, the *hilanderak* (literally, spinners), also danced—something quite unusual for that time and for our young *txistularia* from Berriz. Aldekoa played for that first group of *hilanderak* from Eibar and thereafter also traveled with the same group to Bermeo (Bizkaia) to perform in the inauguration of the local *batzokia* there.

That same year, Aldekoa, now fourteen years old, was invited to Madrid to play the *txistua* for a group of students from Bizkaia. For that special occasion, he went to Bilbao, the capital of Bizkaia, where he had a suit made to measure, vest and all, in a famous store. Once in Madrid, he went to the Recoletos *fronton* (a *pelota*, or Basque handball court). First they danced some numbers of the *dantzari-dantza* and the *soka dantza*. After the dance, they let him play on the court in front of the audience. It was twenty days before his fifteenth birthday, and he could play the *txistua* well enough to perform in front of all these people. The reaction of the audience to this slightly built,

19. Published in *Txistulari* 74, no. 2 (1973): 2040.

20. "I have very special memories of my first performance in Zengotita," Aldekoa told me. With the exception of his time doing military service, he played his pipe and tabor year after year at the fiestas in Zengotita until 1995.

young Basque instrumentalist was warm. They showered him with pesetas (in those days, made of silver), perhaps through surprise at or ignorance about the possibilities the instrument offered. The eight dancers on the court were hardly enough to pick up all the money. Here was a young *txistularia*, away from Berriz for the first time, experiencing a long train journey, not only performing at the Recoletos *fronton* accompanying the dance group, but also achieving great success with his solo performance. It was a memorable experience for the young Alejandro Aldekoa.

Figure 10. Alejandro Aldekoa at the age of fourteen (1934). Photo courtesy of the Aldekoa family.

The Competitive Exams in Bilbao

The first farmworkers' labor union in the Basque Country had its head office in Begoña, a suburb of Bilbao named after the important basilica there. Aldekoa's uncles worked there as caretakers. On the premises, there was a café with a large lounge that was usually full of people, not only those who worked for the union, but ordinary people from the city.[21] The great Martín Elola,[22] a famous *txistularia* from Idiazabal (Gipuzkoa) who held the position of *txistularia* of the Republic (that is, the municipality) of Begoña in Bilbao, used to give recitals there, and this was the main reason why the young *txistua* student from Berriz visited the café once he was thirteen years old. According to Aldekoa, he had never heard anybody play the variations of the "Hiru Damatxo"[23] like Elola. He played effortlessly and so well that he made it all seem so easy, even the parts Aldekoa knew to be difficult. However, Martín Elola was an old man and died on January 7, 1935. His position was left vacant, and competitive exams were announced. It seems that both Laspiur and Arana, Aldekoa's teachers, encouraged him to apply to take the exams for the position in Begoña. They then began to get him ready.

Aldekoa went to Enrique Elola—Martin's son and a qualified piano and harmony teacher—twice a week to improve his knowledge of harmony. At that time in Begoña, the organist was a man named Eduardo Gorosarri, a music teacher and professor of history and aesthetics at the Bizkaia Conservatory of Music.[24] Gorosarri was also a *txistularia* and one of the founder-promoters of the Association of *Txistulariak* in the Basque Country.[25] Modesto Arana had been his student, and because both were also organists, Aldekoa said, they had a very close friendship. Aldekoa was already registered for the exam, along with eight other candidates, when, approximately a month before the exam date, he accompanied Don Modesto to the parish of Begoña so that Gorosarri could listen to the talented young musician from Berriz. For the category of free choice, they had prepared one of Gorosarri's own pieces, the "Idiarena."[26] He did not play it with excessive agility, but his rhythm was good. He had been practicing every day, and

---

21. In the words of Aldekoa: "kaletarrak be egotezien han," "urban people used to be there, too." In Euskara, the dichotomy *baserria-kalea* (farmhouse-street) is used to differentiate the rural environment and its inhabitants from the urban dwellers.

22. Martín Elola Berasategi won various awards as a solo performer (Donostia 1889, Bilbao 1896, Gasteiz 1901). He was director of the Municipal Band of *Txistulariak* of Zumarraga (Gipuzkoa) before moving to Begoña, where he obtained the position of *txistularia*, a position he occupied until his death in 1935. He was also one of the founders-promoters of the Association of *Txistulariak* of the Basque Country.

23. Another of the classic, well-known pieces from the *txistua* repertoire, based on a popular theme with its corresponding variations, published in *Txistulari* 73, no. 1 (1973): 2006.

24. He obtained the position in 1917, coming in first in the competitive exam ahead of eight other contenders. In those days, the position of organist was an ambitious position to hold, and access to it was by means of competitive examination alone. What is more, the position at Begoña was one of the most important in the Basque Country.

25. At the age of fourteen, he held the position of municipal organist and *txistularia* of Sopuerta (Bizkaia).

26. A well-known, popular concert piece that consists of a theme with very difficult variations, especially some in C minor, published in *Txistulari* 21 (1931): 174.

after having played it hundreds of times, his fingers seemed to know how to move by themselves. That it was also one of Gorosarri's own pieces greatly pleased the composer. They entered a hall. Gorosarri put the score on the piano and moved away a little to be able to hear better. Aldekoa played. The delighted composer spoke: "Good, good. Over in Barakaldo [Baracaldo, a town on the left bank of the estuary traversing Greater Bilbao] there's another *txistularia*, but if you play like that, stay calm, and don't lose your nerves, you'll get the position."[27]

Eduardo Gorosarri was one of the members of the jury. Of course, Aldekoa knew that in an examination, anyone could make a mistake and with it lose the position. As the day of the examination drew nearer and nearer, Aldekoa continued to study and prepare himself. The examination consisted of a harmony exercise, a previously unseen piece of music, a set piece, and a piece of his own free choice. His teacher explained the procedure for the unseen piece to him and advised him how to get through it. He would be given four or five minutes to read the score, in which time he had to look for the pitfalls and take as much care as possible. His own teacher gave him pieces he did not know to help him practice first-sight reading. He was almost at the end of the second course on harmony, could handle himself well in transposition, and in general was a brilliant, advanced student. Modesto Arana hoped Aldekoa would study some other instrument to enable him to enter an orchestra or continue with his composition studies. Everything seemed to be running smoothly, but then, a couple of weeks before the examination, the Spanish Civil War broke out. The examination was not held, and all activity in the Basque Country came to a standstill. Aldekoa was forced to stop playing the *txistua*, and although with time he started again, it seemed clear that he had lost the chance to become a fully professional *txistua* player and that he would never be in such a situation again. He continued to practice what he already knew, but without enough dedication, or without the dedication he would have liked. His future as a professional musician was thwarted by the war when he was just sixteen years old.

> Now it's easy to play better than me—you don't have to be anything special. But before I played well, passable, at least. Perhaps I was in better condition. I practiced more. Maybe I should have studied more, but the war started, and that broke me. When I was sixteen, ah! What I could play when I was sixteen! Even nowadays, very few *txistulariak* can play at that age what I played! The truth is that, since then, I haven't learned anything new. I've practiced what I learned then, and through playing and playing I've developed a kind of ease, but it was then when I learned to play the "Idiarena," *Artzain Kantak*, and those pieces, not since. Then the war started, and that was it! Alone with my mother . . . six years away . . . and anyway, I didn't have anyone to play with for ten years . . . that's what shattered my life. If the war hadn't broken out, I'd have carried on studying, I'd have learned things, I'd have played, and perhaps I would have been a professional musician.[28]

---

27. Alejandro Aldekoa, interview by the author, April 12, 1996.

28. Alejandro Aldekoa, interview by the author, April 24, 1996.

Aldekoa and the Spanish Civil War

In Spain, the coup d'état of July 18, 1936, came up against a greater resistance than expected and turned into a long civil war. The PNV fought in defense of the Spanish Republic and democracy. While they were fighting for the Republic, many Basques also felt they were fighting for autonomy, self-determination, and the long-dreamed-of Basque independence.

The advances of Franco's troops, who had concentrated their offensive on the northern front and were sweeping west toward Bizkaia from early gains in Gipuzkoa, were unsustainable, and the delicate situation produced by the war forced the Aldekoa family to take what they could and move to a safer place. They took refuge for almost a month in Gordexola (Gordejuela), situated in the western part of Bizkaia. However, faced with such insecurity and the persecution of all those who had stood out as Basque nationalist leaders in the years of the Second Republic, Ambrosio Aldekoa, Alejandro's father, was forced into exile. His activities as a founder of the *batzokia* and promoter of nationalist cultural activities made him a target for Franco's forces, known as "the nationals." For fear of fascist reprisals, Ambrosio left Gordexola for Santander, to the west of the Basque Country, where he embarked by sea for France. While Ambrosio was in exile in France, Alejandro's older brother, Vitoriano, joined the Kirikiño Battalion of the Basque Army and fought against Franco's forces. He disappeared and was presumed killed in the bombing of Gernika in April 1937, while Alejandro's other brother, Jorge, was among Basque soldiers captured by the enemy.

Aldekoa returned to Aretxandieta with his mother. With his father in France, one brother missing, and the other a prisoner in Santoña, a notorious jail in Santander for opponents of Franco, Aldekoa and his family endured moments of sadness and desolation, with his mother working the land to survive. Fighting back his tears, he told me: "And there I was, alone with the mother. We'd go to the hills, just the two of us, me, with the sickle in my hand, mother crying, one son disappeared, the other in the Worker's Battalion."[29]

There was not much incentive to play the *txistua*, but as if that was not enough, Aldekoa received a prohibition on playing issued by the town council. It came from Felipe Alberdi, nicknamed "The Executioner" by local people. It is not easy to understand with any degree of certainty why such a prohibition was made, because the celebrations of San Pedro's Day and Santa Isabel's Day had not stopped, in spite of the war or the pro-Franco invasion. On November 8, 1937, Hipólito Amezua, the *txistularia* of Berriz, made a formal, official request to be allowed to continue to carry out the duties required of his position.[30] Perhaps the ritual character of the dances and their association with religious festivities explains the lax attitude of the Falangists, Franco's supporters,

29. Ibid. The Worker's Battalion was composed of captured soldiers forced to do hard labor.

30. Fermin Barceló, "Aproximación a las fuentes para el estudio de la música popular en una comunidad local: Berriz," Ph.D. diss., University of Deusto, 1993, 52.

in the maintenance of these traditions. The *dantzari-dantza* of those days was full of contradictory ideas. The old flag of 1700 disappeared, and in its place, the authorities forced the dancers to dance with the Spanish national flag, a symbol of power, domination, and imperialism. Therefore, the prohibition to play the *txistua* in Aldekoa's case could have been influenced by a mix of political and personal reasons the Basque separatist character of the instrument itself and because Aldekoa was the son of Ambrosio Aldekoa, an exiled militant Basque nationalist. Whatever the reason, Aldekoa, like many others, was prohibited from playing.

After the arrival of the "nationals," the situation in Berriz became dramatic, with more than forty arrests and three residents shot, without counting those, like Ambrosio, who remained hidden or in exile until the revengeful fervor of these initial moments had passed. Felipe Alberdi, "The Executioner," commanded the power group of Franco supporters and was the man who governed the destiny of Berriz and its inhabitants and the person who made denunciations against those who, according to Aldekoa, had committed no crime other than that of being Basque nationalists.

> And our father, as a founder of the *batzokia* in Berriz . . . the only thing he did was to help people. Before and during the war, he helped anyone he could. He never hurt anyone, but that was sufficient to be punished, some more and others less. There was no reason to shoot the ones that were shot, either; they'd never done anything wrong in the town, nothing, nothing, but one had been the mayor and the other an autonomous guard working for the regional council . . . their only crime was being nationalist, and they weren't even affiliated to the PNV. They were Basque, and that was their only crime.[31]

Aldekoa the Soldier

Jorge, Alejandro's brother in the forced labor battalion, returned home in 1940, and his father came back from exile one year later, in 1941. Yet the family was still divided, because in 1938, as soon as he was eighteen, Alejandro Aldekoa was called up to fight in Franco's army. His first posting was to Catalonia, where he spent six months on the front line of the Ebro River. When the Ebro campaign ended and Catalonia had been conquered, he was sent to the Madrid front, specifically, to Toledo. He remembered that the offensive to conquer Madrid began on March 27, his birthday. The Moors (North African troops) marched in front, Aldekoa and the rest of his companions behind, covering the second line. They bombed the enemy positions. The Moors ran to take the Republican trenches, but found no resistance, no gunfire—the trenches had been abandoned. On March 28, the military offensive had ended, but since Franco did not give his last dispatch until April 1, the assault on Madrid was not considered officially finalized until that day, April 1, 1939, and with it came the end of the Spanish Civil War. Aldekoa spent his nineteenth birthday on the front. From there, he was sent to Donostia and

31. Alejandro Aldekoa, interview by the author, April 24, 1996.

after a while to the African front, where he spent twenty-seven months with the sappers, mainly digging trenches.

Figure 11. Aldekoa (sitting) in the Spanish Army (1938–44). Photo courtesy of the Aldekoa family.

In that mountain camp, he was under the command of a captain and a second lieutenant—both from Aragón—who had started the war on the Republican side and who had been sent to Africa by Franco's supporters as a punishment. The captain visited them once a week, going up to the camp on Friday and leaving on Sunday. Being a great music lover, he asked one day whether there was anyone there who could play a musical instrument from the military band. Because he had asked for an instrument from a band, Aldekoa did not answer. One of his companions from Catalonia raised his hand, saying he could play the clarinet, and another said that he could play the *bandurria* (a sort of flat-backed mandolin). Both were given two months leave on the condition that, on their return, they brought their instruments back with them. Aldekoa regretted not having said anything. The *bandurria* was not a band instrument, either. When they returned, the captain made them play for him on his weekly visits. A short time after, a friend of Aldekoa's from Bolibar (Bizkaia) who had also been sent to Africa took advantage of some of his leave and went to Aretxandieta, telling Ambrosio that his son had sent him to collect his *txistua.* This was in fact not true, but he managed to take the *txistua* to Aldekoa in Africa. So one Saturday night, to celebrate the return of Aldekoa's friend from Bolibar, the Basques in the camp organized a party at which Aldekoa's *txistua* played an important part. On the following day, Sunday morning, the lieutenant asked:

> "Who was walking around last night being a pest playing some strange instrument?"
>
> "Aldekoa."
>
> I was sent for.
>
> "Was it you?"
>
> "Yes sir."
>
> "When the captain comes, I'll send for you. He likes that kind of thing."
>
> And that was how, after supper, while the commanders were having coffee, I was sent for and told to play. I didn't have a tabor—if only I'd had a tabor. I was told to play outside, in the doorway.
>
> "What do you want me to play?"
>
> "Anything you want."
>
> So, I started to play some passages from an Aragonese *jota.* The captain began to shout from inside:
>
> "Who's that? Bring him in! Bring him in!"
>
> I was serious and they were both laughing. As soon as I went in, he took my *txistua* and asked:
>
> "What kind of instrument is this?"
>
> "A Basque regional instrument sir, it's called a *txistua.*"
>
> "Play it again."
>
> For my second piece, I played the variations of the "Hiru Damatxo." The captain took hold of the *txistua* again:
>
> "How is it possible to play like that with just three holes and make it seem as if there were two instruments playing at the same time?"
>
> He called to his assistant and said to him:
>
> "You can be on your way with your clarinet. I've got someone here who can play more than you with just three holes!"[32]

Aldekoa was discharged from the army after four and a half years of service on the front at the Ebro, near Madrid, and in Africa, with only a short stay in Donostia in between. Just when he thought that everything was over, he was called up again for another two long years to combat the guerrilla revolts that were taking place in some

32. Alejandro Aldekoa, interview by the author, March 1, 1991.

areas by the groups known as the *maquis* and to guarantee peace and stability for the new regime in the face of the fear of a new military revolt.[33] In total, Aldekoa served six and a half years in military service, from 1938 to 1944. He returned home at the age of twenty-four.

After the War

The pro-Franco occupation imposed a dictatorial regime that lasted for four decades. The Basque Country was especially punished for having supported the Republican side, as well as for its "treason" and its anti-Spanish politics.[34] The consequences were terrible: in addition to the thousands of Basques killed in the war, prisoners were sent to forced labor camps, others were recruited by the army to fight on the pro-Franco side, and finally, many thousands of Basques went into exile.[35] Industry in Bizkaia, which suffered little damage during the war, was set to work for Franco's army. During the first few years after the war, the economy was based strictly on the country's own resources, due mainly to the fact that self-sufficiency formed part of Franco's new national policy for Spain and also due to the outbreak of World War II, which stopped any commercial relations with the industrial powers of Europe. Self-sufficiency was imposed, not chosen. Faced with shortages, the government introduced rationing, causing a black market to appear, along with administrative corruption, deterioration in the standard of life, and hunger. Everyone who lived through those times remembers the shortages and the hunger they suffered in the 1940s.[36]

Back Home

When Aldekoa returned home, his brother Jorge was already working in Eibar as a gunsmith. The time had arrived for Alejandro to make a decision: his aspirations to follow a musical career had been crushed with the war, and now, at the age of twenty-five, in the postwar era, he could not sit around pondering his future for very long. He was given an opportunity to learn the trade of gunsmith alongside his brother, working for Ugartetxea, a company specializing in the manufacture of shotguns, and he took it. Until approximately the age of twenty-eight, Aldekoa worked in Eibar, learning his trade.

33. In France, during World War II, the *maquis* was the name given to the guerrilla movement from which the French Resistance grew. The same name was used to denominate the armed anti-Franco resistance force at work in Spain after 1939.

34. Bizkaia and Gipuzkoa were the only two provinces in the Spanish state officially declared "traitorous" by the new Franco regime.

35. Robert P. Clark points to around one hundred and fifty thousand Basques exiled to France during the period 1936–37. See *The Basques: The Franco Years and Beyond* (Reno: University of Nevada Press, 1979), 74.

36. Joseba Zulaika's study of his own village, Itziar (Gipuzkoa), after the Spanish Civil War also demonstrates this: "*Gosia* (hunger) is vivid in the villagers' memory of the postwar situation," a period marked by "a slow return to normal cultural models of behavior." See Joseba Zulaika, *Basque Violence: Metaphor and Sacrament* (Reno: University of Nevada Press, 1988), 34–35.

Then he went back to the *baserria* in 1948, to Aretxandieta, where his father set up a small workshop from which he was able to work for the same company, Ugartetxea. In 1960, he began to build his own home, and in 1961–62, he moved his workshop to the still-unfinished new house. In 1965, he and his wife moved to the new house, although they continued to keep the cattle in the old *baserria* until it was knocked down.

Aldekoa's Wife and Family

Alejandro Aldekoa's wife, María Arriaga Arriaga, was born on May 31, 1924, in Bolibar, in the Atxabal *baserria*.[37] Her mother was taken ill while still young, at the age of forty, but with medical care, she lived until she was eighty-seven. Her father died when he was sixty-six. María was the eldest of six brothers and sisters, three of whom died while still children. Being the eldest daughter, she had to take care of the housework from a very early age. The *baserria* was large, with a lot of land, but few people to work it. Because of the loads she used to bear and all the hard work she had to endure, María had a serious back ailment that in later life prevented her from standing upright.

There was a school in nearby Iruzubieta, but because María often had to work or look after her brothers, she could not attend on a regular basis. At school, the teacher spoke and taught in Spanish, which meant that the children, all of them Basque, could not understand most of the work. To make matters worse, whoever was heard speaking Euskara at school was fined. Nevertheless, despite everything, María learned to read and write in Spanish. Before the war, the catechism had been in Euskara. After the war, with Franco, it was in Spanish. Going to Mass, the catechism and the rosary were all obligatory.

Figure 12. María Arriaga in her garden (April 1996). Photo by the author.

---

37. "Aritzabal," better known as "Atxabal" and "Aitzoal," means "Wide Oak."

The square where dances were held in Bolibar was well known, attracting people from all around the area, from Markina to Mallabia. However, because of the pressure of certain priests, people stopped dancing in the public square and took to the new fashion of dancing in the lounge of the Aroma Bar. The men who attended the dance paid an entrance fee, which was used to pay the musician-accordionist, receiving in return a badge to distinguish those who had paid from those who had not. The women did not have to pay. As a rule, young women began to attend the dances at the age of eighteen. Aldekoa and María met in Iruzubieta, in the dance hall.[38]

María and her friends used to stay until the end of the dance, which always finished with the *trikitia* or *solture* (free or untied) dance such as a *jota* or *arin-arina*. It was at this point one evening when Aldekoa and his friends joined the girls on the dance floor. After the dance had finished, the boys accompanied the girls home. María's friends lived farther away, but they walked halfway together. So did Aldekoa. They walked along, chatting, until they reached Atxabal, the *baserria* where María lived. They said goodnight, and Aldekoa rode off on his bicycle. The following week, they saw each other again and walked home together after the dance. Little by little, their courtship began.

Figure 13. Aldekoa playing at a wedding with his two sons, Jon and Germán (ca. 1975). Photo courtesy of the Aldekoa family.

38. Interestingly, the Basque diaspora community in the United States continued this practice. Lisa Corcostegui observes that Basque boardinghouses there "were filled with music on many occasions and like the *erromerias* of the Basque Country were wonderful places to meet potential marriage partners." See "To the Beat of a Different Drum: Basque Dance and Identity in the Homeland and in the Diaspora," Ph.D. diss., University of Nevada, Reno, 2005, 125.

In 1951, Aldekoa Aldekoa and María Arriaga were married in Bolibar. During almost fifty years of marriage, María never grumbled at Aldekoa's musical obligations. As Aldekoa himself observed:

> My wife never told me not to go and play. She never complained. She left me alone to do my own thing. She respected my interest in music. In Iruzubieta, she never saw how we danced here in Berriz, but she watched me and never made me stay away. "If you have to go, then go," that's what she'd say. Sometimes I used to have to go to weddings or fiestas and get home late, after supper or at two or three o'clock in the morning, and even then, we'd never have a row. It's also true that I never came home offending anybody, always sober. But people gossip, and more than once, they've gone to María with chit-chat, but she's always known how to answer.[39]

They had three children, Germán, Amaia, and Jon. In those days, it was not usual for girls to play the *txistua*, so Amaia could not follow in her father's footsteps, but Germán and Jon learned to dance and play the *txistua* with their father. Both became good dancers and joined the San Lorenzo dance group. Jon, the youngest, won many *aurreskularia* (*aurresku* dancer) competitions as a child in the under-fifteen category. "He could dance the *aurreskua* and the *atzeskua* like the best," recalled Aldekoa. Both accompanied Aldekoa on the *atabala* or *txistua* on important occasions. Today, Jon works in the municipal library of Berriz, and Germán is an industrial engineer working for different companies, specializing in CAD-CAM software. When Aldekoa was ill or when two events coincided, Germán or Jon would substitute for their father, but as Aldekoa told me:

> I don't think either of my boys will take on my position when I'm gone. They fill in for me now because I'm still here, but when I'm gone—no way. They help me keep my position, my job, and they look after my dance group if I have to go perform somewhere, but if I'm here, they leave me to it. A few days ago, we played in a procession together, the three of us, but afterward, on the stage, they left me by myself, although they can play the same as me. The practice sessions, that's my job, too. I always go. If I can't, well then they'll go. But to take on the responsibility of the job, they wouldn't do it, even if they were offered double the money.[40]

However, a year after Aldekoa's death, Germán Aldekoa, his eldest son, did in fact take over the position of *txistularia* in Berriz.

---

39. Alejandro Aldekoa, interview by the author, April 24, 1996.

40. Alejandro Aldekoa, interview by the author, April 12, 1996.

Figure 14. Germán Aldekoa (*txistua*) and Jon Aldekoa (*atabala*), playing in Garai (ca. 1985). Photo courtesy of the Aldekoa family.

The Txistula *Calls Again*

Back home from the army and forgetting the prohibition on playing that he had received some years before, Aldekoa started to play the *txistua* again. In 1949, he was approached by the neighboring town hall of Zaldibar (Bizkaia) through Valentín Lasuen, who at that time was conductor of the Zaldibar Choral Society. The society developed many cultural activities, promoting the creation of dance and theater groups as well as a municipal music academy in which they wanted Aldekoa to teach. Until then, Cesáreo Ezenarro, the municipal *txistularia* of Abadiño, had also held the post of *txistularia* in Zaldibar. However, it seems that, given his technical limitations and his limited ability to read music, he did not meet the necessary requirements for the teaching post in the new municipal academy. The mayor offered the job to Aldekoa, who accepted on the condition that the town hall would come to some agreement with Cesáreo Ezenarro. It appears that the mayor did not keep his promise, and Ezenarro accused Aldekoa of stealing his job. Aldekoa, angered by the accusation, went to see the mayor. The town hall eventually reached a financial arrangement with Ezenarro, settling the issue once and for all. From 1949 to 1995, along with his job as a teacher, Aldekoa the *txistularia* was also in charge of entertainment during the fiestas of Zaldibar and its four parishes: San Martín, Santiago, Santa Marina, and San Lorenzo.

Figure 15. Aldekoa in front of his house (April 1996). Photo by the author.

Aldekoa worked on a piece-work basis making guns for Ugartetxea. This allowed him a certain flexibility in his work schedule, which in turn made it possible for him to help with the farmwork when it was necessary and in the house with his wife, María. It also gave him time to work as a taborer. Nevertheless, his work as a taborer interfered with his profession as a gunsmith. Many of his performances went on until late, often ending in nighttime parties in which the taborer could not refuse to participate. As a result, on the following day, he would be in no condition to work properly. Aldekoa remembered an especially wild celebration on the eve of San Martin's day in Zaldibar:

Every year, a group of young married couples organized a supper in which the presence of a *txistularia* was obligatory. After the supper, we went out partying until the early hours of the following morning—up and down the streets, from bar to bar, playing the pipe and tabor and singing. When I got home, the only thing I could think about was sleep. How was I going to work the next morning? Many times, because of playing the *txistua* here and there, instead of making money, I lost it. It wasn't always the case, but nearly always.[41]

Most people did not know that Aldekoa was a gunsmith. Throughout the County of Durango, in which he had often traveled and where he had become famous, people knew him as a *txistularia.* He was much sought after to play in the villages and towns, at dance competitions, and as a dance teacher. He was the only local musician who could perform competently in so many different kinds of situations. There was no other *txistularia* like Alejandro Aldekoa, and as he said: "People knew me as a *txistularia*, rather than a gunsmith. I could have been a gunsmith or the Bishop of Rome, for all they knew. But they knew I was a *txistularia.* Ah yes, they knew that!"[42]

Txistularia of Mañaria

At a certain moment, most likely after the 1966 fiestas in Mañaria, Serafín Amezua communicated to the mayor of Berriz his intention of leaving his post. Amezua was an old man, he did not have a car, and in the *albonada* (going from house to house), he ended up drinking more than he should.[43] As his replacement, he offered the mayor the name of one of his neighbors who was a good *txistularia* and dance master, Alejandro Aldekoa. The mayor offered the post to Aldekoa, who willingly accepted, knowing that Amezua had recommended him. The following year, on August 15, Andra Mari Day (the Day of the Ascension of our Lady), Aldekoa went to Mañaria early in the morning. To his surprise, he found Amezua was there with his pipe and tabor. On seeing him, Aldekoa hurried to the mayor:

"I thought you said Serafín . . . well he's over there with his pipe and tabor."

"He can't be."

"Well he is," I said. "It doesn't matter. I'll go to Mass, and then I'll go home as if nothing has happened. Let him play—he's been playing in the square for years. It's his place."

At that time, I had a motorcycle, a Lambretta, so I wouldn't have any trouble at all getting home.

"No sir!" answered the mayor. "You're not going home without playing. He said he wasn't coming anymore. I don't know what he's doing here! Last year he told us to look for somebody else. He was the one who gave me your name, and then he goes and turns up."

---

41 Alejandro Aldekoa, interview by the author, April 15, 1996.

42. Ibid.

43. Although Serafín Amezua was not considered a hard drinker or a drunk, most of the people from Berriz who knew him remember that he did have a small drinking problem. This was not unusual for a taborer, who had to play in so many parties and celebrations.

> The mayor managed to sort the problem out diplomatically.
>
> "Well, since you, Alejandro, have rehearsed with the dancers, you can play the '*Agur Jaunak*' after Mass" (Serafín did not know how to play the piece), "and then you play for the dances in the square. After lunch, let him play the *albonada*."
>
> "Alright, but you can tell Serafín. I don't want him to get angry with me!"[44]

The mayor spoke to Amezua, and they played as he had suggested: Aldekoa played first, and they went to lunch together, hand in hand. There was no trouble. They talked with one another about the old times, about Aldekoa's grandfather. After lunch, Amezua went to play the *albonada*. The problem had been resolved. The following year, there was no "misunderstanding." Amezua did not appear, and Aldekoa took over the post in Mañaria, a duty he would carry out for the following three decades.

That lunch with Amezua would be the first and last time Aldekoa stayed to eat at the fiestas in Mañaria. The town halls did not pay the taborers much for their performances, inviting them to lunch as a kind of "extra." Aldekoa preferred to go home for lunch, although it meant having to return to Mañaria in the afternoon to play the *albonada*:

> I've been going to Mañaria for thirty years, but I've always come home for my lunch. If you stay there, you end up drinking, and then it's worse. Right at the very beginning when I started, I told the mayor:
>
> "I'm not staying to lunch. I'll send you a bill for services rendered, with the amount we both agree upon for the chapels and all that, and that's it, finished."
>
> "That sounds fine by me," answered the mayor.[45]

A month after the fiestas, Aldekoa sent his bill to the town hall and received his payment. Apart from the main fiestas in Mañaria on August 15, he also had to carry out his duties in the four parishes there: Santa Cruz, San Juan, San Martín, and San Lorenzo.

"They didn't know any of the rules for the dances in Mañaria," said Aldekoa, referring to the state of anarchy in which he found the dance group on taking over from Amezua as *txistularia*. They didn't know how to dance the *erregelak*, and so they didn't know how to bring the girls out into the chain: "'Go on! Off you go! Get in the chain!' pushing them in any old how. That's not how it's done! You take the girl by the hand, not one, two, or three at a time and . . . in you go, like a flock of sheep! No! Two at a time and with a little more respect!"[46] They did not know when or how to move round the chain after the *aurreskua* and then again after the *atzeskua* in such a way that the leader of the dance would be at the head of the chain, always dancing

44. Alejandro Aldekoa, interview by the author, April 24, 1996.

45. Ibid.

46. Ibid.

in a counterclockwise direction: "I don't know how many times I had to do the chain with the group from Mañaria until it resembled something orderly! What a lot of work for a *txistularia*!"[47]

The lack of any form of choreography in Mañaria caused problems for Aldekoa with one of the dancers in the group who had also been performing the duties of dance master. In the dance number *makil jokoa* (game of sticks), for example, the "master" was showing them how to use the sticks in a way that even the dancers themselves did not see as correct. They consulted Aldekoa, who explained to them how it should be done, much to the anger of the local "master."

> There aren't any dancers there today—it's all over. There's nobody. . . . One of them got angry, then another one. . . . The youngsters don't want to dance anymore . . . they start when they're eleven or twelve and give it up when they're sixteen or seventeen. The same happened in Zaldibar. Twenty years ago, there were two dance groups there. Now there isn't even one![48]

More Posts

Aldekoa replaced Serafín Amezua in Garai in 1968, about the same time as in Mañaria, when Amezua, then an old man, began to give up his posts. The main obligations of the *txistularia* in Garai were the fiestas of Santiago and Santa Ana. He had to play during the procession and attend to the local dance group, a task he shared with Santos Oregi for many years. Santos Oregi was a dance enthusiast and held the position of dance master and director of the local dance group.

At the end of the 1960s, Aldekoa was also approached by the mayor of Durango, who offered him the post of conductor of the Municipal Band of *Txistulariak*. The obligations were many, playing every weekend and at the usual fiestas of the religious calendar, but the pay was low. Aldekoa turned down the offer. Along with his job as a performing musician, he taught the *txistua* to various generations of *txistulariak* throughout the County of Durango and the surrounding area for many years, in Berriz, Zaldibar, Apatamonasterio, and Durango.

In Berriz, Aldekoa took over the post of Serafín Amezua through a rather long and complicated process. In that transition, the role of the master of dances and ritual of the municipal *txistularia* was decisive, as we will see now in an examination of Aldekoa as dance master and the history of his dance group, San Lorenzo.

47. Ibid.

48. Ibid.

Figure 16. Aldekoa playing in Garai during the Santiago Day Procession (July 25, ca. 1970). Photo by permission of the journal *Dantzariak*.

Aldekoa the Dance Master

As noted, after the end of the Spanish Civil War in 1939, little by little, cultural activities were permitted by the new regime. As a result, Segundo Olaeta formed the Artibai dance group in Markina in 1944 and the Oldarra dance group in Biarritz in 1945. Thereafter, the Dindirri group was formed in Bilbao in 1946 and around 1950 the Gaztedi group was founded. From that time on, many dance groups were established all over the Basque Country, and as we will see, Berriz would be no exception. Aldekoa was the leader of the first permanent adult's dance group in Berriz, a group created under the influence of the large urban folklore choreographic groups that had become popular at this time, but with the peculiarity that in Berriz, ritual dances were still alive and dance remained an important part of the cultural life of the town, at least for the native Basque community. However, because of the nature and pace of changes taking place in Berriz, a town that had been transformed into an urban-industrial area in the short space of a few years, a crisis emerged in the traditional methods of transmitting dances. As a consequence, Aldekoa and his San Lorenzo group introduced a new system of teaching and recruitment of dancers—what might be termed the "group system."

Aldekoa's First Dance Group

It was on July 10, 1952, when, on their way back from the fiestas of San Cristobal, a group of young men from San Lorenzo began to comment on the disastrous performance of the local dancers at the San Pedro's Day celebrations that year and how they could learn to dance and do it as well, if not better. They already knew Aldekoa and therefore knew of his ability as a dancer and taborer, and so, without a moment to spare, they went to Aretxandieta that very same night to talk to the *txistularia.* They told him what they were thinking of doing after having witnessed the disaster of the dance group at the fiestas and asked him if he would be willing to teach them how to dance. They wanted to be ready to perform in the neighborhood in the festivities of San Lorenzo on August 10. Therefore they only had four weeks to learn the *dantzari-dantza* and the *soka dantza.*

They started to practice right away on the road behind the *baserria*—in those days, there was hardly any traffic. They started with the *banangoa,* and as Aldekoa later told me, it was not easy for some of them. Aldekoa persisted, and little by little, one by one, they began to learn the steps. Later, they would meet at the chapel of San Lorenzo. Next to the chapel there was a small square, but they preferred to practice on the road, where the paving was smoother and easier to dance on. They ran a cable with a light bulb from the *baserria* next to the chapel so that they could continue to practice after dark. The practice sessions were long and hard. The majority of the boys were complete beginners. They did not even know how to turn around in the *banangoa,* and they wanted to perform on San Lorenzo's Day! Nevertheless, they were twenty years old, fit, and they wanted to dance. When they made a mistake, the dance master would shout, "Again!" and they would repeat and repeat until they got it right. The effort left many of them bruised. The dancers in this group were Patxo Alberdi, Ismael Aldekoa (no relation to Alejandro), Jesús Arriaga, Iñaki Gorrotxategi, Iñaki Uribe, Javier Urkijo, Angel Zabala, and Sabino Zabala.

Figura 17. Aldekoa with his first group of dancers in 1952. Photo by Iñaki Uribe.

They paid for their own dance costumes and tools and asked the town hall for a flag. That year, the town hall had ordered a new flag, since the original one used by the dance group had disappeared in 1936. Instead, from 1936 to 1952, the dance group had used the Spanish flag, and so the town hall gave the new dance group from San Lorenzo this flag, instead of a new flag of Berriz. At the last moment, reluctant to dance with the Spanish flag, they decided to dance without any flag whatsoever. They bandaged the arm of the *banderari*, or standard-bearer (Patxo Alberdi), making out that he had had an accident and could not carry or wave the flag. Word of the San Lorenzo group's boldness in refusing to dance with the Spanish flag thereafter spread throughout the whole vicinity.

At that time, Serafín Amezua was the official *txistularia* of Berriz, and it was his duty to play in the parishes, including that of San Lorenzo. As a mark of respect toward the municipal *txistularia*, Aldekoa thought that Amezua should play for the group. Aldekoa and his group of dancers rehearsed once with Amezua and performed for the very first time on August 10, 1952. The official municipal *txistularia* was grateful for having been given the honor of playing for them. On the following Sunday, at what is known as the "repetition," the participation of the municipal *txistularia* was not obligatory, and so Aldekoa himself played for his group for the first time in public. The enthusiastic reception they received and the experience in general were such that they decided to continue dancing together. The San Lorenzo dance group, Aldekoa's group, had been formed.

Figure 18. Aldekoa playing for the first San Lorenzo dance group (1952). Photo by Iñaki Uribe.

San Lorenzo Begins to Dance in the San Pedro Fiestas

In the years that followed, Amezua was in charge of organizing the group of dancers for the patron saints' day celebrations of Berriz, San Pedro's on June 29 and Santa Isabel's on July 2, while Aldekoa maintained his own group, which danced in other places and on other occasions, mainly in the district of San Lorenzo. Amezua had somewhat neglected the training of new dancers and was faced with the difficulty of finding enough of them for the San Pedro and Santa Isabel celebrations. Around 1954–55, Amezua approached Aldekoa to ask him for two dancers he needed to complete the group for that year.

Aldekoa said there was no problem and told Amezua to come along to the rehearsal that day and ask the dancers himself.

That day at noon, after having a quick drink in Karteru's Bar, the two *txistulariak* made their way to the rehearsal at the chapel, where they found all the dancers waiting. Aldekoa recounted what happened:

> "All ready to rehearse then?"
>
> "Yes."
>
> They were all there, underneath the oak tree, some sitting, others standing.
>
> "Well, um, this year I need two dancers for the San Pedro fiestas, so two of you, one of them you, Laizkue [a pseudonym for Ismael, "Laizkue," taken from the name of his *baserria*], have to come with me," said Serafín, somewhat abruptly.
>
> "That's if I want to! Now that you need people, you come to us. . . . We were here before, as well you know!" answered Laizkue.
>
> That was true. We'd been functioning as an independent group for years. We never tried to dance in the town square . . . it had never occurred to us. Serafín had his group, and we traveled around. If there was a performance in Mungia or Fruiz [Frúniz, both in Bizkaia] we'd go, but we never tried to dance in the square . . . never![49]

The following days were filled with negotiations and arguments. Aldekoa acted as intermediary between Amezua, his dancers, and the mayor, who did not seem to understand the problem very well. The San Lorenzo group's first proposal was that each group should send four dancers. However, the problem then for Amezua concerned what he was going to do with the rest of his dancers. The San Lorenzo group's response was terse: "Send them home!"

The next proposal was to send two dancers to make up the eight Serafín needed for the *dantzari-dantza* and another two to dance the *aurreskua* and the *atzeskua.* The mayor thought that the addition of two extra dancers would increase the expenses for the lunch too much, because at that time, the dancers were paid with food. The dancers were told they would have to dance for free, and they agreed.

The day of the performance arrived, and Amezua played. When the *dantzari-dantza* ended, the other two dancers came out to dance the *soka dantza,* after which the deputy mayor, who was presiding over the act, ordered them to go eat with the rest of the group, contradicting the arrangements made by the mayor.

For several years, Aldekoa's dancers continued to reinforce Amezua's group, in spite of the reluctance of some of them and the tensions between the two groups. Each *txistularia* contributed four of the eight dancers to the celebrations. I do not know if Aldekoa received some kind of payment from the town hall or from Amezua himself as part of the agreement. The town hall paid the dancers 100 pesetas to dance at midday and in the afternoon on San Pedro's Day and on Santa Isabel's Day, a total of four dances plus

---

49. Ibid. "To dance in the square" refers to the main fiestas in Berriz, the San Pedro and Santa Isabel day celebrations.

the rehearsal on the eve of San Pedro's Day. On top of this, there was food and drink for lunch and supper following each performance: lunch and supper on June 29 and lunch and supper on July 2. According to Aldekoa, one year before he took charge of the San Pedro celebration, the dancers had taken excessive advantage of the free food, spirits, champagne, and cigars. The extra expense and the behavior of the dancers were such that Angela Olabegoia, the proprietor of the restaurant, vowed that she would never "feed the dancers again."[50]

> Angela was embarrassed when she presented the expenses for the celebrations that year. Worse was yet to come, when the head of the group and another two started to complain about the food. They said that the hake, which she had ordered specially from Ondarroa [a well-known fishing town in Bizkaia famed for the quality of its fish], was not hake at all, but cod. . . . She was very upset.[51]

The bad feelings surrounding these events resulted in the replacement of the dance master. The underlying reason for the change was the crisis in which the dance group found itself under the leadership of Amezua and Aldekoa's desire to take over. It seems that faced with the problem, the town hall decided to put the dance budget for the San Pedro festivities out for bids. Some comments seem to indicate that Aldekoa obtained the post thanks to his contacts in the town hall, but most agree on the fact that at that time, he had no rival as a musician and dance master. He had a solid dance group of his own, and his dancers had helped Amezua complete the official dance group for the past few years. In any case, Aldekoa, who was not interested in banquets or partying, presented a low budget quote, one much more austere than in previous years, with no lavish meals included. The town hall would have to pay only the agreed sum for the performance and nothing more, and the municipal authorities were pleased with his offer.

The data on this period of transition are confusing. During these years of crisis, the town hall even contracted the services of a nonlocal dance group for the San Pedro's Day fiesta.[52] In spite of numerous inquiries, we do not know what the exact, official procedure was of the transition between Amezua and Aldekoa, or perhaps it would be better to say between the Patxiku family and Aldekoa, since Hipólito Amezua stayed in active service as a *txistularia* until 1954, the year in which he died. We do not know the exact date of Hipólito's retirement, and in 1942, he still appeared on the personnel list of the local council. Given the critical situation of the official dance group in the mid-1950s and his own personal interest in the post, Aldekoa gradually began to make an impression in the town hall until he managed to get his own group to dance in the San Pedro

50. Angela Olabegoia was one of the women from Berriz who had danced in Madrid in the Recoletos *frontón* with Aldekoa when he was fourteen years old. They were very good friends. Jabier Urkijo, one of the dancers from the first San Lorenzo group, who later danced with Amezua, was at that lunch. According to him, the excesses were intended to annoy the town hall. The dancers were tired of what they considered the bad conditions arranged by the authorities.

51. Alejandro Aldekoa, interview by the author, April 23, 1996.

52. In 1965, the Andra Mari dance group from Galdakao danced in the fiesta of San Pedro in Berriz.

festivities in the 1960s. If this is so, Amezua acted as dance master for only a very short time in his career as municipal *txistularia* in Berriz. According to many, it was a period of decline, both in the choreography and in the general organization of the group. Although Amezua kept the post of *txistularia* and played in the parishes until his death in 1973, the intrusion of Aldekoa's group, seeing himself relegated to playing on the outskirts, and losing his place in the official fiestas must have made Serafín Amezua feel uncomfortable.[53] However, this was later all forgotten.

Dance: The Following Generations

When Aldekoa started up his first San Lorenzo group and was thinking about the future, he began to teach and to prepare a group of children. They were going to form his second group, the second generation, a pool of young dancers who would gradually take over from the original group. By the end of the 1950s, the generational change had been completed. The group was made up of those born around 1944,[54] and many of them remained active for a long time, some dancing with the San Lorenzo group for twenty-five years, such as Jose Luis Zabala, Rikardo Albizuri, and Valentín Gorostiza. With this second group, Aldekoa participated in numerous festivals throughout the whole of the Basque Country. Later, Aldekoa stopped working with his second group and began to select young people from the dance group at the *ikastola* (a school where instruction is carried out entirely in Euskara) in Berriz, preparing them, little by little, to take over from the second generation. With this, his last group, Aldekoa reached his peak insofar as choreography was concerned. As he told me: "The first group was good, the second was better, but the third is the best."

In his relationship with his dancers, not everything was easy, although he never had any serious problems. He would complain about their lack of availability to rehearse or the little enthusiasm or interest that some showed, but not much else:

> I remember one occasion when we were asked to take part in the fiestas in Mallabia. They were going to pay us some 50,000 pesetas. Money isn't everything, but you have to get paid. We didn't have much money in the bank, but once in a while, we'd all get together and have a meal and spend it. That is, all the money we were paid went into the kitty, whether you danced or not—the money was for everybody. Well, when I asked who was willing to go to Mallabia, a couple of the dancers had doubts:
>
> "If somebody else can go, all the better," one said.

---

53. Roberto Maiztegi told me that when Iremiñe was founded in 1969, they asked Amezua to play a couple of times, because Valentín Lasuen, their *txistularia*, was sick. Amezua understood that it was a good chance to retake the post of dance master in the official fiestas, because he was still the official taborer, and Iremiñe could be his group, the alternative to Aldekoa's. But the members of Iremiñe did not want to get into more trouble, especially with Aldekoa, and they turned down Amezua's proposal.

54. "They'll be all about fifty-two now," Alejandro told me when I interviewed him in 1996. He was not wrong. One of the dancers, Roberto Maiztegi, was born in 1944.

"With that attitude, there won't even be four of us. We have to know for sure if you can come or not," said Alejandro.

"I don't think I can," another one said.

That was a month before the performance. At the next rehearsal, Alejandro proposed:

"The ones that go will get paid, cash in hand. Instead of putting the money in the kitty, we'll share it out among us all."

Those who had said no before suddenly changed their minds and said yes. So you see, I've had to play those kinds of tricks to keep out trouble.[55]

Other than that, Aldekoa was pleased with his dancers:

> With the ones I have now, I've never had any problems. They're good kids, nice people. They consider me as a second father. We've always got on well, all of us, without exception. Karmelo, the flag bearer, and his brother-in-law are the best dancers, exceptional people. . . . They don't drink either, none of them. Smoking, one of them smokes, but not the others. No liquor, a little wine once in a while. One of them always drinks milk, even when we rehearse after supper, only milk. In the evenings, they practice some kind of sport, running or cycling in the mountains or something; they're always doing some kind of sport. They're healthy people, and that shows. They don't have any breathing problems. The *dantzari-dantza* is hard exercise.[56]

Iremiñe

The creation of the Iremiñe group from within the ranks of Aldekoa's San Lorenzo group had enormous repercussions on dance in Berriz. In fact, this division is the most important key to understanding the contemporary situation of dance in the locality, as well as to understanding the personal and social interests and pressures that interacted during a very important part of Aldekoa's life in the late twentieth century. It is for this reason, and also because it was Alejandro's wish,[57] that here I give a detailed chronicle of the events leading to the division and the establishment of Iremiñe. I will thereafter contrast Alejandro's detailed version with that of Roberto Maiztegi, another of the main protagonists in this story.

According to Aldekoa, Roberto Maiztegi, a member of his second dance group ("the second generation," as he termed it), went to see him to tell him about a *soka dantza* competition that had been organized in Iurreta, a nearby town in Bizkaia. Each participating couple was to be given 2,000 pesetas, and he had thought of entering with Otsue as his

55. Alejandro Aldekoa, interview by the author, April 9, 1996.

56. Ibid.

57. What to many observers may appear as a simple misunderstanding or personal dispute between two neighbors, was, especially for Aldekoa, a problem of vital importance. "I could stop talking about a lot of things, and that's what I've done, but not before clearing up the matter of Iremiñe."

partner.[58] He wanted to know in what order and how they should bring the girls out into the ring. Aldekoa told them that before, when they brought the girls out for the *aurreskularia* and the *atzeskularia*, they always danced the *banango zaharra* (the old *banangoa*), and that if they wanted, he was willing to teach them the dance. They refused to learn the *banango zaharra*. Thereafter, Aldekoa asked his son Germán and Rikardo Albizuri if they wanted to participate in order to raise 2,000 pesetas for the local *ikastola*. They accepted his proposal to take part in the competition and to learn the *banango zaharra* dance for that occasion.

> They came and learned the *banango zaharra*. For those who know how to dance the *dantzari-dantza*, it's easy. You only have to remember the jump and do the *grabilleta* [a dance step] with the left leg. The day of the competition arrived, and we went. I played for both couples, and the rest of the San Lorenzo group accompanied them all to complete the *soka* [rope or chain], because Roberto didn't have a group of his own and there wasn't another group in Berriz. They danced very well, especially Otsue [Rafael Albizuri], and they did the *soka dantza* just as I told them, bringing the girls out first, one by one and then two by two, going round the rope when they should, with the girls on the outside . . . they did it all well. They included all the details, just as we do in Berriz. However, I played the normal *banango* for them when they brought the girls out. The others, they did the *banango zaharra*, and they did it well. That's what happened. First prize went to Roberto and Otsue, second, those from Iurreta, and third, my group. They didn't give much importance to the *banango zaharra*.[59]

Maiztegi's version of the story is different, however. Two couples, two *sokak*, representing the San Lorenzo dance group, entered the competition in Iurreta: On the one hand, Otsue and Maiztegi, and on the other, Ricardo Albizuri and Jose Luis Zabala. They rehearsed together without any problem. When they arrived there, the other couple (Albizuri and Zabala) danced a *kontrapas*. This was a dance that, in the past, had been danced by a certain Pedro Juan Gaztelurrutia in which the dancers enact a kind of challenge between themselves. Throughout the whole interview, I asked Maiztegi about the *banango zaharra*, but he denied the story and insisted on the *kontrapas*. What had offended Maiztegi, what he did not think was right, was the fact that two couples from the same group were participating in the competition and that the others had presented that item of dance without saying anything beforehand. In Maiztegi's words, "They did it behind our backs, a betrayal. We lost our tempers, and it was all over. We won the prize for best *aurreskularia*, best *atzeskularia*, and best *soka*, which only added more fat to the fire: that we'd robbed them of the prize and all that."[60]

---

58. Otsue means "The Wolf" and was Rafael Albizuri's nickname. According to Aldekoa, he was one of the best dancers ever in Berriz.

59. Alejandro Aldekoa, interview by the author, April 12, 1996.

60. Roberto Maiztegi, interview by the author, March 5, 1998.

After what had happened, the personal relationship between the two turned sour. According to Aldekoa's side of the story, out of hate or spite, Maiztegi started to form another dance group, subsequently named Iremiñe. And from the moment Iremiñe appeared in 1969 on, there was constant friction and tension between the two groups, due increasingly to the aspirations of the Iremiñe members to dance in the Berriz town square on San Pedro's and Santa Isabel's days. In other words, the group claimed its right, as dancers and members of the community of Berriz, to dance in the most important festive celebrations of the town. Only two or three years after the group had been formed, it publicly demanded this right and continued to do so year after year since then. Iremiñe argued that traditionally things had been different. Before, it had been the job of the *txistularia* to select the dancers from among all the inhabitants of Berriz, and there had been no lack of arguments, negotiations, or town hall meetings.

> Before as well, although you don't know, when Patxo, Sabino, and company were dancing in San Lorenzo, and they'll all be about sixty-five years old now, a lot older than you, well, I had my group and Serafín had his. We never even tried to dance in the square on San Pedro's Day. Serafín was the official *txistularia*, and his group had preference. I never even tried to do it. When Serafín couldn't keep up the group, the town and the town hall called me, and that's how I started playing and dancing on San Pedro's Day. Here's the document conceding me the post.[61]

The then mayor, not wanting to change the situation laid out in the document naming Aldekoa as official town *txistularia*, left things as they were: that is, the San Lorenzo dance group would continue to dance on San Pedro's Day. That is how things remained. However, that year, while Aldekoa's group danced in the square, Iremiñe, as a point of protest, did the same, a little farther up the street, in front of a bar. The situation was extremely tense. The matter at hand was the most deeply rooted traditional festive celebration in the town. Everybody wanted to take part, everybody was right, and everybody defended tradition. Claims to the town hall were continuous from that point on, dividing even more the supporters of both sides. Many things had changed since the times when the taborer could select the dancers:

> What do you want me to do? Send the boys who've been dancing with me for ten, eleven, twelve years home and put some others in their place? Is that what you want? Well I won't do it, I can't do it! They'll carry on dancing with me as long as they want to. When they leave, that's it, it'll all be over; but until that day, I'm not going to kick anyone out and put somebody you want in, and that's that![62]

---

61. Alejandro Aldekoa, interview by author, April 12, 1996. At the meeting held on June 16, 1975, the town hall, in full session, agreed to give the post of *txistularia* for life to Alejandro Aldekoa Aranburu and so passed the selection of the dancers into his hands.

62. Alejandro Aldekoa, interview by the author, April 12, 1996.

In Berriz, Alejandro Aldekoa had introduced the whole dance group system, with its group dynamics, its internal leadership relations, its cohesion and loyalty, and its collective identity within the local community and the rest of the groups. It was a new way to learn and to practice dance, a new way to establish who was to represent the community in the festive celebrations and rituals.

Aldekoa the *Txistularia*

Although Alejandro Aldekoa's work as dance master was certainly the most important function of the municipal *txistularia* in Berriz, there were other contexts where the *txistularia* played an important role, such as *albonadak* (goings from house to house), weddings, dance competitions, *erromeriak* (open-air dances), or as conductor of big concerts of *txistulariak*. Some of these events were among the duties of the municipal *txistularia* and clearly defined in the written regulations of the town council. Others were engagements that Aldekoa did on his own initiative, freelance. But in all of them, he was preceded by his prestige as *txistularia* of Zaldibar, Mañaria, Garai, and above all, Berriz. Although he was not acting officially as municipal *txistularia* of Berriz, for the people, the audience, and the organization of the event, he was "Alejandro Aldekoa, the *txistularia* of Berriz." In many ways, one might say that he used the reputation of his post to get extra work. Sometimes it was the town council of Berriz or one of the councilmembers who called Aldekoa to play in certain events that might be classified as semiofficial. All this makes it difficult to define the limits of his duties as municipal *txistularia* and his freelance work.

The Official Taborer in Berriz

The relevance of the post of taborer in Berriz is shown in the following document, where the pipe and tabor player is named as one of the eleven municipal employees of the town council of Berriz in the 1920s, a municipality with 2,048 inhabitants at that time:

> *Regulations for Municipal Civil Servants in the Town Council of Verriz* [sic].
>
> —*General Regulations*—
>
> Art. 1: The town council of Verriz [*sic*] will pay from its funds, the hereafter mentioned professional and administrative employees named in accordance with the current regulations, and for good service rendered.
>
> Art. 2: A secretary, an accountant for the municipal corn exchange, an accountant for the slaughterhouse, a deposit taker, bailiff, park ranger, gravedigger, taborer [*tamborilero* in the Spanish original], doctor, pharmacist, and veterinarian being the different employees who lend their services to this municipality.
>
> Art. 3: The prime duty of all the aforementioned posts is to treat the neighbors and inhabitants of this municipality with all due respect and consideration, being courteous at all times even when, for reasons pertaining to the post, they must approach the inhabitants in order to read them their rights, issue them with a warning or apprehend them for an offence.

—*The Taborer*—

Art. 70: For greater entertainment in the fiestas and *erromeriak* of the locality, a taborer will be paid from the municipal funds: being understood beforehand, that any further expense for the payment of an accompanying drummer will be paid for from the salary assigned to the aforementioned taborer.

Art. 71: He will have the duty to entertain at all the fiestas and *erromeriak* traditionally celebrated in the locality, which will be specified by the town council on his appointment.

Art. 72: It will also be his duty to direct and make enjoyable the *ezpata-dantza* in the fiestas for the celebration of San Pedro's Day: patron saint of this town council.

Art. 73: He will be punctual on his arrival at all the *erromeriak* and fiestas assigned to him.

Art. 74: He will report his absences in advance to the town council, taking care to find a substitute in charge of fulfilling his obligations.[63]

By the end of the 1970s, Aldekoa was the undisputed leader of the *txistulariak* in both Berriz and the County of Durango as a whole. He had already been in charge of the dance group for the fiestas in Berriz for a number of years, when, after Amezua's death in 1973, he took over the rest of the functions and obligations of the municipal *txistularia* in Berriz. He was not, however, appointed as a civil servant. The last taborer to hold civil servant status in the town council of Berriz was Hipólito Amezua. When his son, Serafín, reached the age of retirement and went to claim his pension, he discovered that he was not included on the list of municipal civil-service staff and had to continue playing as long as he could.

As well as organizing and maintaining the dance group for the San Pedro's Day celebrations, the municipal *txistularia* of Berriz also had to play in the fiestas of the nine chapels in the municipality:

January 17: the fiesta of San Antonio Abad in the parish of Olakueta.

Forty days after Easter Sunday: the fiesta for the Ascension of our Lord in the parish of Urdaia.

June 24: San Juan Bautista in the parish of Murgoitio.

The first Sunday following June 29 (San Pedro's Day) in Ereña. Because this fiesta coincided with the fiestas in the parish of Berriz, it would be postponed until the following Sunday. Then it was popularly known as San Pedro Txiki (Little Saint Peter).

July 10: San Cristobal of Gorliz.

August 10: San Lorenzo in the parish of Mendibil.

August 15: The Ascension of our Lady in the parish of Andikona.

September 29: San Miguel in the parish of Okango.

October 14: San Fausto in the parish of Eitua.

---

63. Fermin Barceló, *Ajelandro Aldekoa Berrizko txistulari zahar-berria* (Berriz: Berrizko Udala, 1993), 30–31. Even though the document is not dated, Barceló is certain that it is from 1924 or 1925. See Barceló, "Aproximación a las fuentes para el estudio de la música popular en una comunidad local: Berriz." Ph.D. diss., University of Deusto, 1993, 33.

This was the festive calendar of the main performances of the *txistularia* of the town council of Berriz. In the past, the parish fiestas and the *erromeriak* were famous, attracting crowds of people, but later, with industrialization and modernization, customs and the festive calendar changed. Indeed, today, many of the previously important fiestas are no longer celebrated. The introduction of a new, rational, modern, European calendar moved all festivities to the Sunday immediately following the actual feast or saint's day.

> Before, we used to dance after Mass, but that custom has disappeared now. Whatever the case, you still have to be there, even if only to play the "Agur Jaunak" [a popular hymn sung as a greeting] during Mass. The "Agur Jaunak" was never played before; Serafín didn't know how to play it. After Mass, you play a few *fandangoak* in the square, and even if the people don't dance, the *txistularia* has still got to fulfill his duty.[64]

In 1996, at the age of seventy-six, Aldekoa confessed that the effort of attending all the celebrations was not worth the money he was paid by the town hall:

> I've already told the lads in the group: "I'm still doing all this for you. If you tell me you've had enough or that you're tired and you want to give it up, we'll send a letter to the town hall requesting termination of employment, and it's all over and done with. They can find another *txistularia*. I'll give it all up." I'm still here for the lads, for their enthusiasm, and because they're damn good dancers! I feel sorry for them.[65]

Albonadak

Curiously, Aldekoa distinguished the *alborada* from the *albonada*. The *alborada* was "music to be played at dawn, in the morning," whereas the *albonada* was one of the traditional obligations of the *txistularia*, when the mayor sent his taborer to play for the inhabitants of the town as a form of greeting on festive days. I do not know the reason for such a distinction and have not found any document or reference to the term *albonada*. Normally, what Aldekoa referred to as *albonada* was given the name *alborada*, because it was usually in the morning when the taborer honored the inhabitants with his musical recital.

Aldekoa stopped playing the *albonadak* in Berriz, a custom that Amezua had maintained.

> The *txistularia* before me played the *albonadak* in all the chapels and on all the festive days, San Antonio's Day [Saint Anthony Abad, January 17] in Olakueta, Santiago's Day up there. Serafín used to come to our house on San Lorenzo's day, the festive day in our neighborhood. That day, all our family and friends would get together at our house. As a boy, I remember the *txistularia* coming and my father and my aunt going out to dance in the street. In those days, the *albonada* was played in nearly all the houses. Nobody went without a dance, a *fandango,* or an *arin-arina*, especially if there was a dancer in the family,

---

64. Alejandro Aldekoa, interview by the author, April 12, 1996.

65. Ibid.

> like ours, or a woman in the house who liked to have a dance without needing a partner. Then, when the working calendar was changed, if the festive day fell on a working day, it was moved to the following Sunday. The *txistularia* didn't come then—he only played on the actual festive day, the saint's day. Then, as the years went by, Serafín stopped coming altogether, and I didn't take over the *albonadak* in Berriz. In Zaldibar, however, I played them up until two years ago [1994]. Last year I didn't go. That's it, it's over. Alejandro's finished and the *albonada*'s finished. It's a shame to lose old customs.[66]

Aldekoa had many anecdotes to tell about his years playing the *albonadak*. On one occasion, as he was approaching one *baserria*, he heard the son of the house say, "Here comes a beggar," so he walked straight past and did not play for them. Later, the young boy apologized for what he had said. On another occasion, in the Santamañe neighborhood, the wife of a family of Spanish immigrants who had come to live in an abandoned *baserria* saw how her neighbors had given something to Aldekoa. The *txistularia*, fulfilling his obligation, went to the woman's house to play for her. The woman was in mourning. She came out to listen, and when he had finished, the following exchange took place:

> "Good day madam! See you next time."
>
> "What? Don't you charge anything?" She had the money ready in her hand.
>
> "No, I have no obligation to charge, only to play."
>
> "Really? Why do you do it then?"
>
> "Because that's the way it is . . . the town hall, the hierarchy sends the *txistularia* to greet the inhabitants at their doors on festive days. I go from door to door, greeting everybody."
>
> "Is that so? What a lovely custom!"
>
> She offered me seven pesetas.
>
> "No, no thank you."
>
> "Yes, here you are."
>
> I liked what that woman did. She asked me and I explained. Not like in the other *baserria*, where they took me for a beggar. The seven pesetas that woman gave me meant more to me than the money from quite a lot of other people.[67]

Weddings

For centuries, marriage ceremonies in the Basque Country have always required the presence of a taborer and his music: "in the town where there lived a taborer, no wedding was celebrated without him having been called to play."[68] Aldekoa played at a great many weddings throughout the County of Durango. After his official obligations as municipal *txistularia*, weddings were probably his most frequent performances. Nowadays, the wedding ritual has changed, accommodating customs from outside the area, some of which

---

66. Alejandro Aldekoa, interview by the author, April 17, 1996.

67. Ibid.

68. Juan Ignacio de Iztueta, *Gipuzkoako dantza gogoangarrien kondaira edo historia* (1824; Donostia: Euskal Editoreen Elkartea, 1990), 69.

are not well accepted by the native population, such as throwing rice on the newlyweds as they leave the church, the bride and bridegroom opening the dance, and the auctioning of the bride's underwear or the groom's tie.

As a rule, Aldekoa would start by playing a piece of music as the couple entered the church, usually a *zortzikoa*, a well-known type of Basque melody and rhythm pattern usually transcribed in 5/8 (not be confused with the *zortzinangoa*, the second dance of the *dantzari-dantza* dance suite).[69] During the ceremony, after the offertory, he would play the "Agur Jaunak." He would then wait at the door for the ceremony to end, the register to be signed, and the taking of photographs to finish and would play again as the couple left the church. His playing signaled to those waiting outside the moment when they could throw rice, flowers, or whatever—that is, when the bride and groom were on their way.

As the bride and groom left the church, he would play another *zortzikoa*, if possible, different from the one at the beginning. He would continue playing for quite some time, until everyone had greeted each other and had their photographs taken. The wedding ceremony ended here, but Aldekoa would frequently be invited to the banquet, where he would continue playing between and after each course. That said, Aldekoa told me that he preferred to go home for his lunch:

> Whether you went to the lunch or not, they paid you the same, so I preferred to go home. If you stay for the banquet, you have to play afterward. The church doesn't take up much time. When the wedding was that of somebody you knew, from the neighborhood or a friend, well then I didn't mind staying. However, when it's a group from Bilbao, they take you to the restaurant, and they say, "Sit here," and you don't know anybody, it's not a very good atmosphere. I've never had any trouble making conversation, but it's not the same. You never know what kind of music to play. They could ask you to play the Spanish national anthem, and you wouldn't know where to start.[70]

There always has been great controversy about playing the Spanish national anthem on the *txistua.* Because they were not allowed to show their ideological reasons to avoid playing the piece, one of the reasons more frequently argued by the *txistulariak* was that there is not an issued score of the Spanish national anthem for *txistua.* Although this is not true, it seems that this excuse worked most of the time and was used by Aldekoa himself.

The question of whether the people felt Basque or Spanish was one of the problems Aldekoa had to face when selecting his repertoire for a wedding. At present, Basque society is a complex mixture of people with different feelings and ideas about the Basque political problem and with different ways of feeling and living their "Basqueness." At a wedding, Aldekoa might encounter different types of people, from Basque indigenous

69. As an example of the *zortzikoak* that he played on such occasions, Aldekoa cited the following: "Mendi bazter," by Isidro Ansorena, published in *Txistulari* 7 (1934): 400; and "Semiaren etorrera," by León Laspiur, published in *Txistulari* 59, no. 3 (1969): 1576.

70. Alejandro Aldekoa, interview by the author, April 23, 1996.

people who had forgotten their language, to right-wing pro-Spanish people in politics who requested the *txistularia* because it was a tradition and it made for a nice picture, to Castilian-speaking immigrants now integrated in Basque culture who spoke Basque and who were even Basque nationalist sympathizers.

As soon as he saw they were Basque, he would relax and start playing whatever they asked for, or he would suggest well-known Basque songs or play whatever came into his head at the time. When he did not know what kind of people they were, he would play a *zortzikoa*, a *fandangoa*, or a *kontrapasa* by Santos Intxausti,[71] a virtuoso piece for his public to appreciate while he waited for them to start singing so he could find out what they liked. When he did not know what they were singing, he would stop playing and wait for the next song.

Aldekoa said that during the 1970s, orchestras came into fashion for the dances at weddings.[72] The *txistularia* would play at the table, and the orchestra after the meal. At some weddings, where guests preferred to dance without holding their partners, the orchestra would give way to the *txistularia*, who would play a *fandangoa* and *arin-arina*, but generally, the *txistularia*'s work was done once the orchestra started to play. Another custom that became popular was for the wedding march or hymn to be played while the bride and groom cut the cake. Although this was normally done by the orchestra, Aldekoa did do this at some weddings, especially where the bride and groom and the guests were Basque. The pieces of music he would play were "Gora Euzkadi," "Eusko Gudariak," and more frequently, "Gernikako Arbola."[73]

Dance Competitions

Alejandro Aldekoa played for many dance competitions, especially in Berriz, where he was the musician for the *Jota* Dancing Championship of Bizkaia held in the town every year between 1954 and 1974. The promoter of these *jota* competitions in Berriz and many other cultural activities was Eduardo Urzelai. In January 1940, during the festivities of San Antonio Abad in the parish of Olakueta, the sixteen-year-old Urzelai had organized the first competition of *jota* dancing in Berriz. Despite the problems he had with the Guardia Civil, the Spanish Civil Guard, that first year, he continued organizing the dance competition year after year. Perhaps because the *jota* is a dance known in other regions of Spain and not identified with excessive pro-Basqueness, the authorities allowed the event

---

71. Santos Intxausti composed five *kontrapasak* for virtuosos. They are well-known pieces in the *txistularia* repertoire. Edited in different publications, they can be found together in Jose Inazio Ansorena Miner, *Txistu Ikaskizunak* (Donostia: Euskadiko Kutxa, 1978), 87–92.

72. These orchestras consisted of two or three (and even sometimes four) musicians. Mainly, they played the accordion (although more recently other keyboard instruments were introduced) and a drum set by the name of *jazbana* (derived from the English term "jazz band"). Sometimes they were accompanied by a wind instrument (frequently a saxophone or a clarinet) and sometimes by a guitar or a double bass.

73. All three themes can be considered patriotic Basque hymns.

to be celebrated. In 1954, Urzelai decided to reconvert the competition into the official championship of Bizkaia.

> Competitions had been held before, in different places, but it was Eduardo Urzelai who had the idea of organizing a Basque *jota* championship, some thirty years ago now. He consulted the Basque Dance Federation, and they decided that because it was going to be a Basque *jota* competition, they'd have to change the accordion for the pipe and tabor. That's how they came to me, and I told them I'd be willing to play. I could play well in those days. I was only thirty or forty years old then.[74]

Aldekoa, like the good *txistularia* and dance master that he was, was accustomed to following the dancers. He is remembered by all of them as the best *txistularia* ever to have played for them. If a dancer made a mistake, Aldekoa followed him, covering up the error to allow the dancer to shine in front of the public. So as to avoid any problems and so that all participants could dance to the same music, Aldekoa and Eduardo Urzelai established a new way of playing for competitions: Aldekoa would play with his back to the dancers, so that there could be no doubt about his impartiality. In those marathon competitions, Aldekoa would sometimes have to play the same piece of music twenty-two times. To avoid confusion, he played from a score. "In a competition, you can't change anything in the slightest. You have to play the same for everyone—exactly the same, and if at all possible, with the same rhythm and at the same speed, not faster, not slower, exactly the same. I don't think I ever got it wrong: when I get a rhythm on the tabor, I keep it up to the end."[75]

He did, however, have a problem on one occasion when the number of bars in a piece of music he played did not fit with the dance and some of the participants complained. Later, thanks to an error found in the score, Aldekoa was freed from any blame. When reading music, he respected the score. The score was paramount.

Erromeriak

The *erromeria* is a fiesta celebrated around the chapel on a saint's day. Its initial religious and devout character, however, later gave way to a lively, popular outdoor party, with picnics, teas, games, and dancing. To speak of dance in the Basque Country is to speak of the pipe and tabor and, to a lesser extent, the *dultzaina* (shawm) and the *alboka* (hornpipe). This was the case at least until the end of the nineteenth century, when the accordion appeared and became increasingly popular. Dance was such an important aspect of the *erromeria* that today, for many people, the term is synonymous with open-air dance.

When Aldekoa was young, the accordion was already fashionable and present in nearly all the dancing arenas, but the *txistua* still had an important role in the *erromeria* and in fiestas in general. The taborer would play his music for the people, and they

74. Alejandro Aldekoa, interview by the author, April 19, 1996.

75. Ibid.

would dance to it. Everyone appreciated and enjoyed dancing to the sound of the pipe and tabor. The *txistularia* played the *solture* or *trikitia*, and especially the *jota*, *arin-arina*, and *biribilketa*. He also played the *aurreskua*, in great demand among young people. The taborer would start to play his music early, at about five or six o'clock in the evening, giving way to the accordion after dusk: "The *txistua* has never been a night instrument, a partying instrument as they call them. The *txistularia* always leaves at the appropriate time, a couple of notes after dark and then home"[76]

One of the priests in Berriz, originally from Gautegiz Arteaga (Gautéguiz de Arteaga) on the right-hand bank of the Gernika estuary in Bizkaia, hired the services of Aldekoa for the fiestas of San Antolín (September 2). The fiestas were to be celebrated in a neighborhood on the slopes of Mount Ereño, from where a view of the whole town could be obtained. The fiestas were to last for three days, and so Aldekoa stayed at the priest's house. On the eve of the fiestas, he played a *pasakallea* (*passacaglia* in Italian), and the following morning, another *pasakallea* through the entire town and then to Mass with his *txistua*. After Mass, before lunch, he played for the people to dance in a small square at the side of the chapel. That day, there were also a couple of *dultzaina* players, with whom Aldekoa took turns at playing.

> I don't know who started playing first, but from twelve o'clock, when Mass was over, to two o'clock we played nonstop, the three of us. The people danced all the time. When we thought that that was it, that was enough, somebody always shouted, "Hey, play a *fandangoa*! We want to dance a *fandangoa*!" There were only us three musicians, but there were many dancers. They took it in turns to dance, and we played nonstop. At lunchtime, the whole place was filled with cases [packed lunches people would take to eat outside, especially in the *erromeriak*, often old shoe boxes, tied up with string], the town hall looked after my case, and I was their guest. We had lunch, then a coffee and a drink—everyone was happy. The fiesta and the dance continued at the lunch table. In the evening, at about six or seven o'clock, we had supper and then went down to the town for another *pasakallea*, all of us together, forming a long chain. On the way down, we stopped at two or three bars for a few wines from the *porrón* [a vessel with a long thin spout, used for drinking wine] and the *bota* [a leather wine bottle]. We got wine all down our shirts . . . a bit like the San Fermines in Pamplona [the famous bull-running fiestas]. There was a good atmosphere, a very good one. Happiness. They don't have fiestas like that anymore.[77]

Aldekoa, Soloist and Conductor

When the Association of *Txistulariak* of the Basque Country was permitted to resume activities in 1955, thanks to the initiative of Juan Lasuen and the unconditional support of a group of *txistua* enthusiasts, the first concert by *txistulariak* from the County of Durango was held on March 19, 1956 in Abadiño. The concert's main objective was to spread and

76. Alejandro Aldekoa, interview by the author, April 15, 1996.

77. Alejandro Aldekoa, interview by the author, April 17, 1996.

promote the instrument among the younger generations in an attempt to attract as many new students as possible—the future *txistulariak* of the area. A decision was also made to celebrate the Durangaldeko Txistu Eguna (Day of the *Txistua* in the County of Durango) every year on March 19, San José's Day. With the exception of the period from 1972 to 1978, when the celebration was not authorized, the event has been held annually to this day.

Figure 19. The first Day of the *Txistua* in the County of Durango in 1956. Photo by Juan Antonio Aroma.

For many years, Juan Lasuen was the event's promoter and organizer, in charge of relations with the town hall and of negotiating with the authorities for the permits needed for the events. Lausen was a great lover of the *txistua* and of Basque culture in general, but his ability to play the instrument was limited. He would play only in the *pasakallea*, but thanks to him, the events were held even through those politically difficult years. An institution, acting as guarantor, was necessary at the time for obtaining permits and completing other bureaucratic formalities. The Asociación Cultural Geredíaga, the Geredíaga Cultural Association, legally sponsored the first concerts. Permission had to be asked from the town hall in the location where the event was to take place, then from the Ministry of Information and Tourism, and finally, from the police. For permission to be granted, all scores, titles, and lyrics (if there were any) had to be presented. Even so, permission was nearly always granted at the very last minute. The town hall hosting the event was asked to help with the expenses of the meal offered to the *txistulariak* taking part. Gradually, Juan Antonio Aroma and Antón Alberdi, both *txistulariak* from Durango, began to take over from Juan Lasuen in the organization of the concerts.

Eight *txistulariak* participated in that first 1956 concert in the Abadiño *frontón*, including Aldekoa. There were no music stands, so one of the participants from Otxandio took a boy with him to hold his score sheets during the concert. In those days, this was nothing new or strange.[78] Luis Albizu—known as Luis Txiki (Little Luis), a *txistularia* himself and conductor of the Municipal Band of Ermua—conducted the concert. Indeed, Luis Txiki conducted the concerts for sixteen consecutive years, until 1971. During this time, Aldekoa participated as the first *txistularia* and also, on some occasions, as a soloist. He would interpret variations of well-known pieces such as "Idiarena" or the "Vals" by Federico Corto,[79] either solo or accompanied by a second *txistua* and *silbotea* (a three-holed pipe longer than a *txistua*). Aldekoa was not a member of any stable, regular band. It was only in concerts of this type that he played within the general classical formation of a band of *txistulariak*, consisting of first *txistua*, second *txistua*, *silbotea*, and *atabala*. The concert repertoire was kept simple and accessible so that more people could join the group. The soloist or a reduced group of performers played variations of the more complicated concert music. There was also dancing, and on more than one occasion Aldekoa played the *erregelak* so people could dance.

For seven years (1972–78), including the last few years of Franco's life, these concerts were not legally authorized by the Spanish authorities. In 1979, after the death of Franco and with a new political regime in the town halls, Mañaria was the first place where the *txistulariak* went and where the first concert conducted by Aldekoa was held. In fact, Aldekoa conducted the San José's Day concerts there until 1995. Juan Antonio Aroma thought up the programs and prepared the scores, always under the watchful eye of Aldekoa. The score sheets would then be distributed among *txistua* teachers and students in the area. Each teacher would prepare the program with his students and then, after only one general rehearsal, the concert would be held. Given this schedule, it was impossible for Aldekoa to make any changes or corrections during the general rehearsal. This, for all intents and purposes, was usually held on the same day as the concert itself. Some *txistulariak* had problems reading the music, while others either had problems of a more technical nature or they had not studied enough, making Aldekoa's work as conductor very difficult. Some say he conducted a little too slowly, but the fact is that the group could not play any faster.

The connection between the concerts, teaching, and the diffusion of the *txistua* was evident, but Aldekoa was not convinced about including students who were either too young or who could not play with a minimum degree of expertise. Some *txistulariak*

---

78. As children, my father and his friends used to hold the scores of music for the musicians in the band in exchange for a little money.

79. Federico Corto composed at least two waltzes with variations that became very popular. Both are edited in Ansorena Miner, *Txistu Ikaskizunak*, 105–10.

understood that a concert was a good way to encourage the younger players to study—a way to motivate them—but Aldekoa was clear on this question: "That's not the point. The concert is the concert. It's something serious, only for those who are capable of producing something minimally decent. If you're not ready, then wait until next year; and if you're ready then, well, you'll play."[80]

Gradually, music academies and schools were set up in the surrounding towns. The students' musical standard got better, which in turn contributed to a progressive improvement in the quality of the concerts. As Aldekoa observed, "The improvement has been remarkable. At least now, after years and years, they can read music quite well, some of them very well."

Figure 20. Alejandro Aldekoa conducting the Day of the *Txistua* concert in the County of Durango (1993). Photo by Juan Antonio Aroma.

Not only did the quality of the *txistulariak* improve, but their number also increased. From the original eight who played in 1956, the number had risen to seventy-two in 1995 at the concert held in Mallabia. And of these, 72 percent were under the age of twenty-five.

Table 1 shows the dates and places where the Day of the *Txistua* in the County of Durango was held, as well as the name of the conductor and the number of players taking part in the concert.

80. Alejandro Aldekoa, interview by the author, April 22, 1996.

Table 1. Day of the *Txistua* in the County of Durango

Date	Place	Conductor	Players
03-19-1956	Abadiño	Luis Albizu	8
03-19-1957	Ermua	Luis Albizu	unknown
03-19-1958	Berriz	Luis Albizu	unknown
03-19-1959	Zaldibar	Luis Albizu	unknown
03-19-1960	Bolibar	Luis Albizu	unknown
03-19-1961	Otxandio	Luis Albizu	unknown
03-19-1962	Durango	Luis Albizu	unknown
03-19-1963	Mallabia	Luis Albizu	unknown
03-19-1964	Zaldibar	Luis Albizu	unknown
03-19-1965	Berriz	Luis Albizu	26
03-19-1966	Abadiño	Luis Albizu	unknown
03-19-1967	Apatamonasterio	Luis Albizu	unknown
03-19-1968	Durango	Luis Albizu	unknown
03-19-1969	Garai	Luis Albizu	32
03-19-1970	Axpe	Luis Albizu	unknown
03-19-1971	Izurtza	Luis Albizu	unknown
1972-1973-1974	Permission denied by the authorities		
1975-1976-1977-1978	Permission not requested		
03-19-1979	Mañaria	Alejandro Aldekoa	22
03-23-1980	Elorrio	Alejandro Aldekoa	40
03-22-1981	Otxandio	Alejandro Aldekoa	47
03-19-1982	Mallabia	Alejandro Aldekoa	40
03-19-1983	Zaldibar	Alejandro Aldekoa	31
03-19-1984	Bolibar	Alejandro Aldekoa	30
03-19-1985	Abadiño	Alejandro Aldekoa	unknown
03-23-1986	Berriz	Alejandro Aldekoa	41
03-19-1987	Apatamonasterio	Alejandro Aldekoa	33
03-19-1988	Garai	Alejandro Aldekoa	38
03-19-1989	Ermua	Alejandro Aldekoa	66
03-19-1990	Iurreta	Alejandro Aldekoa	61
03-19-1991	Izurtza	Alejandro Aldekoa	58
03-19-1992	Elorrio	Alejandro Aldekoa	66
03-19-1993	Mañaria	Alejandro Aldekoa	49
03-19-1994	Otxandio	Alejandro Aldekoa	58
03-19-1995	Mallabia	Alejandro Aldekoa	72

The objectives proposed in the 1950s by Luis Albizu, Juan Lasuen, Alejandro Aldekoa, and others, including Julian Azkarate, Moises Gorosabel, Julian Pildain, Alejandro Zubizarreta, and Amantzi Zurikarai, who were, likewise, seminal in promoting *txistua* concerts in the County of Durango, had been accomplished. Of all these people, however, Alejandro Aldekoa stood out as the most charismatic *txistularia* and *txistua* conductor, and his leadership served as a model to a whole new generation of *txistulariak*, as demonstrated by their growing number in table 1.

Figure 21. Alejandro Aldekoa in his garden (April 1996). Photo by the author.

CHAPTER TWO

Some Historical Context: The Pipe and the Tabor

Alejandro Aldekoa's *txistua* and *danbolina*, the pipe and tabor, a combination instrument, has a long history. Although it is difficult to ascertain the exact origin of the instrument (there is still much to be investigated and discovered about the origin and history of instruments in general), Jeremy Montagu, former professor of historic organology at the University of Oxford and an expert on the ancient history of the tabor, cites the origin of the pipe/tabor combination as being clearly European. The appearance and diffusion of the instrument throughout the whole of Europe at the beginning of the thirteenth century could point to an Oriental or African origin similar to that of other instruments that arrived during the same period, such as the guitar, psaltery, tambourine, or shawm, but there is no known proof of the pipe/tabor combination being used in Islamic or Middle Eastern countries, which seems to confirm its European origin.[1] On the other hand, some authors claim its pre-Columbian origin in South America, where it still forms part of various musical traditions today. However, the most probable and widely accepted theory among most observers is that the instrument was taken to the new continent by the Spanish conquerors and settlers.

Nevertheless, what does seem clear is that in the Middle Ages, the tabor pipe was used more in Europe and was one of the favorite instruments employed to accompany the dances of the time. Iconography showing the pipe/tabor combination was at its most glorious in the Gothic period. A great amount of documentary evidence has been found in the Basque Country from that time. The instrument probably reached the peak of its popularity around the middle of the fourteenth century, although it must have continued to be fashionable until at least the sixteenth century, as indicated in the *Orchésographie*, a treatise published in 1589 by Thoinot Arbeau (an anagram of Jehan Tabourot) to aid the learning and practice of dancing: "In our parents' time, the tabor, accompanied by a long

---

1. Jeremy Montagu, "Significación del conjunto flauta y tamboril: ¿Dónde comenzó? ¿Ha sido siempre tal y como la conocemos ahora?" *Txistulari* 172, no. 4 (1997): 70.

flute or other instruments, was used because one musician could do the job of two. He could play both instruments simultaneously, the melody and the accompaniment, without the additional expense of other musicians such as violinists or the like."[2] As Arbeau pointed out even then, the main reasons why the instrument has survived until today in some form or another are its ability to provide melody and rhythm simultaneously; its economic character, requiring only an individual, not a group; and its suitability as an accompaniment for dance.

The *Orchésographie* can be considered the first printed method for pipe and tabor and is one of the best sources of information on the instrument and its repertoire of period dance. Besides giving us valuable information on the instrument and its repertoire, it clearly states the principal use of the pipe/tabor as an accompaniment for dance, giving precise instructions on the relationship between music and dance. Indeed, the *Orchésographie* and the study of Renaissance dance in general "reaffirm that music and dance are inseparable, just as popular tradition has known how to preserve that relationship until today."[3]

Despite the pipe and tabor being very popular and widely used, especially to accompany dance, very few early music groups of today use the three-holed pipe and the tabor. Not even the most rigorous purists among music lovers of ancient instruments have dared to incorporate this instrumental combination. Experience seems to show us that it is the organological singularity of the pipe/tabor combination that has imposed a barrier on its use and expansion into areas other than that of traditional folklore. Percussionists who have tried to use the tabor have had problems with the pipe, and flute players who have tried both the pipe and the tabor have found that they could not coordinate the instruments well. They could not even follow the simple beats that Arbeau suggests in his *Orchésographie*. In this regard, things have not improved in recent years, due undoubtedly to the absence of an example to follow, the lack of instruments with a minimum quality of sound and tuning, and the ignorance of many ancient-music-loving musicians of the pedagogical and musical possibilities of the instrument. Except for a few honorable exceptions (the work of Carles Mas as a performer and teacher of the tabor in the Centre de Musique Médiévale de Paris and the Compagnie Maître Guillaume group, for example), the world of early music still has to address the question of the pipe and tabor.

From the sixteenth century onward, the pipe and tabor suffered a setback as far as its presence and social status were concerned. The expansion and popularization of the violin seems to be one of the causes that contributed to the general decline of the taborers, but there were still exceptions. In the eighteenth century, ideas arising from Rousseau's plea for "natural" music and the aristocratic fashion of copying traditional

---

2. Thoinot Arbeau, *Orchésographie* (1589; Langres: Dominique Guéniot, 1988), 24.

3. Carles Mas, "La danza antigua y la pedagogia musical," *Txistulari* 157, no. 1 (1994): 15.

(especially pastoral) customs brought about what we might term the "Golden Age" of the pipe and tabor (*galoubet* and *tambourin*) in France. The *galoubet-tambourin* was used quite frequently in the orchestra of the Paris Opera and even became fashionable among the nobility, who went to have lessons in the academy of Le Chateminois, a famous virtuoso player. The *tambourin* also gave its name to a type of dance that appears in some French Baroque suites.[4]

While the eclipse of the tabor as a "universal" European instrument seems to clearly date to the seventeenth century, at least as far as its importance, diffusion, and geographical extension within the general panorama of music on the Continent are concerned, the instrumental combination of pipe and tabor continued to play an important role as a "regional" European instrument, a part of local, regional folklore. Indeed, it is in this area where the instrument still shows us its musical, technical, and expressive possibilities today. In some regions of southwest Europe, the pipe and tabor has survived, in one form or another, within local traditions: in Aragón (*chiflo-salterio*), Asturias (*xipla-tamboril*), Bearn (*flûte à trois trous-tambourin*), Castile (*gaita-tambor*), Catalonia (*flabiol-bombo*), Extremadura (*pito-tambor*), Huelva (*flauta rociera*), Gascony (*flabuta-tamborin*), Ibiza (*flaúta-tambor*), Majorca (*fluviol-tambori*), the northern Basque Country (*txirula-ttun-ttuna*), Provence (*galoubet-tambourin*), the southern Basque Country (*txistua-danbolina*), and Trás-os-Montes (*flauta-tambor*).

In other regions, people have started playing the instrument again as part of a collective effort to revitalize old, long-lost traditions where the violin, and, more recently, the accordion and the concertina have usurped the position of the pipe and tabor, even in local folklore. This is the case in England, where the instrument fell into disuse in the nineteenth century. In 1912, George Butterworth, while researching Morris dances in Oxfordshire, England, found a pipe and tabor in the possession of a man who could still play a few simple tunes. He was the last living exponent of past practices. However, a subsequent craze to revive folklore in those countries where it had disappeared led to an unfortunate reinvention of both the tradition and the instrument.[5]

In more recent times, the panorama has changed, thanks to the contact between traditional tabor players from different regions in meetings and courses. Indeed, there now exists an interesting exchange of knowledge between musicians of different traditional cultures and students and experts working on ancient music.

---

4. Maurice Guis, Thierry Lefrançois, and René Venture, *Le galoubet-tambourin: Instrument traditionnelle de Provence* (Aix-en-Provence: Edisud, 1993), 113–47.

5. "The early revivalist pipes sold by the English Folk Dance and Song Society in London were cylindrical brass tubes which were much too wide in bore to work effectively. Their tuning was poor and, to make them easier to play, a fourth hole was added, for the ring finger. This made it impossible to hold the pipe in the normal way, and so a ring was added for the little finger." Montagu, "Significación del conjunto flauta y tamboril," 71.

Between the Sixteenth and Eighteenth Centuries: A Time of Transition

Gradually, the pipe and tabor ceased to be a "universal" European instrument and began to be absorbed into the traditional culture of the Basque Country. This was a period of indigenization and acculturation that probably appears strange to us today. Its precise chronological demarcations are difficult to define, beginning some time around the beginning of the eclipse of the instrument as early as the seventeenth century and ending toward the end of the eighteenth century, when tabor players began to feel the influence of new ideas associated with the Enlightenment.

Although tabor players and other secular musicians of the time did not enjoy a particularly high social status, they did practice a recognized trade demanded by society in general and by the official authorities in particular. Consequently, as well as dancing to the sound of their music, people also began learning how to play it. During this new period of change, however, the social position of the *juglar* (minstrel) became especially problematic,[6] because the Enlightenment idealization of universal nobleness and a democratic, egalitarian past for the Basque Country did not match the socioeconomic reality of the eighteenth century.[7] Instead, the Basque Country was becoming increasingly stratified by cleavages that divided the society along lines of class and social, political, and linguistic allegiance. In Berriz, for example, the percentage of tenancies rose from 30 percent in 1700 to 50 percent in 1800, concentrating the wealth more and more into the hands of a few families, an oligarchy that also controlled local institutions and political power in general.[8] This increasing differentiation between the elite and ordinary people was reaffirmed by various forms of behavior and a series of symbolic acts that ranged from special religious celebrations only for the rich to the increasing use of Castilian (Spanish), which most people in the town could not speak.[9] Music and dance were not untouched by this situation, so while the townsfolk danced to the sound of the

---

6. *Juglar* is a Spanish term that frequently was used in the past to refer to the taborer.

7. Due to limitations of time and space in this work, I cannot explore this theme in great detail. Anyone wishing to understand more fully the role of taborers during the Enlightenment should consult Carlos Sánchez, *Del danbolin al silbo: Txistu, tamboril y danza vasca en la época de la ilustración* (Pamplona: Euskal Herriko Txistulari Elkartea, 1999); and Jose Inazio Ansorena Miner, "Iztueta eta Albéniz-en musika bilduma," *Txistulari* 163, no. 3 (1995): 10–27.

8. To give some an idea of the levels to which the manipulation of municipal power reached, in the mid-eighteenth century, only 0.72 percent of the inhabitants of Donostia (San Sebastián) and 1 percent of the population of Azkoitia, Gipuzkoa, had access to high positions in their respective town halls. Juan José Madariaga, "Municipio y vida municipal vasca de los siglos XVI al XVII," *Hispania* 39 (1979): 546.

9. In 1707, for example, the inhabitants of Berriz protested "against the ostentatious funerals and nine-day mourning celebrations in church when there were many indebted peasants who could hardly honor their dead." Felipe Andrés García, *Berriz: Estudio histórico-artístico* (Bilbao: Diputación Foral de Bizkaia, 1997), 107. Also in the eighteenth century, Carlos III promoted the use of Spanish through a massive literacy campaign to give a sense of unity to the Spanish empire. As a consequence of this process, the traditional language, Euskara, was marginalized and even persecuted, causing a feeling of shame on the part of the population with respect to their own language. On the linguistic question at this time, see José María Jimeno, *Navarra, Gipuzkoa y el Euskera: Siglos XVIII* (Pamplona: Pamiela, 1999).

tabor, the upper class celebrated its soirées to the sound of violins and other musical instruments.[10]

In this situation, the taborer was discriminated against, along with other declassé trades, despite the notion of *hidalguía universal* (universal nobility)—something that all Basques were supposed to assume. As a decree dated 1760 proclaimed: "This decree . . . agrees to request the council assembly never to permit active or passive voice in elections to any tabor or drum player, butcher, or town crier in any of the town councils. This refers not only to those exercising such trade at the time of elections, but also to those who have exercised such trade at any time in the past."[11]

The tabor player was even refused Holy Communion in church. Indeed, his position was so low that certain localities experienced extreme difficulties in finding a taborer, as demonstrated in the following testimony in Balmaseda (Valmaseda), Bizkaia, in the sixteenth century: "They were therefore very rare those devoted to the tabor and the pipe believing their nobleness [*hidalguía*] to decline with it."[12] This would explain the existence of numerous Romani or Roma (also known as Gypsy) tabor players, as in many other areas of Europe, where itinerant musicians were often Romani or other nomadic peoples due to the fact that not many other people were willing to become taborers because of the low status of the profession. Yet in spite of everything, the tabor was still the most widely used instrument in festivities and traditional celebrations in the Basque Country. Indeed, Juan Ignacio de Iztueta observed that "there has never been created nor will ever be invented an instrument as merry to the Basque people as the pipe and tabor."[13]

In addition, despite social dynamics that fostered the social marginalization of the tabor player (and perhaps also because of them), when the ideology of the Enlightenment reached the Basque ruling class, it brought with it an interest in the traditional music and dance of the original inhabitants of the region. The idea of a return to nature, for example, made popular traditions fashionable again, and anything "pastoral" or "rustic" aroused the interest of the upper class. However, this interest was a double-edged sword, and the valorization of these activities equally entailed their regulation. Within the paternalist policy of town control and codes of public life linked to so-called enlightened despotism ("Everything for the people, but without the people"), the dominant class exercised control over leisure and entertainment, avoiding anything that could be considered too wild, superstitious, or subversive.

---

10. "Here it is said that the soirée is the dance and entertainment which both men and women celebrate together during the night in the great houses, these being open to any of them [the upper classes] whether they be of the house or not." Fray Bartolome Santa Teresa, *Euscal Errijetaco Olgueeta ta dantzeen Neurrizco Gatzozpinduba*, ed. Patxi Altuna (1816; Bilbao: Universidad de Deusto, 1987), 76.

11. Domingo Ignacio de Egaña, *El guipuzcoano instruido en las Reales Células: Despachos y Ordenes que há venerado su Madre la Provincia* (San Sebastián: Lorenzo Riesgo, 1781), 91.

12. Martín de los Heros, *Historia de Valmaseda* (Bilbao: Excma. Diputación de Vizcaya, 1926), 396.

13. Juan Ignacio de Iztueta, *Gipuzkoako dantza gogoangarrien kondaira edo historia* (1824; Donostia: Euskal Editoreen Elkartea, 1990), 67.

Figure 22. *Soka dantza* in Elorrio (County of Durango), eighteenth-century engraving. Engraving by permission of the journal *Dantzariak*.

Consequently, it was deemed necessary to impose some kind of order and morality on public dancing in order to rid it of any hint of indecency.[14] Although the influence of the church was notable, it was not religious scruples that mattered, but the control and order of social behavior by conditioning public dancing within the framework of courtship, gallantry,[15] initiation, social cohesion, and hierarchic boundaries. The handkerchief was introduced in the *soka dantza* (chain dance) to separate the hands of men and women, while the last part of this dance, known as *culadas* (to bang dancers' hips together), or anything characterized by the close physical contact of the dancers, was suppressed.[16] The place and time of the dance was closely controlled and always under the supervision

14. This was a matter of great importance, as described later.

15. The most radical churchmen proposed the total elimination of dance. This was not a very satisfactory solution, as illustrated by the fact that wherever the dance was successfully repressed, the number of illegitimate births in the locality rose, obliging the authorities to reinstate the dance. Manuel de Larramendi, *Corografía: O descripción general de la Muy Noble y Muy Leal Provincia de Guipúzcoa* (1882; San Sebastián: Sociedad Guipuzcoana de Ediciones y Publicaciones, 1969), 240.

16. Writing in the early 1930s, Violet Alford describes the scene: "He, then, the perspiration pouring down his face, presents her with one end of a handkerchief, himself holds the other end and leads her into the circle. The separating handkerchief was introduced by the priests some hundred years ago. One supposes it was felt that some reform was needed, but it was certainly accepting the mountain while reforming the mole-hill." "Ceremonial Dances of the Spanish Basques," 472–73. For a contemporary description of the dance, see Lisa Corcostegui, "To the Beat of a Different Drum: Basque Dance and Identity in the Homeland and in the Diaspora," Ph.D. diss., University of Nevada, Reno, 2005, 187–89.

of the local authorities. The Basque dances were thus transformed into something said to be essentially "pure" and "honest."[17]

The authorities ultimately resorted to controlling the tabor players as a means of controlling dance. It was much easier to watch over and keep the poor tabor players subordinate by means of various types of threat (fines, jail, or exile) than to control the community directly. This is how the tabor player, who until then had been "of the lowest rank in the community,"[18] curiously became responsible for ensuring moral, decent behavior in dance. Severe rules were promulgated that the tabor player had to observe and make the community follow. Sometimes these rules were clearly stated in their contracts. Most of the town councils of the country at this time equipped themselves with wage-earning tabor players. Because the wish of some municipalities to contract their own "minstrel" was confounded by the difficulty they had in finding tabor players, due to the service's bad reputation, as an incentive, the tabor players were sometimes offered communal, municipal land as part of their remuneration or as an alternative form of payment.[19] Temporary contracts were extended to ever-increasing periods of time,[20] but the wages were still so low that the tabor player also frequently had to do the job of bailiff, town crier, postman, or even gravedigger, and sometimes he had to pass his hat around to collect money after the dance. It was quite common for the taborer to be the local organist, as well, and sometimes he was also responsible for the musical education of the young.[21]

---

17. In the above process of transformation within these dances, the role of Juan Ignacio de Iztueta was extremely important. Iztueta tried to combine Enlightenment ideas with a pro-Basque apologetic tone. He was responsible for the invention of a certain Basque tradition created in order to preserve the antiquity of the dances and to legitimate their hierarchical and honest character as inseparable from the original Basque dances. Although his work did not exert a great deal of influence at the time it was published in the early nineteenth century, in the twentieth century, it became a kind of bible for dance studies, because it was both old and its apologetic tone in favor of Basque culture was convenient for the mythology assumed by the growing Basque nationalist movement. On Iztueta, see see Juan Madariaga Orbea, *Anthology of Apologists and Detractors of the Basque Language*, trans. Frederick H. Fornoff, María Cristina Saavedra, Amaia Gabantxo, and Cameron J. Watson (Reno: Center for Basque Studies, University of Nevada, Reno, 2006), 508–13.

18. Francisco Antonio de Palacios, *Viva Jesús: Respuesta satisfactoria del Colegio de Misioneros de N. P. S. Francisco de la Noble Villa de Zarauz, con ocasión de una proposición sobre bailes equivocadamente atribuida á dos Misioneros del Sobre Dicho Colegio en la Misión que últimamente predicaron en la mencionada Noble Villa. Y de paso una disertación sobre lo lícito ó no de los bailes regulares de las Plazas, y Saraos* (Pamplona: Josef Longás, 1791), 21.

19. In 1649, the town council of Hernani in Gipuzkoa contracted Joanes de Bizcarrondo for two years, offering him three yugadas of land or two hundred reales. A yugada was a piece of land that a pair of yoked oxen could work in a day, while a real approximated fifty pesetas of that time. In 1657, the same taborer continued working in this position, strengthening his relationship with the town hall through land exploitation contracts. Patxi Apezetxea, *Hernani eta txistua: Bere txistulariak / Sus txistularis* (Donostia: Kutxa Fundazioa, 1992), 49–50.

20. In the same municipality of Hernani, the first news of a fixed contract for a taborer came in 1799. See ibid., 55.

21. I will cite only a few cases from the County of Durango: Roque Amilburu (1862–1925), organist and *txistularia*; Santiago Maiagarai (1869–1939), town crier, *txistularia*, organist, music teacher, and director of the Municipal Band of Ermua; Pedro Abaitua (1870–1919), blind organist and *txistularia* of Berriz; José María Pradera (1893–1947), *txistularia* and organist of Mallabia, music teacher, and director of the parish choir, as well as composer of small religious pieces; and Valentín Lasuen (b. 1934), organist, *txistularia*, and choir director of Berriz.

So now the function of the municipal tabor player was not limited only to dance; he was also obliged to accompany the authorities in solemn acts such as processions, parades, and other celebrations. He acted as herald to solemnize, by means of music, the exercise of municipal authority in public acts. Another of the tabor player's obligations was to play the *alborada* (dawn song) on festive days—in other words, to wake up the population. The tabor player had to brighten up the streets and play the *alborada*, knocking on the doors of those notable and well-off people who deserved being entertained with the music of the minstrel. He was not allowed to play the *alborada* for servants, temporary farm workers, or day laborers. The tabor, therefore, became a symbol and means of social differentiation that was manifested on every festive day.

The conversion of the tabor player into wage earner, his ever-closer relationship with authority, his use by the statutes of the power to control dance and entertainment, to solemnize public acts, and to reinforce authority and social difference were undoubtedly the main reasons for a progressive change in his social condition. The tabor player was now nothing less than the representative of the society's fundamental institutions and the guardian of music and traditional dance, which, in the wake of the Enlightenment reform of the original traditional dance, was now declared to be essentially pure and honest.

As society gradually came to consider tabor players to be musicians, the *txistularia* began to develop repertoires of highbrow Western music introduced by the upper classes. Gradually, pipe and tabor players began to play duos together with a drum accompaniment. Soon, a third voice was needed, giving rise to the appearance of the *silbotea* (a longer, three-holed pipe played without tabor, a kind of bass *txistua*), and with it, the beginnings of the formation of the typical band of *txistulariak*, consisting of *txistua* 1, *txistua* 2, *silbotea*, and *atabala* (drum).[22] Changes were made to the instrument's tuning to respond to the new musical requirements imposed by the erudite music that the tabor players imported and adapted (redowas, mazurkas, polkas, country dances, and so forth). The use of chromaticism was extended, and the range of notes made by the instrument increased. Some composers, and the instrumentalists themselves, even began to compose music exclusively for the *txistua*. If improvisation had been important in older music, now *txistulariak* were valued by their ability to compose.[23] Thus, new genres of music were created, such as *idiyarenak* (music for the bullfights) and *alkate soiñuak* (literally, "mayor's tunes," hymns performed by the *txistulariak* in honor of the municipal authority, the mayor), consequences of the convergence between traditional and erudite and foreign music, between the indigenous styles of the instruments and the aesthetic preferences of the time.

---

22. In 1802, in the so-called "Humboldt Papers," observations of Basque culture written by the famous German scholar, Wilhelm von Humboldt, pieces for *txistua* duets were noted. It was observed that "a longer *txistua* was used, and it was tuned in chapel tone playing a second voice." Aita José Antonio de Donostia, *Cancionero Vasco* (San Sebastián: Eusko Ikaskuntza, 1994), 1535. The *silbotea* would have been tuned in C (now usually in B-flat) and the *txistua* in G (now usually in F).

23. One of the tests in the exams for the position of taborer, especially in important municipalities, was the composition of music for the *txistua*. In some of these positions, the taborer was contractually obliged to compose a determined number of musical pieces a year.

Figure 23. The Municipal Band of *Txistulariak* of Iruñea-Pamplona.
Photo by permission of the *Txistulari* journal archives.

The panorama outlined here reflects one part of the reality of the tabor players in the eighteenth and early nineteenth centuries—that of the literate, municipal wage-earning, urban musicians. At the same time, there were still rural, musically illiterate tabor players, who, as we will see in the case of Berriz, maintained their role down to the present day by remaining nearly always bound to the spheres of traditional dance and the oral transmission of music.

The Association of *Txistulariak* of the Basque Country

At the end of the nineteenth century, the panorama of traditional music, especially that of dance, was altered by the arrival of new instruments and new forms of dancing. If until then the only music that the inhabitants of the small towns had heard was that of the tabor player or the church organ on festive days, now, musical bands and, above all, the accordion were making inroads into the *erromeriak* (open-air dances) and festivities of the Basque Country. A feeling grew that one's own had to be protected from these foreign incursions, and the tabor player increasingly was seen as the musician of clean, decent, secular traditions standing against these foreign, lustful innovations.

To put it another way, in the face of this "invasion," ordinary people had to be made aware of the wealth of their own culture and folklore. With this idea in mind, Antoine d'Abbadie promoted composition and playing competitions for the *txistua* in the *euskal jaiak* (Basque festivals) that he organized.[24] The first of these competitions was held in Urruña (Urrugne) in Lapurdi (Labourd) in 1853.[25] Moreover, Sabino Arana's nationalism, in need of signs of identity, included the *txistua* in the group of elements that were said to define a certain Basque aesthetic (dances, gait, clothes, and so on). Nationalism associated the *txistua* with the virility and spirit of Basque dancing soldiers, reversing some of its generally accepted qualities: from being an instrument of a sweet and soft tone, it became warlike, loud, and bittersweet.[26] Indeed, it was a group of enthusiastic nationalists who, during the dictatorship of General Primo de Rivera, created Euskal Herriko Txistularien Elkartea, the Association of *Txistulariak* of the Basque Country, in 1927.

Since he was born in 1920, Alejandro Aldekoa's life as a tabor player thus coincided with that of the association, of which he was already a member at the age of thirteen, before the Spanish Civil War stopped all cultural activities of the Basque Country. From its foundation, the Association of *Txistulariak* led and organized the world of the tabor players. The vast majority of *txistulariak* in the Basque Country

---

24. On Abbadie, see Madariaga Orbea, *Anthology of Apologists and Detractors of the Basque Language*, 581–87.

25. For example, in the *euskal jaiak* celebrated in Durango in July 1886, the winner of the *txistua* playing competition was Roque de Ansola (1821–1911), who had already won the prize in the *euskal jaiak* in Markina 1882. Angel Berguices, "Dos siglos de música culta y tradicional en el Duranguesado (1800–1986)," unpublished ms., 1986, 24–25.

26. Similarly, as Corcostegui notes, in reviving Basque dance, "of all the available Basque dances to choose as a national icon, virile and combative dances were chosen" by early Basque nationalists. "To the Beat of a Different Drum," 231.

(myself included), whether professional, amateur, or simply fans of the instrument, belong to this association, and today, it has close to two thousand members. For *txistulariak*, it is "The Association," and the truth is that almost everything concerning the *txistua* in recent times (publications, competitions, concerts, and so on) has passed through the hands of this group of tabor players. During this time, the *txistua* has seen the cultural apogee of the 1920s and 1930s, the disaster of the Civil War, the prohibition of any cultural manifestation suspected of being Basque, and the dictatorship of Franco, when the *txistua* became one of the main symbols of identity for the Basque people.

One of the main objectives of the association was to conserve, spread, improve, and extend the repertoire of tabor players in the Basque Country, for which it created the journal *Txistulari*. As well as publishing the traditional dances and repertoire of the *txistulariak*, composers of the stature of Jesus Guridi, Pablo Sorozabal, and Jose Antonio de Donostia have passed through its pages.[27] *Txistulari* has published more than six thousand pages of music, and the repertoire of the *txistularia* now is certainly wide and varied. In the journal, one can find anything from the simplest of melodies and dances to the most complicated variations on a theme in which, more often than not, the virtuoso performance surpasses the musical intention. In addition to its pages of music notation, *Txistulari* has included all kinds of articles on the music, folklore, and literature of the Basque Country, as well as on other aspects of social and traditional life. As a result, *Txistulari* "became the most popular, widespread, modern, and complete testimony of Basque music and folklore."[28]

Consequently, through the years, the association has had a very strong influence on the *txistulariak* of the Basque Country. To be a taborer has been synonymous with being a member of the association, whose judgments and opinions became law for many *txistulariak*, including Aldekoa. On many occasions, these judgments and opinions were reflections of the members' own individual thoughts and feelings, but on others, they were the fruit of the ideological propaganda of its founders and executive body. As such, an analysis of the Association of *Txistulariak* and its ideology is fundamental if we are to understand Aldekoa's way of thinking and his career as a taborer.

Although it may seem complicated to establish the ideological guidelines of an association, a collective made up of people from all walks of life, this is not the case with the Association of *Txistulariak*, due to the existence of the journal *Txistulari*. To this principal source of information, I will also add my own observations and thoughts after several years experience as a member and collaborator of the Board of Directors and as editor of the journal *Txistulari*.

---

27. For a brief biographical note of these composers, see *The New Grove Dictionary of Music and Musicians*.

28. Jose Luis Ansorena Miranda, *Txistua eta Txisulariak: El txistu y los txistularis* (San Sebastián: Fundición Social y Cultural Kutxa, 1996), 45.

Figure 24. Some front covers of the journal *Txistulari*.
Photo by permission of the *Txistulari* journal archives.

The Association as a Labor Union

In its initial stage, from its foundation in 1927 to the outbreak of the Spanish Civil War in 1936, the aims of the association were defined in Article 2 of its statutes:

> The aims of the Association are to promote artistic progress and to defend economically the *txistulariak*, by and with all means deemed necessary and appropriate, especially the following:

> Artistic progress: a) to enrich the musical repertoire of the *txistua*; b) publicity to encourage the study of the *txistua*, creating classes in which the instrument is taught; and c) to consolidate the post of municipal *txistularia* in all the municipalities of the Country.
>
> Economic defense of the *txistulariak*: d) to protect the *txistulariak* in cases where it be deemed necessary for the intervention of the Association: and for the creation of a *Txistularia* Fund.

As we can see, at its inception, the association created a kind of labor union, which even included an emergency aid and pension fund. This fund consisted of money collected as a membership fee from each member and was destined to be used for pensions or aid in cases of need (illness or death) for the members and their families. The interest made on the fund's capital was distributed by the Board of Directors among those who applied for help, after having presented the report of the parish priest, receipts of medical expenses, and/or a death certificate. Half of the interest was destined for relieving ill health and the other half for death benefits: "Economic aid, in the case of death, will be distributed among the widow, children, or heirs, in accordance with the current civil law in force in the municipality in which the deceased last lived." At the Congress of Donostia on July 19, 1931, it was also agreed that in the case of death, a fee of five pesetas per member for the family and a contribution of two hundred pesetas from the association would be established in order to "pay for the cost of a decent funeral."[29]

The association gained authority among the *txistulariak*, and its judgments becoming law. In the pages of *Txistulari*, we find all kinds of instructions and advice, from what posture to adopt while playing the *txistua*, to rules of how to wear the *txapela* (Basque beret), to how to share the money collected in the *alborada*. It also defended the interests of the *txistulariak*, appealing to the authorities in difficult cases and working hard to promote the profession. Today, however, the association is not able to confront serious problems, such as the future of the *txistua* within the new plans for education.

Religion and Morality: Agur Arrateko Ama *(Greetings! Virgin of Arrate)*

> At the start of our active life, fulfilling the mandates and agreements of the memorable Congress of Eibar, we are obliged, first of all, to invoke the name of our Patron the Virgin of Arrate, dedicating to her the first thoughts of *Txistulari*, and offering to her our labor for the sake of wholesome Basque art, and whose help in this task we implore. Receive as a thanksgiving, something which sounds sweeter to the ear than the cascades of harmony we dedicate at the door of your chapel, *a prayer*.

These are the first lines of the first issue of the journal *Txistulari* for March–April 1928. The congress of Arrate took place on September 20, 1927. Among the promoters

---

29. *Txistulari* 31 (1933): 5–6.

of the association were Sandalio Tejada,[30] as well as Eduardo Gorosarri,[31] a priest, *txistularia*, and musician-organist in the Basilica of Begoña (Bilbo), who, under the pseudonym of Zaraya, composed several pieces of music specifically for this first assembly, and conducted the concert of the *txistulariak* himself. Priests and monks (such as Aita Donostia and Aita Hilario) have always been present, in some way or another, in the comings and goings of the association, and today, the organization still has its own chaplain. The association still celebrates Mass at its annual congress and at special commemorations or celebrations, even though there are some members who oppose this and have suggested that the religious connection of the association be revised, alleging that it is time to separate cultural activity in favor of the *txistua* from religious activity. Whether it be through inertia or for the fondness and respect the members have for Jose Luis Ansorena, the current chaplain, the fact is that the association still has a chaplain and still celebrates Mass. Times have changed, and many things have changed with the times, but one has to be very careful to confess one's opposition to these religious practices openly if one wants to remain on friendly terms with the *txistulariak*, especially the older ones. Criticism is frowned upon, and discussion of religion is taboo in the association. For some, to be a *txistularia* is still synonymous with being a good Catholic, even though the church will not allow the *txistua* to be played at funerals.

Obviously, nowadays, religious influence is notably less, and the positions of the church have also changed, but let us look at some of the notes published in the journal that were considered almost "sacred" and that still exercise their influence today. Apart from a few articles that dealt with similar moral questions, notes written in bold type and with a highly moral content were inserted here and there in the journal: "**For a dance to be authorized, it is necessary and of utmost importance that no inconvenient gesture, no indiscreet contact, no intimate proximity between adults of the opposite sex, no dishonest posture, no union nor embrace which could incite carnal passion, should ever take place.**"[32]

Sandalio Tejada and the rest of the ideologists who collaborated in *Txistulari* managed to impose their moral code, reinventing history and tradition and constantly calling on the naive goodness and irreproachable Christian morality of the Basque people and the *txistularia* as a model of Christian and civic virtue.[33] A fervent *txistularia*, believer in God, respectful of ecclesiastical and civil authority, faithful to his mandate and norms,

---

30. Sandalio Tejada (1893–1971), sensing the need to coordinate relations between the *txistulariak* through an association, became the main catalyst and driving force behind the Association of *Txistulariak*. In his professional life, he was a lawyer and secretary of the Bar Association in Bilbo. An active militant in favor of Basque culture, he died in Caracas, in exile, in 1971.

31. Eduardo Gorosarri's biography and the catalogue of his work can be found in *Txistulari* 129, no. 1 (1987): 6–7.

32. *Txistulari* 1 (1928): 3.

33. Sandalio Tejada is the author of the article "La romería vasca ha desaparecido," *Txistulari* 3 (1928): 9, one of the most complete and interesting documents of propaganda published in the journal.

stands high in these texts as the guardian of virtuous customs, vested with the power to stop the dance on observing the slightest deviation from correct behavior.

Despite the fact that these claims today seem like old-fashioned nonsense and more often than not provoke laughter among the *txistulariak* themselves, the fact is that nearly all the *erromeriak*, or dance occasions "animated" by a *txistularia*, are still basically an exhibition of "pure," "chaste" dancing: the *jota*, *arin-arina*, *biribilketa*, and *mutil dantza*.[34] And woe betide anyone who tries to perform a foreign, impure dance such as the paso doble.[35] When I asked if he had ever played a waltz or paso doble, Alejandro replied:

> No, my teacher gave me strict instructions about things like that, and I've always kept in mind that the *txistua* isn't for playing *loture* [dances where the couple holds on to one another]. You know, the priests promulgated the idea that it was a mortal sin. Maybe that's why I never played them. Although once . . . I remember one day in a neighborhood I was asked:
>
> "Would you play a *loture* dance?"
>
> I thought I'd try, and so I played one.
>
> "Hey, why don't you usually play like that?"
>
> "Not in the square."
>
> On another occasion, after supper, during the fiestas in some neighborhood or other, we threw a little party. Quite a lot of people came, and at around midnight, under the arches, someone asked me to play something different, and so I played. Playing the notes by ear, you can play almost anything. In those days, the paso doble "Ay! Mari Cruz!" was in fashion.

> But never in public. It has never been considered that the *txistularia* can play that kind of music, and anyway, the association, the congress, or the Board of Directors would never allow it. I remember how a player from Markina was reported to the association for playing "La Gallina Turuleta"[36] early in the morning. The association sent him a letter, and he gave the instrument up. He didn't play anymore, and he was young.

34. All of these dances today are danced without any physical contact between the men and the women.

35. The paso doble (*pasodoble* in Spanish) is a dance for couples where physical contact is made. Men and women dance holding on to one another. It was very popular due to its rhythmic and choreographic simplicity. It was also played as a musical accompaniment at bullfights. Maybe for this reason, along with the fact that the titles and lyrics of famous *pasodobles* such as "España Cañí," were full of Spanish overtones, certain Basque nationalist sectors considered them to be emblematic of Spanish culture.

36. "La Gallina Turuleta" was a children's song, very popular for a time because it was sung by the Spanish clowns Gaby, Fofo, and Miliki on their TV show.

Jaungoikoa ta legizarra: *God and the Old Law*

Because the *txistulariak* had been absorbed into the institutions of social control in the Basque Country, under the Association of *Txistulariak*, the boundary between the interests of the church and those of the civil authorities or political powers is, at times, difficult to determine. The influence of the church over civil authority in the Basque Country, however, seems clear and manifest. Even the nationalist ideology promulgated by Sabino Arana and his followers chose as its slogan "Jaungoikoa ta legi zarra," "God and the Old Law."

Whatever the case may be, I would underscore the proximity of the association and the *txistulariak* to power and specifically to the machinery of power, whether it be ecclesiastical or civil. For example, after the praise of our Patron the Virgin of Arrate, the following text is printed on the first page of *Txistulari*:

> Alkate soiñua. ["Mayor's Tune," a hymn performed by the *txistulariak* in honor of the mayor. Most of the time, it is a kind of taborer minuet, played in 3/4 time, classical, solemn, and slow.]
>
> To the Authority; Secondly, we turn to the Authority to publicly ratify what has already been said in private, without and under no suspicions. We were born for art, and only for the art of which our thousand-year-old skill is paramount.
>
> The *txistularia* has always been the official keeper of the customs of the town. His post was and is at the immediate command of the Authorities. For this double importance, for the transcendency of our step, we have today, more than ever before, to work so that those customs that were the stamp of honor and peace in our towns do not disappear; but that, on the contrary, they reemerge strengthened by their purity and honesty and their particular character. In this task, the collaboration of the Authorities will be the main factor; making respectful use of this tie of immemorial dependency on the same [authorities], we ask for that efficient collaboration necessary to meet our aims, which by their character are beneficial to and for the public.
>
> Civil Governors, Provincial Councils, Town Halls of all the Basque Country, the *txistulariak* greet you!

Because of their traditional condition as municipal employees (civil servants), the *txistulariak* and their association have always been sure of who has the power and the resources to pay for their services. Since the association was founded, the sponsorship of culture in general and of the taborers in particular has always been and continues to be in the hands of public institutions, mainly town halls and a few councils, through their municipal bands of *txistulariak*.

Today, the Association of *Txistulariak* continues to collaborate with the various institutions that govern the Basque Country. The publication of monographs or journals dedicated or related to a specific area helps to improve relations with the town hall, council, or government most directly concerned with the subject studied. Sometimes, financial support is forthcoming from the autonomous and municipal governments through the sale of copies of the journals, but, above all, the idea is to strengthen the standing of the instrument and its bond with the people and their governors, as well as to promote and spread knowledge and research about the topic at hand. *Txistulari* opens its doors to the mayor and councilmen, putting the first pages of each issue of the journal at their disposal for them to write eulogistic, laudatory speeches on the virtues of the *txistua*, the *txistulariak*, their repertoire and dances, and, above all else, to show their unconditional support for the *txistularia* movement. Significantly, some politicians are or have been *txistulariak* or have a close relationship with the *txistua* through family ties.

The Association of Txistulariak *under Franco*

The editorial in the issue of *Txistulari* for March–April 1931 (number 19), published a few days after the proclamation of the Second Republic in Spain on April 14, shows the position taken by the association and the *txistulariak* regarding the issue of Basque nationalism. In other words, with the coming of a new more liberal Spanish political regime, the association was able to clearly state its Basque nationalist sympathies:

> After the evolution [*sic*], our love for VASCONIA [another name for the Basque Country] grows more and more.
>
> There has never appeared, in the pages of *Txistulari*, an article that reflected political tendencies; our apolitical position has always been paramount, we leave all politics to one side. All, except one: the defense of everything Basque, keeping the flames of the sacred fire of our love for our traditions, our customs, our laws, and our rights alight. This was our policy, a policy of love for the things that are ours, a policy of hope for the reintegration of all that was ours. We understood that such behavior was basic and principle of the conduct of all Basques in any aspect of life, especially if it involved maintaining and fomenting our traditions.
>
> *Txistulari* cannot remain indifferent to the change of regime in Spain. If the regime were exactly the same as the previous one in its principles regarding the Basque Country, little would it matter. We would have to continue with a distant hope, yearning for all that was taken from us and that the generations of today, except for a few, have never even known; but this is not the case; daily it is declared that this present regime will be the one to give back our autonomy, and at the least ease the way for the integration of the *fueros*. This is to say that the Republic established in Spain has to be the way for the Basques to recuperate all that we have lost.
>
> The *txistulariak* are not politicians; we should not write about politics on these pages, it is not our place nor our mission to do so, we, who only attend to the Basque folk musicians. But we do want to make one policy: the union of all Basques. We have been divided by fights for many years, some of them fratricidal, watering the green fields of our country with the blood of our brothers, fighting one against the other. The moment has arrived for us all to unite, to look for and achieve together our one and only ambition, our liberation in the interest of national union. First and foremost, we are Basques to achieve what we want, reclaiming all that was taken away from us by those who were confident of the divisions between us. Let us divide later, at a more appropriate time so that the criteria each one of us holds may prevail; not now, when the circumstances demand the union of all of us who love our country, this Basque Country, once again witness to the rise of its great spirit to make our traditional demands.

> We offer this sermon to all our readers:
>
> Let us be Basques, Basques for ever more. Let us unite to achieve the wish of a lifetime and make our country the pride of the peoples of the peninsula for its administration or for its wholesome and honest politics, worthy of the successors of those just men who set the greatest example of democracy ever, under the oak tree of Gernika.

Needless to say, as events soon proved, this optimism about the prospects for cultural and political autonomy in the Basque Country was premature. After the defeat of the Republic and the rise to power of General Franco, the prohibition of all and everything that represented Basque culture was severe: to speak in Euskara or to play the *txistua* were reason enough to be punished. Persecution varied, depending on the criteria of the local authorities. The Municipal Band of Donostia began to play again immediately after Franco's troops had taken over the city, given the desire of the new authorities for municipal life to get back to normal as soon as possible. Despite the war, the Municipal Band of Gasteiz never stopped playing, but in Bilbao, the band had to wait until 1956 to renew its activity. In small towns, it was a very different story, with prohibitions of all kinds. Some taborers hid their instruments, played in secret, or stopped playing altogether. Gradually, folkloric performances were permitted again, but always within the established order and system. Under the orders of governmental authority, the *txistulariak* were obliged to play for Franco, including the "Cara al Sol," a fascist hymn obligatory in public ceremonies, schools, theaters, cinemas, dances, and any kind of celebration and one of the main symbols of Franco's dictatorship, at the unveiling of the monument to Juan Telleria, composer of the hymn, in the display held in Zegama (Cegama), Gipuzkoa, in 1957.

Nevertheless, other developments underwrote a continued emphasis on the *txistua* within the enclaves of Basque nationalist ideology during the Franco era and lent support for a return of the Association of *Txistulariak* as a popular public institution. Racial anthropology took the first steps to configuring and differentiating the Basque racial type.[37] The task that was continued by two local scholars, Telesforo Aranzadi and José Miguel Barandiarán, who, on the basis of skulls found in Urtiaga (Itziar) in Gipuzkoa, interpreted and established the hypothesis of the evolution of the Basques. According to this theory, the Basque race is a direct descendant of the Cro-Magnon through a biological evolution in situ. Racial anthropological discourse had a decisive influence on the development of ideas about the origins of Basque culture, with the skull of Urtiaga converted into the symbol and fetish of Basque anthropology, and of the ideology of differential Basque identity.[38] In a similar way, the timely appearance of what became known as the "*txistua* of Izturitze" strengthened Basque nationalist racial ideas, this time in the area of culture and music. As an article entitled "The Basques, the First Taborers, the First Musicians" claimed, the *txistua* was said to be not only the oldest straight flute in the world, but also the first musical instrument ever known.

---

37. Figures involved in this work included Anders Retzius, Paul Broca, and Georges Hervé.

38. Joseba Zulaika, *Del cromañon al carnaval: Los vascos como museo antropológico* (Donostia: Erein, 1996), 21–30.

In the main ancient civilizations of Assyria, Babylonia, Egypt, and Greece, they played the straight flute, technically the same as the *txistua* of the Basques, although different in size, rings, and other accidental details.

One can assume, for now, the priority of the Basque *txistua* over its similar counterparts, which appear on the bas-relief of tombs of the fourth and fifth Assyrian dynasties (2700 B.C.), or some of the forty-five flutes found in Egyptian tombs (2500–1000 B.C.) and now conserved in the museums of Florence, London, Leyden [Leiden], The Loret Collection, Maspero, etc., and also the straight flute of Greece, whose invention was attributed, in mythology, to the goddess Pallas and the satyr Marsyas.

There is a document of unappreciable value that shows us the singular, chronological primogeniture of the Basque *txistua* over all other flutes and musical instruments of humanity.

It was discovered by the learned archaeologist from the University of Strasbourg, Mr. [Emmanuel?] Passemard. . . .

Among the series of extremely interesting discoveries of bones that honor the art of those ancient ancestors of the Basques, Professor Passemard found a thick bird bone, with three holes made on one of its sides at proportional distances, and which, according to the discoverer, could not have been made for any other purpose other than that of producing sound.

Unfortunately, it is broken just above the superior hole, and we have not been lucky enough to find the missing piece for us to see what the shape of the mouthpiece was like.

Nevertheless, according to the archaeologist, we are looking at the oldest instrument in the history of mankind: the straight, three-holed flute or "*txistua* of the cave of Izturitze."[39]

Figure 25. The "*txistua* of Izturitze." Photo by permission of the *Txistulari* journal archives.

It is therefore not surprising that, starting from this premise, the existence of taborers in other parts of the world or the ancient iconography of taborers were interpreted from an evolutionary, ethnocentric perspective by those who wrote in *Txistulari*. Could this similarity be due to the emigration of Basques in ancient times? Despite the fact that

39. Father Hilario Olazaran [Alejandro Olazaran Salanueva], "Koreografia," *Txistulari* 2 (1933): 14–15.

subsequent research has shown the chronological estimates and dating of the skulls of Urtiaga to be wrong and that the "*txistua* of Izturitze" was not a *txistua* at all,[40] the myth had already been created and lives on to this day. Who else, other than a Basque, could be capable of inventing something as Basque as the *txistua*?

It was in this atmosphere that, in 1952, coinciding with the date of the silver anniversary of the founding of the association, Isidro Ansorena—using the excuse to gain authorization for the event that they were celebrating the silver anniversary of the proclamation of the Virgin of Arrate as patron of the *txistulariak*—organized a new convention of *txistulariak* in Arrate, a neighborhood of Eibar (Gipuzkoa). Memories of the association were revived, inspiring the unanimous decision and desire of all present to do what was in their power to restart the association. Their wish came true in 1955.

In this second phase, initiated in the middle of Franco's rule, the emblematic and symbolic value of the association and its journal and the symbolic value of the *txistua* as a patriotic Basque instrument reached new, hitherto unimaginable heights. To be *euskalduna* (literally, someone who possesses the Basque language, that is, a Basque speaker, but also meaning Basque in general), one had to be a *dantzaria* (dancer), a *hilandera* (spinner or female dancer), or a *txistularia*. To be a *txistularia* and a member of the association or simply to see one's name published on the list of new members of the association was like being invested as a *txistularia* in itself. It was like receiving a Basque passport. Indeed, groups of *txistulariak* and *dantzariak* grew so much, that if a survey were to be carried out today, there would probably be very few Basque households in which a *txistua* has not been played at some point or another. The association achieved a widespread distribution of the *txistua* unknown until then. The objective was quantity, and in such a process, it was inevitable that quality would be sacrificed. At one point, it had thirty-five hundred members, many of whom were only patriotic supporters of the association, while others were more *txistudunak* than *txistulariak*—owners, rather than players of the *txistua*.

Post-Franco: The Txistua *in Conservatories*

During the post-Franco years, another decisive factor in the recent history of the *txistua* was its official recognition as an instrument for study in the Superior Conservatory of Donostia (San Sebastián) from the beginning of the academic year 1978–79. The consequences of creating this first professorship of *txistua* were evident: a detailed method of learning was designed, created, and published; the making of instruments, as far as both sound and tuning were concerned, was developed and improved, making it more accessible; and positions for teachers of *txistua* in numerous conservatories and schools of music were created. In short, the number of professionals of the instrument increased significantly.

40. José Antonio Arana raises his doubts about the "*txistua* of Izturitze" due to the fact that it has three holes all on the same side, whereas the *txistua* has one hole at the back (for the thumb) and two at the front (like the vast majority of three-holed flutes). But Arana continues to use the term "*txistua* of Izturitze" and of course does not doubt that it is "the oldest instrument of its kind in all the cultures of the world." José Antonio Arana, *Música Vasca* (1976; Bilbao: Caja de Ahorros Vizcaína, 1987), 32.

By the close of the twentieth century and the beginning of the new millennium the *txistua* thus began to occupy different fields of playing from those in which it had traditionally appeared. The performance of *txistua* accompanied by orchestras and other instruments, concerts of groups of *txistulariak*, and the participation of tabor players in diverse musical events were activities of a new style that, little by little, became more normal in Basque society.

Today, the *txistua* is and continues to be one of the main symbols of identity associated with traditional Basque culture. At the same time, its horizons extend to a future full of new possibilities. Indeed, at present, the *txistua* leads three-holed flutes in Europe in matters such as pedagogical means and method, teaching staff, training programs, pipe and tabor makers, the quality and refinement of instruments, the creation and periodic publication of repertoire, and performance techniques.

Folk and Traditional Dance

In 1927, during a decade when Basque culture and autochthonous folklore were promoted quite assertively, Segundo Olaeta created what might be considered the first choreographic dance group in the Basque Country, Elai Alai, made up of children and young people. Thereafter, two adult groups were formed to stage Basque dances, scenes, and choirs: Saski-Naski in Donostia (1928) and Oldargi in Bilbao (1930). The shows presented by these new groups included dances from all over the Basque Country, giving the public access to dance repertoires until then unknown, or at least not frequently seen. These shows were not based on the simple repetition of everything traditional, but required a great amount of creative work on the part of the choreographers to mantain the traditional folkloric language and at the same time be innovative. For example, in 1930, José Franco—a conductor and composer of music for brass bands who was awarded prizes in many competitions—composed *Las cuatro estaciones* (The Four Seasons) in a brass band version, which, under the Basque name of *Lau Urtaroak*, was transformed into a ballet by Olaeta. Also at this time, in Bilbao, Euzko Gaztedi (EG, the Basque Youth Movement, the youth wing of the PNV) began to organize dance displays, and many groups of *ezpatadantzariak* (sword dancers) were formed around the numerous *batzokiak*, the PNV centers or clubs, in the Basque Country. Moreover, in 1928, the Academy of *Txistua* and Dances was founded in Donostia, with the backing of the city hall and under the direction of the Society for Basque Studies, with professors of the standing of José Olaizola, Hilario Olazaran, and Luis Urteaga, who were inspired by the example of recent events in Europe:[41] "Now we can be glad to have an organization, similar to that

41. José or Joseba Olaizola Gabarain was organist of Santa María de Donostia and a composer. In 1956, his opera *Olezkari* premiered in Donostia. He won various competitions as a composer and wrote music for the journal *Txistulari*. Hilario Olazaran was the religious name of Alejandro Olazaran Salanueva. He was an organist, *txistularia*, composer of many pieces of music for the *txistua*, and the author of the first method for *txistua* ever published. For many years, he was chaplain of the Association of *Txistulariak* of the Basque Country. Luis Urteaga was a composer and organist in Zumaia (Gipuzkoa) and Donostia. His prolific production for *txistua* earned him various awards.

of English society with The English Folk Dance Society and other foreign collectives, which, blessed with all kinds of guarantees, takes into its care the conservation and full reconstruction of our music and dance."[42]

Competitions of *ezpatadantzariak* were held to promote the dance, and in 1928, the town hall of Zumaia (Gipuzkoa) created an official group of *ezpatadantza*, an example that was followed by other town halls throughout the whole of the Basque Country.[43] Groups of *ezpatadantza* were formed around schools, especially in working-class and rural areas, inspired by the model of the PNV's Euzko Gaztedi. The journal *Txistulari* echoed the initiative to form an *Ezpatadantza* Federation, whose main aim would be to organize great dance displays and concentrations of dancers, as well as to attend to the conservation of Basque choreography, imitating the role of the Association of *Txistulariak*.[44]

However, the outbreak of the Spanish Civil War of 1936 caused nearly all activity in the dance groups to come to a halt. Segundo Olaeta was forced to seek exile in Paris with his group Elai-Alai. Activity in other dance groups also disappeared, with the exception of a few local, autochthonous traditional dancers, who, as in the case of Berriz, were authorized by the local administration to continue with their traditional customs.

Figure 26. The group Elai-Alai in Gernika (ca. 1930).
Photo by permission of the *Txistulari* journal archives.

---

42. "Se crean en Donostia la Academia de Txistu y Danzas," *Txistulari* 3 (1928): 11.

43. Julian de Bedialauneta, "Resurgimiento consolador. Los 'nidos' de txistularis: Los cuadros de ezpatadantza," *Txistulari* 3 (1928): 3.

44. *Txistulari* 22 (1931): 11.

Figure 27. The group Elai-Alai performing in a theater (ca. 1935).
Photo by permission of the *Txistulari* journal archives.

After the war, in 1944, Segundo Olaeta formed the group Artibai in Markina (Marquina), Bizkaia, and began to prepare a choreographic version of the dance of San Miguel de Arretxinaga, substantially different from the traditional version, for the Congreso Eucarístico de Bilbao (Eucharistic Congress of Bilbao). In 1945, Olaeta also founded the dance group Oldarra in Biarritz (Lapurdi).[45] In 1946, the group Dindirri was formed in Bilbao and around 1950, a group named Gaztedi appeared, of which the well-known dance masters or choreographers Joseba Arrieta, Kepa Artetxe, José Luis Etxebarria, and Txomin Unzalu were members and dance masters. With the creation of the Txinpartak group, Basque theater and choir music were added to the dances, and shortly after, groups like this began to appear throughout the whole of the Basque Country.[46]

---

45. "Oldarra was a [semiprofessional folk ballet] and toured extensively. They inherited a tradition that began in the 1920s of taking folklore to the stage in a balleticized form modeled after Russian Folk ballet companies." Moreover, Oldarra was founded by Basque exiles from Hegoalde (the southern Basque Country), for whom "dance played an important part in identity maintenance." Corcostegui, "To the Beat of a Different Drum," 59, 61.

46. José Antonio Arana, *Enciclopedia Histórico Geográfico de Vizcaya*, vol. 4, s.v. "Folklore de Vizcaya" (San Sebastián: Hiru Editor, 1984), 314–15.

In the 1960s, the idea of creating a National Association of Dancers contributed to the reconsideration of the affirmation of Basque culture. The political-legal problems involved in forming an association that attempted to include the seven Basque provinces seemed insurmountable. Xabier Gereño, through his tenacity and hard work, tried to convince the Spanish authorities that if the Association of *Txistulariak* of the Basque Country had been legalized, the same could be applied to an association of dancers. However, failure to convince the authorities led to the creation of an association of dancers, EDB, Euskal Dantzarien Biltzarra (the Basque Dancers' Association), in Baiona (Lapurdi), where the French authorities were more tolerant.

Meanwhile, groups in the southern Basque Country organized themselves by provinces and held common meetings to discuss their work. Xabier Gereño founded the magazine *Dantzari*, and in total, twelve issues were published.[47] Coinciding with the Aberri Eguna, the Day of the Basque Nation,[48] in 1967 in Biarritz, the first postwar Dantzari Eguna (Dancers' Day) was celebrated with the participation of groups from all over the Basque Country.

However, in May 1968, all activity in France was brought to a halt by the demonstrations and uprising in Paris. Meanwhile, the assassination of police inspector Melitón Manzanas in August that same year by the ETA increased the repression of the Basque Country in Franco's Spain, paralyzing all activity of the EDB. However, in November 1969, the Association of Dancers and the Federation of Basque Dance Groups (Euskal Dantzarien Biltzarra) was legalized in the southern Basque Country through the Society of Friends of the Basque Country. And in 1977, after Franco's death, the Dantzari Eguna was once again held, this time in Donibane Lohizune (Saint-Jean-de-Luz) in Lapurdi. Many groups participated in the display, and following the 1978 convention in Iruñea, enthusiasm for the initial project was recuperated. In other words, dance rallies, courses, and classes were organized, and the magazine *Dantzariak* was once again published. Indeed, between August 1970 and July 1995, fifty-two issues and approximately twenty-five hundred pages of the magazine were printed. Without question, then, the momentum gathered in the 1960s for reviving interest in Basque folklore, music, and dance was given new impetus as a result of the political changes in the 1970s.

47. On *Dantzari*, see Corcostegui, "To the Beat of a Different Drum," 66–67.

48. Celebrated every year on Easter Sunday, the Day of the Basque Nation is the fiesta of Basque nationalism. Prohibited during the dictatorship of Franco, it was celebrated clandestinely.

CHAPTER THREE

The Ritual Dances of Berriz

The *dantzari-dantza* and the *soka dantza* (the latter is also known as *erregelak* or *aurreskua*) are two very different dance suites that are always danced together on saints' day celebrations in Berriz. The *dantzari-dantza* requires eight dancers, whereas the number of dancers in the *soka dantza* varies. Clothes and "tools" (as the dancers often call this paraphernalia—swords, sticks, the flag, and bells) play an essential part in the choreography and execution of the *dantzari-dantza*, while the *soka dantza* can be danced without any special attire or tools. The setting for each dance is also different. The *dantzari-dantza* is danced exclusively in the most important celebrations and on certain specific dates.[1] On the other hand, the *soka dantza*, as well as being danced in the town or village square, can also be danced in the *erromeriak* in a lighthearted, relaxed atmosphere. There are the exceptions of a few sporadic, informal exhibitions or when young people dance part of the *dantzari-dantza* suite for fun, but whatever the case, they are recognized as exceptions and transgressions of the norm. If it were possible to establish a ritual-ceremonial barometer, the *dantzari-dantza* would be more ritual-ceremonial than the *soka dantza*, or the *soka dantza* could be said to have a double setting or location, one ritual-ceremonial in the square on festive days and the other that of the *erromeriak* in a more relaxed, ludic atmosphere.

The production and ceremonial processes of the *dantzari-dantza*—and even more so the *soka dantza*—are extremely complicated due to the plethora of small details that give the ritual its meaning. Without reaching the extreme of having to repeat the whole ritual every time a mistake is made, there is a feeling of sorrow and frustration every time the dancers change the order, protocol, or ceremony of the dance. Here, I am not referring to the casual errors dancers make now and then during the dance, something the public accepts as normal and inevitable, but to the deliberate alterations in the way, the order, and the "correct" style the dance should be executed. When this happens, the ritual itself is changed and manipulated. The way in which the chain of dancers moves around the square, the order in which the women join the dance, the way in which they are introduced into the dance, the beats of the tabor between each dance number, and the way the

1. According to Aldekoa, in the old times, "the dancers danced only in the fiestas. That was it. Twice a year."

dancers join and leave the chain are all important parts of the ritual that are sometimes forgotten, omitted, or changed by the dance group. Aldekoa complained that even the dancers of his own group, San Lorenzo, had forgotten and/or changed some of the details in the ritual, despite the objections of their dance master. This discrepancy becomes clear if one compares the description of the dances with their performance as shown in the DVD of the fiesta of San Pedro (June 29, 1990) that accompanies this work.

The *dantzari-dantza* lasts for about twenty minutes, although in some performances, such as weddings, it can be shortened by omitting some of the dances. The order of the nine dances making up the *dantzari-dantza* is as follows.

1. *Agintariena* (literally, of the authorities) or *banderiena* (literally, of the flag)—an introductory salute
2. *Zortzinangoa* (eight-by-eight dance)
3. *Ezpata joko txikia* (small game of the swords)
4. *Banangoa* (one-by-one dance)
5. *Binangoa* (two-by-two dance)
6. *Ezpata joko nagusia* (main game of the swords)
7. *Launangoa* (four-by-four dance)
8. *Makil jokoa* (game of sticks)
9. *Txontxongilloa* (the finale of the suite)

The *soka dantza* lasts about ten to fifteen minutes. A shorter version is usually danced for weddings and other celebrations, with only two dancers performing a selection of dances, commonly the *aurreskua*, *atzeskua*, and the *banango zaharra*, although I have seen many other combinations. The order of the dances is as follows.

1. *Aurreskua* (the hand in front, or the first hand)
2. *Atzeskua* (the hand at the rear, or the last hand)
3. *Andra soiñua* (women's melody)
4. *Banango zaharra* (the old *banango*)
5. *Andra soiñua* (women's melody)
6. *Banango zaharra* (the old *banango*)
7. *Zortzikoa* (of eight), *seiak* (sixes), or *kunplitzekoa* (to compliment)
8. *Jota* or *fandangoa* (a dance in triple time)
9. *Arin-arina* (fast-fast or very fast) or *porrusalda* (literally, a thick leek soup)
10. *Biribilketa*, *martxa* (march), or *bidekoa* (of the road or of the street)

The correct execution of the whole ritual requires the skillful hand of the master of ceremonies and ritual specialist: the *txistularia*. It is the *txistularia* who must establish the guidelines and the general order and preparation of the events. He is the one who corrects errors and makes the necessary changes in the face of any unanticipated setback.

With all this in mind, it is clear that Aldekoa was one of the last great masters of the ritual. His knowledge and authority, as far as music and dance were concerned, were accepted by everyone—friends, enemies, and detractors alike.

Here, then, is an outlined description of the ritual of the *dantzari-dantza* and the *soka dantza* through the eyes of Alejandro Aldekoa. Other accounts of these dance suites could be cited, but because Alejandro Aldekoa is the primary focus of this study, I consider it appropriate to base my account on his point of view.[2] In order to illustrate the work in a more effective way, the text is accompanied by transcriptions of the dances and the DVD images of the fiesta of San Pedro held on June 29, 1990.

As a kind of introduction to the description of the ritual dances of Berriz, the first section below deals with the process of learning the dances and the recruitment of dancers in the context of changes that occurred during Alejandro Aldekoa's life and career.

Dance Training and the Recruitment of Dancers in Berriz

As we have seen, the teaching or transmission of dance in Berriz has been conducted following various different procedures. In an idealized past, everyone learned to dance at home, within the family unit. Parents who were dancers taught their children the noble knowledge of the dance ritual, passing it down from one generation to the next. The task of the taborer and dance master was to select the best dancers in the town or village for the main fiestas. Once the composition of the group had been decided, his job was to coordinate the execution of the dances, organize and practice the choreographical movements as a group, something that had obviously been absent in the individual teaching of the *baserria*, teach the use of the tools (flag, swords, and sticks), and refine any small detail and improve what is generally called "style."

However, after inquiring among the dancers and the general population in Berriz, I discovered a more complex reality, one that does not exactly correspond to that idealized image of a town in which all the inhabitants are dancers. Before the war, in the times when young people were supposed to learn to dance at home, many youngsters in the County of Durango went to the home of the Amezua family to be taught by Hipólito or Serafín. Even though they were taught outside, in a shady area near the house, those classes would not have been so different from classes or rehearsals today. Transmission through the family worked in some *baserria* environments, but it cannot be typified as general. Within this context, the role of the taborer and his intervention in the process of teaching the dances was also diverse and changeable.

---

2. A full description of the dance, with all its steps and variations, requires space way beyond the limits of this present work. For a detailed choreographic description of the ritual dances of Berriz, see José Luis Etxebarria, *Danzas de Vizcaya: Bizkai'ko Dantzak* (Bilbao: La Editorial Vizcaína, 1969).

Autodidactic and Academic Learning

Any attempt to establish a closed classification of the different methods used to teach the dances in Berriz is impossible, due to the great variety of situations and different ways each individual dancer was taught. Initially, one might establish two typological limits of the learning process that would help us to situate ourselves when faced with the diversity of all the learning processes involved in the dances of Berriz. At the one extreme is the process of pure, autodidactic learning. In other words, the individual learns by imitating what he observes in his surroundings in order to practice later on his own. In this case, there is not a specific framework or situation dedicated to the learning that could be classified as a class or rehearsal.[3] At the other extreme, we find the purely academic process of learning. This is instruction regulated in a determined number of hours and times, in a specific place, with the dance master or teacher to guide the learning process of the student at all times. In the case of the traditional folk dances of Berriz, this type of education—which in other environments takes place in schools or dance academies—is carried out in dance groups. Although dance groups do, on occasion, organize courses and classes, the majority of the instruction sessions within the group are in the form of rehearsals. Despite the term "rehearsal," these sessions constitute, in practice, authentic dance classes, at least while the learning process lasts. Real rehearsals, in the pure sense of the word, begin only once the necessary minimum knowledge has been acquired to be able to dance in public.

Of course, the majority of people learn, to a greater or lesser extent, through a combination of both systems, establishing a continuum between the two extremes: dancers who have learned to dance by themselves, but have received, at a given moment, instructions from a dance master or from another more experienced dancer, or students of a dance group who have practiced, at a given moment, by themselves or who have learned particular steps or variations of a step by observing other dancers.

Whatever the case, there are many people in Berriz who have learned to dance by themselves and are self-taught dancers. In the case of *solture* dances, the *jota* and the *arin-arina*, we could say that even after the founding of the first dance groups in the postwar period, formal instruction to dance *solture* did not exist. Instead, everyone learned to dance in the same square, at the *erromeria*, by imitating and copying others. From the 1950s on, and throughout the whole Basque Country, the proliferation of dance classes by dance groups and the "academization" of *solture* or *trikitia* had a counterproductive effect, one that is still noticeable today, on the *erromeriak* in the towns. The square was no longer a place to dance or a place to learn to dance, but a place to exhibit the choreographic abilities the dancers learned in the dance groups. The *jota* stopped being a free, improvised dance that everyone danced according to their own ability and skill

3. See on this John Baily and Veronica Doubleday, "Patterns of Musical Enculturation in Afghanistan," in *Music and Child Development: Proceedings of the 1987 Denver Conference*, ed. Frank Wilson and Franz Roehmann (St. Louis: MMBV Music, 1990).

and became an academic exhibition, no longer open to the participation of everyone, but only to specialists who showed off their art in the square. As a consequence of this hermeticism, many people stopped dancing *solture*, most likely as a result of feeling inadequate compared with the "specialists." And many others (myself included) never learned to dance, despite having an interest and the capacity to do so. When a *jota* is played at an *erromeria*, many stand aside to let the ones who have learned the dance in the local group take to the stage.[4]

Until not so long ago, *loture* dances were learned by "following the music" and your dance partner at the *erromeria*, that is, in an informal, autodidactic way of learning. Nearly all of us learned to dance this way, with our parents when we were young, with our brothers and sisters, but above all, in the square, at the *erromeria*. It is only comparatively recent that ballroom dancing lessons have proliferated, attracting, so it seems, a lot of people.

As far as ritual dance is concerned, there is a high percentage of self-taught dancers, especially among the older generations. Aldekoa himself learned to dance by watching his brothers, who were taught by their father. Florencio Berrojalbiz (Serafín Amezua's son-in-law) told me that he learned to dance the *dantzari-dantza* and the *erregelak* by watching others and then practicing by himself. Roberto Maiztegi (the founder of the Iremiñe dance group) learned the rudiments of the *dantzari-dantza* by accompanying and watching his cousin at rehearsals and sometimes dancing as a substitute in the group. Later, he completed his formation through a more "formal" instruction with a dance master, in this case, Alejandro Aldekoa. This mixture of self-teaching through imitation of the choreographic model, followed by a more formal formation, was the case for many people. In other cases, the learning process was more informal and less orthodox: between friends, while hiking in the mountains, and so on. The closer we get to modern times, the more the imitation/self-taught process diminishes and the academic process, with a teacher or dance master, in a class or rehearsal, increases. The latest generations of dancers in Berriz have learned to dance in classes/rehearsals in the dance group at the *ikastola* or with the Iremiñe dance group.

Aldekoa Teaching and Selecting Dancers

Faced with this panorama, in the beginning, Aldekoa began to teach the dances from first principles. This was the case with his first group of dancers, whom he taught to

4. See also Lisa Corcostegui's comments on the changing nature of dance among Basque diaspora communities in the United States. Attending an *erromeria* for the San Inazio festival in Boise, Idaho, in 2004, she observes, "As I looked around, I thought how different things were now. I thought back to Jimmy [Jausoro]'s words from our interview, 'Gradually we're losing it. Let's face it, we're losing it.' He was referring not to dance performance, but to social dancing that was once so popular. Over the years he noticed that young people, although they have continued to dance in the context of Oinkaris [the Boise dance group] and performing, have lost the tradition of dancing for pleasure. He noticed over the years from his bandstand, that they did not know how to do many dances and the dance floor slowly started to fill up with people just standing with drinks in their hands." See "To the Beat of a Different Drum: Basque Dance and Identity in the Homeland and in the Diaspora," Ph.D. diss., University of Nevada, Reno, 2005, 164.

dance in eighteen sessions, and his second group (the second generation), with whom he began to work when they were children only eight years old. Little by little, Aldekoa gave up this type of work and left teaching in the hands of others. The dancers of the last generation with whom he came into contact—his third group—came to him after having received their basic training with other instructors, at the *ikastola* or in Iremiñe. Gradually, Aldekoa took up the role of selector again, like the taborers of old, only this time, the basic work of dance learning had not been carried out in the *baserria*, in the family unit, or through self-teaching, but through other dance groups that worked with children. The people teaching in these dance groups were (and are) older dancers who do that work as volunteers. Sometimes they are not the best dancers or the most qualified for teaching, but those who are ready to do that kind of voluntary work. Because of this, I do not believe they can be given the name of dance "master" as it is applied to Alejandro Aldekoa.

> I've always been patient teaching what I'd learned. When you're teaching the first steps of a dance to the dancers, you, yourself, have to dance a lot, to teach this one, then that one, then all of them. Later, when one from the group has learned to dance well, he can help you a bit with the rest, but until then, to teach them all, you have to jump and dance from one to the other if you have to, and me, when I was forty, I was still quite agile, and if I had to repeat the same step ten times, well, I'd repeat it, but now, as the years go by, you get clumsier.[5]

Age and the gradual physical deterioration associated with growing old may have been one of the reasons why Aldekoa gave up the initial teaching of dance, but why, then, did the dancers formed in other groups want, at any given moment, to join Aldekoa's group?

> The first were good, the second were better, and the ones now are first class, the best. That's what Artetxe [the dance master in the Andra Mari group from Galdakao] says as well. And we don't rehearse much . . . but while other groups spend time dancing different dances from Navarre, Gipuzkoa . . . we only do our own. You can see that in the style of dancing. [Juan Antonio] Urbeltz [folklorist and director of the Argia group in Donostia] once said to me:
>
> "We can't dance like you. We have good dancers, well trained, agile, and athletic but the character you give to the dance . . . we can't get it, that style, we have an extensive repertoire with different dances. That, you can tell."[6]

Aldekoa was conscious of the quality of his group and of his leadership in the dances of Berriz and the County of Durango. On the one hand, they were the guardians of the old customs that Aldekoa had learned from his father, and on the other, they were the

---

5. Alejandro Aldekoa, interview by the author, April 12, 1996.

6. Ibid. Corcostegui mentions the fact that Urbeltz and the Argia group learned the *dantzari-dantza* directly from Aldekoa. See "To the Beat of a Different Drum," 58.

only ones who conserved the true style of the *dantzari-dantza*, thanks to their specialization, dedicating themselves exclusively to their own dances. They were the best. They received recognition and confirmation of their quality from all sides, from prestigious choreographers and folklorists alike. His group was not called "the first division" for nothing.[7]

> Now I have three dancers from that group that split up [Iremiñe]. First I put a kid from the *ikastola* into the group, when he was a little older, fourteen or so. He still couldn't beat time with his feet very well in the *dantzari-dantza*, and he couldn't dance the *eskasak* well, either. With time, he learned like the rest of the group, and some two years later, when he came in, another dancer said:
>
> "There he is, the one from your group, you see, in the first division. Is there a difference or not?"
>
> All of them want to come here, to the first division. They've learned to dance with my disciples [a reference to Roberto Maiztegi and the rest of the dance masters of the Iremiñe group], but they've still got a lot of detail to learn.[8]

Aldekoa also complained of not having the energy necessary to maintain two groups: "I can't admit everybody into the group. If you have eight dancers in the group and another six reserves, that's fourteen. That's enough to be able to work. If I were forty again, I'd have a second group, but the years keep adding up, and I can't."[9]

Another of the possible reasons why other dancers were interested in dancing with Aldekoa may have been opportunism. San Lorenzo was the official group of the town hall, and because Aldekoa was the master of ceremonies for the ritual of the main fiestas, he decided who would dance. It was a question of dancing in the square, taking part in the real ritual, not a display or a performance of any old type. Aldekoa's group held a position of great prestige, and this gave it a kind of power.

The Dance Groups Today

As Aldekoa observed, the movement to form dance groups, principally an urban phenomenon, gave way to an inevitable, progressive abandonment and omission of the traditional forms and styles that they were supposedly trying to represent and maintain. The creation of dance displays in which all kinds of stage resources are used and the original choreographies are mixed or changed is a symptom of the decline in the original forms and functions of dance. Besides, even though traditional forms may, at times, be preserved with as much detail and as faithfully as possible, really the only thing that is achieved is the creation of a kind of museum of choreographic forms or the representation or copying of the dances separated from their true environment and social context.

---

7. This phrase is derived from the world of soccer, a very popular sport in the Basque Country.

8. Alejandro Aldekoa, interview by the author, April 12, 1996.

9. Ibid.

In this sense, the social implications and repercussions of dance become more and more scarce. Now, only a few people dance in the square.

Lately, however, the popular diffusion of dance as a ludic and/or socially cohesive element seems to have aroused interest in some dance groups, musicians, and Basque researchers alike. Indeed, the first steps are being taken toward interactive dance initiatives through the organization of events in which the public is the actor and dances alongside the dance masters. In other words, the present system of choreographic folk dance groups is beginning to be questioned.

Requirements for Dancing

Traditionally, as I've noted previously, to dance in the square, to be a *plaza mutilla* (a young man eligible to dance in public), one had to be at least seventeen years old and a bachelor, but with Aldekoa, all of this changed. Boys under the age of seventeen and married men danced in his San Lorenzo group. Belonging to a group thus was imposed on the old criteria for selection. In the 1997 fiestas, after Aldekoa's death, the town hall again called on all unmarried men over the age of seventeen to present themselves for selection to dance by the taborer, provoking the anger of the San Lorenzo dance group, some of whose most prominent dancers were married.

Everything seems to indicate that bachelorhood was not an indispensable requirement to dance established by law, but something logical, given that the role of ritual dance in Berriz was the initiation and presentation in society of its young men. Obviously, though, the meaning, importance, and functions of dance have changed and adapted to new times and new sociocultural tendencies. Despite the fact that Berriz can be considered traditional when compared, for example, with Bilbao, even there, new types of families and marital statuses emerged to complicate the selection of the dancers. For example, now there are many different ways of living as a couple and having a family, without being married or without the situation having been legalized. What about divorcees, or, in the still hypothetical, but nevertheless possible case of homosexual dancers living together as a couple?

Defenders of the established selection criteria, among them the mayor, Rosa Mari Ostolaza, allege that, although the system may be far from perfect, it at least assures or facilitates the rotation and renewal of the dancers. If this were not so, a few prominent dancers would dance year after year. This is the case of the *banderaria* (flag waver) in Aldekoa's group, Karmelo Angiozar, bailiff of Berriz, one of the leaders of the San Lorenzo dance group and one of the main voices of protest against the move to reintroduce the "old rules" of recruitment.

The Selection of the Dancers

The selection of the dancers who were to take part in the festive celebrations of San Pedro's Day and Santa Isabel's Day in Berriz was in the hands of the municipal taborer. The selection took place in the fields of Iremiñe or Idemiñe in an act whose solemnity

Figure 28. Germán Aldekoa as official taborer with the selected dancers on Santa Isabel's Day, July 2, 1997. Photo by the author.

and importance varied according to the circumstances.[10] During the golden years, when the number and quality of the dancers allowed, the selection was an important part of the ritual, because it marked the moment to decide who was going to dance and represent the town of Berriz in its most important fiestas. After the Civil War, a period of decline began. There were not enough dancers, and the *txistularia* (Serafín Amezua) had problems completing the group. With Aldekoa, the selection process was abolished, and his own group danced in the fiestas. After Alejandro, his son Germán returned to the previous selection system, due in the main part to pressure from the Iremiñe dance group, who reclaimed the right of all the dancers in Berriz to be selected to dance.

Under the present system of selection since 1997, hardly anything is decided, and it is the dancers of the Iremiñe dance group who participate in the fiestas. This is for two reasons. On the one hand, there are the tensions and problems between the two local dance groups (Iremiñe and San Lorenzo), and on the other, Germán Aldekoa has refused to exercise his authority as municipal taborer and impose his own criteria for fear of

10. The place of selection is the reason why, in 1969, when Roberto Maiztegi founded a new dance group from within the ranks of Aldekoa's group, he chose to name it Iremiñe.

creating more problems and hard feelings. The importance of the selection system today is purely symbolic. It represents the end of the hegemony and monopoly of Alejandro Aldekoa and his group and the return to the old system of selection, open to all dancers in Berriz.

Selection Criteria

What are the characteristics of a good dancer? What criteria are followed at the time of selecting the group? Despite the subjectivity of appreciation and the fact that criteria are almost as numerous and various as there are opinions on the subject, with the guidance of Aldekoa, I believe it is possible to outline some of the criteria by which the people of Berriz judge dance and dancers. Under no given order of priority, here are some of those criteria.

To Keep Time

A good dancer has to be able to keep time without losing step.

> Steps are notes marked on the ground with your feet to the same time as the music, that is, beating the rhythm with your feet. Within a beat, you can put in more or fewer notes, just like with an instrument. That is, the steps in a dance are the notes in music. To keep time is just that: follow the time with your feet without losing the beat. In a beat, you can put in the double amount of steps or halve them, but you must always keep time. When you dance with a *txistularia*, you have to follow the rhythm of the *txistua* in every step you make, beating time without losing control or making a mistake. That's it: that's good.[11]

Strength and Agility

Physical fitness is another virtue of a good dancer. Aldekoa valued the agility of some dancers who conveyed speed and confidence with their movements. In others, he praised their strength, their power, and their resilience. He also made it clear, however, that to be a formidable athlete did not automatically convert one into a good dancer of the *dantzari-dantza* and the *soka dantza.*

Repertoire

Another factor Aldekoa valued was knowledge of the whole repertoire—to know how to dance all the dances well. The ideal dancer has to know how to dance in all the positions of the *dantzari-dantza*, whether it be the *aurreskua* or the *atzeskua*. In the *banango zaharra*, he has to be able to do the *grabilleta*, making circles in the air with the foot, just as well with his right leg as with his left, and of course, he must dance with grace and style.

---

11. Alejandro Aldekoa, interview by the author, April 15, 1996.

Demeanor

Aldekoa also valued the dancer's demeanor in front of the public—his powers of concentration and behavior.

> In my first group, there was a dancer who learned all the dances with enormous ease. He was very quick—the first, always the first. But when we had to dance in the square, he was also the first to be distracted by the public. At the beginning of the *banangoa*, for example, the rest of the dancers started to dance, and he just stood there . . . he always used to do that kind of thing. Instead of concentrating on what he was doing, he'd get distracted by the public. Other than that, he was a very good dancer, a fast learner, but he had that problem.[12]

Physical Appearance

Despite the present tendency to avoid discriminating against people in terms of their physical appearance, the height and build of a dancer is still a characteristic to be valued for selection today. One of the characteristics remembered of the famous and celebrated group of dancers who performed in London and Paris in the 1920s was the height of its members. If a dancer is agile and strong, if he can do the *grabilleta* and raise his leg well, and if he keeps time, then he is a good dancer. However, if he is also more than 180 centimeters (5 feet 10 inches) tall, so much the better.

Families of Dancers

A family's commitment to dance may also influence selection. There are many families whose members seem to possess a marked predisposition for dance, which is passed down from generation to generation. To be the son or grandson of a well-known, predominant dance figure creates a certain expectation among the public, anxious to compare the new generation to the old while at the same time remembering the past. For example, in Berriz, some of the dancers who performed as the *banderaria* in the 1990s were brothers from the Alberdi family. Their father, Miguel, and their grandfather were also *banderariak.*

Style

Related to all these characteristics is what might be termed "style." It is a compendium of a number of characteristics, such as range of gestures, speed of movement, decorations, and details that make the dances and dancers of Berriz different. Without any doubt, there is a certain unique style in the way the *dantzari-dantza* and the *soka dantza* are danced in Berriz. As Aldekoa pointed out: "Not even the most agile, professional ballet dancers of some folk dance groups, with their powerful techniques and physical fitness, could dance the *dantzari-dantza* like the boys from Berriz."[13] Scholars of dance in the Basque

---

12. Alejandro Aldekoa, interview by the author, April 9, 1996.

13. Ibid.

Country also speak of a unique style of movement and gestures typical of people from rural areas. Their movements are acquired through their culture, a style impossible to achieve through classical ballet techniques.

Whatever the case may be, it is obvious that the dancers of Berriz have maintained their own special way of dancing and that, apart from the countless personal variations that exist, they share many common characteristics distinctive of their local style. To give an example, let us see what has happened to two of the most characteristic steps of the dances of Berriz, the *puntapioa* or *artazia* and the *grabilleta.*

Many dancers, influenced to a certain degree by the more academic style of dance from Gipuzkoa that has become very popular in folk dance groups throughout the Basque Country, lift their leg straight up in the air with their foot extended when they do the *artazia* or *puntapioa* (The following illustrations are by Txomin Unzalu.):

In Berriz, however, a good dancer lifts his leg in the air with an *ostikoa,* a term which means literally "a kick." First he kicks his leg up into the air with his knee bent, and then, from this position, extends it as energetically as possible.

At the top of the upward movement, the tip of the foot is supposed to be bent backward, stretching the calf muscles: "when the dancer is good, you should be able to see the sole of his espadrilles from the back."[14]

The *ostikoa* is a much harder step than the simple *artazia* and requires good physical fitness and a lot of effort to execute. Because of its abruptness, it is the cause of frequent injuries to the muscles and/or ligaments. Very few dancers are capable of dancing the whole *dantzari-dantza* dance suite and then proceeding immediately to dance the *aurreskua* with an *ostikoa* in each *puntapioa*. In the *aurreskua* alone, the leg is raised (*puntapioa*) about twenty-four times. According to Karmelo Angiozar, one of the best and most prominent *aurreskulariak* to have danced with Aldekoa: "It is very difficult, if not impossible, to dance the *dantzari-dantza* and the *aurreskua* in the rehearsal on the eve of San Pedro's Day and then repeat it in the performance the following day, both at noon and then again in the evening, doing the *ostikoa* in each *puntapioa*. Nobody can do it . . . not without injuring themselves."[15]

Nevertheless, Aldekoa complained of the progressive deterioration of the dances and of how the dancers made less of an effort to execute the dance steps correctly than in the past.

The *grabilleta* consists of the dancer drawing a circle in the air, usually with the right foot,[16] at the same time that he spins around on his left foot, which he uses as a support.

In Berriz, the *grabilleta* is performed by raising the right knee and then drawing a high, wide circle: "the older dancers say that for the dancer to be considered good at

14. Alejandro Aldekoa, interview by the author, April 23, 1996.

15. Karmelo Angiozar, interview by the author, June 20, 1999.

16. The exception being the *banango zaharra*, where the right and left feet are used alternatively.

performing *grabilletak*, he has to dirty his trousers with his espadrilles just above the *sapak* (bells) that are worn below the knee."[17]

The dancers from Iurreta draw smaller circles at a much lower height when executing the *grabilleta.* For this reason, they have time, in some steps, to draw two circles,[18] whereas in Berriz, they have time for only one. Since the *dantzari-dantza* became popular as the Basque national dance, diffused by the PNV and Euzko Gaztedi under the name of *ezpata-dantza*, it was established that the *grabilleta* would be executed from behind, bending the knee some 90 degrees backward and drawing a flat, almost vertical circle in the air. The dancers of Berriz never fully understood the reason for such a change.

The Dance

After the dancers had been selected, rehearsals for the fiestas began. The character of these rehearsals developed in a similar way to that of the system of transmission and teaching of the dances and the selection process. As we've seen, in the past, the taborer played an active part in his role of dance master, and the rehearsals served to coordinate the group of chosen dancers. During his time, Aldekoa exercised fully this role of dance master, directing his own group, which was to perform in the fiestas, while today, his son Germán limits himself to playing for the dancers of the Iremiñe dance group without ever exercising the role of dance master. The dancers learn the dances and rehearse in their group, and the *txistularia* plays for them on one or two occasions before the performance.

Despite the fact that Germán Aldekoa is more than qualified, both as a taborer and dance master, to direct the group of dancers and correct their mistakes, a lack of time, the fact that the dancers belong to Iremiñe (the rival dance group), and maybe a lack of will and interest in leadership on Germán's part turn the rehearsals into a merely symbolic act.

---

17. Alejandro Aldekoa, interview by the author, April 23, 1996.

18. The tempo of their music is also slower.

Figure 29. The rehearsal the day before San Pedro (1998).
Photo by Jordi Urioz.

The Flag

The flag of Berriz is one of the most important symbols of the ritual, and as such, it is kept securely locked up in the town hall. On the day of the ritual, the dancers walk in procession, carrying the flag, from the town hall to the town square. There, it is the central symbol of the first item of the *dantzari-dantza* dance suite, known as the *agintariena* or *banderiena*. Once the dance has ended, the bailiff takes the flag from the *banderaria* and keeps it until the end of the ritual, when he gives it back to the *banderaria* for the return procession to the town hall.

The dancer responsible for carrying and waving the flag, as well as being strong, is usually one of the best dancers in the group. The position of *banderaria* is one of the most prestigious ones in the ritual. The handling of the flag has its own technique and is an art in itself. According to Aldekoa, Patxo Alberdi's father was so good and the public so appreciative of the way he made the flag "dance" that, even after he stopped dancing, as an old man, the dance group would call on him to accompany them only to wave the flag in the first number of the *dantzari-dantza*.

Figure 30. Waving the flag at the 1998 rehearsal. Photo by Jordi Urioz.

It appears that the old flag of Berriz, dating from 1700, disappeared during the Civil War. In the postwar period during the Franco dictatorship, the authorities forced the dancers to dance with the Spanish flag until, in 1952, a new flag, very similar to the old one, was ordered for the dancers. Since then, various flags, all copies of the old one, have been sewn. As noted (see chapter 1), the first performance of Aldekoa's group in 1952 was notable because on asking the town hall for the new flag of Berriz, the mayor sent them the Spanish flag. At the last moment, the dancers decided that they were not going to dance with a symbol that represented Spanish domination and, with the excuse that the *banderaria*, Patxo Alberdi, had sprained his wrist (they bandaged his arm to support their claim), they danced without any flag at all.[19]

19. On this occasion, the omission of one of the fundamental symbols of the ritual and the primordial choreographic element of the first number of the dance suite acquired a greater relevance than if it had been present.

Figure 31. The flag of the dancers of Berriz made in 1994. Photo by Jordi Urioz.

The Dancers' Clothing

The clothes worn by the dancers of Berriz have changed only slightly over the years, following the tendencies and fashion of Basque folklore. "When I was twelve," remarked Aldekoa, "the men who are now [in 1996] eighty, eighty-three, eighty-four years old, danced all dressed in white, but our parents, twenty years older than them, danced wearing a vest."[20]

It appears that the growing influence of Basque nationalist folklore at the beginning of the twentieth century also affected the clothing worn by the dancers. The vest was abandoned, and, in general, not much importance was given to the dancers' clothing. To be able to dance, it was enough just to wear white pants and a white shirt, of any style and material, white espadrilles, a wide red belt, and a red beret. It was a way of trying to make things easier so that all the Basque Country could dance the *ezpata-dantza*, the

---

20. Alejandro Aldekoa, interview by the author, April 23, 1996.

national dance. The return of respect for local tradition and the attempt to rescue and preserve the old style of dance also influenced the clothing worn for dance, and so, at the end of the 1950s, when Aldekoa began working with his second group, he reintroduced the vest. Since then, this piece of clothing has become popular among the rest of the dance groups in the Basque Country. Later, the Andra Mari dance group from Galdakao (with whom I have worked) chose to wear white linen pants and shirts like the ones used until the nineteenth century, and Aldekoa's group did the same.[21]

The clothing worn by the dancers of Berriz today consists of the following items.

- White espadrilles with red ribbons and white socks. The soles are made from esparto grass, but on some occasions (never for the main festive celebrations), rubber soles may be used.
- White linen pants without a fly or belt loops, open at the back and tied with a ribbon, a copy of those worn traditionally.
- A wide red belt.
- A white longsleeved linen shirt with no buttons except on the cuffs, embroidered on the chest.
- A dark-colored vest, usually black or gray.
- A red beret.
- On the vest pocket, the dancers wear a *sienprebibea* (*Helichrysum stoechas*). It is a small yellow flower that keeps its appearance even when dry, hence its name *sienprebibea* (*sempervivum*, or everliving).

If any of the dancers were in mourning for a family member, both he and his partner (in the row next to him) would dance with black ribbons on their espadrilles, a wide black belt, and a black beret.

Paraphernalia

The dancers' paraphernalia, or tools, consist of the *sapak*, *ezpatak*, and *makillak*. The *sapa* (mane) is the name given to the cushion or piece of fur or leather placed on the foreheads of yoked oxen to prevent the strap that ties them to the yoke from rubbing. The same name is given to the set of sixteen bells on a piece of leather that the dancers who are to dance the *dantzari-dantza* wear just below the knee. According to Aldekoa, the old bells were made of bronze and were much heavier than the ones worn today.

Ezpatak are swords. The town hall of Berriz owns a set of old *ezpatak*, the origin of which is unknown. In Aldekoa's opinion, the swords of the town council of Berriz are special, not only for their historic and aesthetic value but also for the sound their metal makes when they clash during the dance. The swords of Aldekoa's San Lorenzo group

21. There has always been a very good and fluent relationship between Aldekoa's group and the Andra Mari group of Galdakao.

and most of the dance groups in the Basque Country are made by local welders who are frequently members of the group or friends and who know how to work with iron. The quality of these swords is not very good, at least compared with that of the old ones kept in the Berriz town hall: "The swords of the town hall have a special sound, a certain ring when they clash. You can't compare the high-pitched, crystalline sound of those old swords with ours."[22]

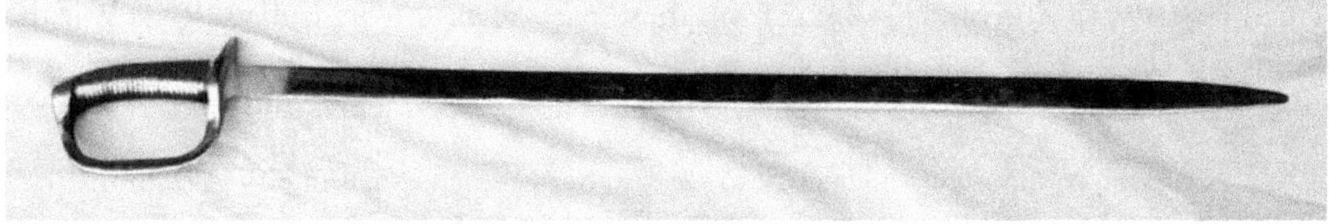

Figure 32. One of the old swords from Berriz. Photo by the author.

The sticks, or *makillak*, used by the dancers are usually made from turned beech or ash wood. Aldekoa had heard that, in the past, the old dancers used to go to the mountains and make their own sticks. One time, with the help of a friend from the neighboring town of Garai, he chose a few straight hazelnut trees, cut them down, peeled off the bark, cut the wood into sticks, allowed them to dry, and then varnished them. According to Aldekoa, these sticks are lighter and more resistant than the others. They do not splinter, and the sound they make is much more powerful than that of most sticks.

Figure 33. Detail of the reverse side of the flag of the dancers of Berriz (1994), with a picture of a *txistua*, *danbolina*, *atabala*, a pair of drumsticks, and the dancers' paraphernalia: an *ezpata*, a *makilla*, and a pair of *sapak*. Photo by the author.

---

22. Alejandro Aldekoa, interview by the author, April 23, 1996.

The Txistularia*'s Clothing*

The clothing worn by the taborer in Berriz is not subject to the strict rules that apply to the dancers. In general, the taborer can dress as he pleases. The same is true for many other dance groups, where the immaculate and well-cared-for clothing of the dancers contrasts sharply with that of the *txistularia*, who performs dressed in any old way. Yet Aldekoa liked to dress with a certain dignity and decorum. However, "If it was hot on San Pedro's Day, I would just wear a shirt, not a jacket. What's the point in suffering when it's so hot? The old *txistulariak* from these parts always wore jackets. That was the fashion then."[23]

When asked whether he thought the beret obligatory, Aldekoa said:

> No, I don't suppose it's obligatory to wear it, but it's the normal thing to do. In the past, everybody wore a beret, especially a *txistularia*. I never saw a *txistularia* without his beret, except for the ones from Markina. My teacher didn't wear one, but when he had to perform, he used to put it on. My sons don't wear it—it's not the custom anymore—but us old men, we only take it off for Mass and when we go to bed.[24]

Donien-aretxa, Donienatxa, Txopue

On the eve of San Pedro's Day, June 28, the dancers meet in the town square to put up the *donienatxa* (maypole) or *txopue* (poplar tree). Nowadays, printed programs of the fiestas, published by the town hall, are distributed, giving details of timetables of all the events. Before, none of that was necessary, because everybody knew the order of the dancers' performances.[25]

The *donien-aretxa*, or "oak of the saints," is the local name given to the maypole, one of the central symbols of the ritual. In the past, the young dancers from the town would find the highest tree in the vicinity and cut it down to place in the center of the square for the fiestas.[26] These days, however, the trunk is kept from one year to the next, hanging under the porch of the church. This not only saves a lot of time and hard work going to find, cut down, and bring a tree to the square, but also makes it easier to put into place, because the tree is a lot lighter, since it is dry. Flowers and recently the *ikurriña* (Basque flag) are placed on the top of the trunk before it is put into place. Using ropes and a ladder, the dancers raise the trunk into position, placing it in a hole in the middle of the square especially dug for the purpose. Once the trunk is in place, wooden wedges are put around the base to secure it. The square is now ready, and the rehearsal may begin.

---

23. Ibid.

24. Ibid.

25. Ibid.

26. In the municipal archive of 1654, it states that the mayor called on the service of the dancers to prepare and put the *donien-aretxa* into place, paying them twenty-three reales for their work. Vicente de Urquiza, *Antigüedades de Berriz* (Bilbao: Caja de Ahorros Vizcaína, 1988), 70.

A long time ago, in my father's time, no sooner had the trunk been put into place [than] the rehearsal began. In the *aurreskua*, the priests' maids were invited to dance in the chain. At that time, there were some four priests living in the curate's house, and each one had his own maid. They were usually *neskazaharrak* [literally, old girls, meaning spinsters]. After the rehearsal, there was a kind of *erromeria*, but that's disappeared now. Each dancer went to the rehearsal dressed as he pleased. The only thing they had to wear were the espadrilles, the *txapela* [beret], and the *sapak* [bells]. Other than that, they could wear what they liked, even a track suit—anything. The flag and the tools belong to the town. After the *dantzari-dantza*, they dance the *aurreskua* if there are people about. They usually need girls, so if there's nobody about, then they don't dance the *aurreskua*.[27]

Figure 34. *Donien-aretxa*, June 28, 1998. Photos by Jordi Urioz.

San Pedro and Santa Isabel

As already mentioned, the patron saints' days of Berriz are June 29 (Saint Peter the Apostle) and July 2 (the visit of Our Lady to Saint Isabel). The official saint's day of the parish of Berriz, however, is that of Saint John the Evangelist, December 27. Because the

27. Alejandro Aldekoa, interview by the author, April 23, 1996.

summer is a better time of year to celebrate fiestas, the municipality must have decided many years ago to change its patron saint. Nowadays, only a few people actually know that Saint John the Evangelist is the official saint, and even the church is known as San Pedro's Church.

Until about 1968, the festive celebrations began with the procession of the dancers and the municipal authorities from the town hall to the church, where they attended Mass with the rest of the parishioners. The taborer accompanied the procession, playing the "March of San Ignacio," Ignatius of Loyola, the patron saint of the Basque Country. Before the religious ceremony began, the priest and altar boys would leave the church by the main door to welcome the municipal authorities and begin the religious procession. Together, they would walk around the outside of the church, passing in front of the curate's house, until they arrived back at the porch. Here, they would stand until the *txistularia* had finished playing the "March of San Ignacio," linked up to the final part of the *agintariena* (in 3/8 time), with the *banderaria* waving the flag in honor of the saints. Once this part of the ceremony was completed, the authorities and priests would enter the church, again to the sound of the "March of San Ignacio." The dancers, with the help of the bailiff, would collect all their tools and leave them under the porch of the town hall before returning to church to take their places for Mass. Inside the church, the authorities would sit in the first row, with the dancers behind them. After Mass, the dancers went back to the town hall, from where they walked in procession to the town square to dance the *dantzari-dantza* and the *soka dantza.*

This is the point at which the festivities begin today. The procession to Mass was withdrawn from the festivities with the movement of ecclesiastical renovation in the 1960s and when the new Basque priests sent to Berriz decided to stop all favoritism and distinction toward the authorities.[28]

Nowadays, the dancers meet at the town hall at midday, where they dress. At one o'clock, after Mass, the mayor, accompanied by another representative of the town hall, walks in procession with the dancers from the town hall to the square. At the front of the procession, the *txistularia* plays the march *agintariena.* Behind him walk the dancers in two lines of four, the *banderaria* carrying the flag of the dancers of Berriz, and at the rear follow the authorities. On arriving at the square, the dancers form a corridor for the authorities to pass through, leading them to the church porch, where they are to preside over the dance. Before, the mayor, deputy mayor, the marquise of Berriz, and the priest used to sit down, but when Rosa Mari Ostogain became mayor in 1991, she always remained standing, even though chairs are placed in the porch for the authorities—her way of showing the profound respect she had for the dance ritual and the dancers. From the porch, the mayor presides over the *dantzari-dantza* and, after a short break, the *soka dantza* or *aurreskua.*

---

28. We do not know to what extent this development was influenced by the political situation at the time, when the majority of the Basque clergy was Basque nationalist and the municipal authorities were pro-Franco.

Figure 35. San Pedro's Parish Church in Berriz. Photo by the author.

The Dantzari-Dantza

As mentioned above, in order to illustrate and complete the description of the dances, a DVD with video samples of the *dantzari-dantza* and *soka dantza* from Berriz, recorded on San Pedro's Day in 1990, accompanies this work. More detailed information about the DVD can be found at the end of the book. For a more comprehensive approach to the dances, in addition to the text and the video, the prescriptive transcriptions of the dances are included in Appendix 1 at the end of the book.

In order to facilitate the access to these different items, a description of each dance, the tracks on the DVD, and the transcriptions are numbered in the same order and labeled conveniently.

01 *Agintariena* or *banderiena.* The *txistularia* stands to one side of the authorities, still playing the *agintariena,* while the dancers position themselves again in two lines of four, facing the authorities. In this position, they begin to mark out the steps on the ground with their feet without moving from their places, waiting for the music to begin da capo. Then, and only then, they walk in formation to salute the mayor, one by one, with their swords held high. Every dancer carries a stick in his left hand and a sword in his right, except the *banderaria* and his partner. The *banderaria* carries the flagpole on his left shoulder, holding one of the ends of the flag and his sword in his right hand. With both hands occupied, it is his partner who carries his stick for him. The *banderaria* is the last to salute the authorities. Once again in their positions, the dancers put their sticks to one side, and the *banderaria* moves to occupy the central position. At the end of the *agintariena,* the *txistularia* plays a cadence with a pause. At this point, the *banderaria* throws his beret into the air, the rest of the group kneel, and the *banderaria* waves the flag, three times to the left, three to the right, and then three to the left again, in time to the music. This part of the dance ends when the flag has been furled. Although the choreography of this dance number is very simple, it is one of the most emotive for the people of Berriz, and it is rarely excluded from a performance of the *dantzari-dantza* dance suite.[29] The approximate duration of the march in 2/4 time is about fifty seconds and that of the final in 3/8 part is fifteen seconds.

02 *Zortzinangoa. Zortzinangoa* means "eight-by-eight dance." As soon as the *agintariena* has ended, the taborer begins to beat the rhythm known as the *ezpata-dantza,* on the tabor:

29. In some performances, for example at a wedding, some of the nine dances that make up the dance suite have to be excluded for obvious reasons of time. The first and last dances, due to their importance and significance, are rarely excluded.

In the meantime, the dancers wait in their positions until the *banderaria* has recovered his beret and picked up his sword. Once they are all ready, the taborer begins to play the melody on the *txistua*. The first time he plays, the dancers remain still, waiting for the last bar of the whole melody, the point at which they begin to dance, before the *txistularia* starts to play the melody again. The dancers dance, changing places with each other, to end on the third round of the melody, back in their original positions. The approximate duration is fifty seconds.

03 *Ezpata joko txikia. Ezpata joko txikia* means "small game of the swords," in comparison with the eighth dance of the *dantzari-dantza*, *ezpata joko nagusia*, "main game of the swords," so called because it lasts longer and the choreography is much more complex. Aldekoa insisted that the original name for this dance was *jokoa* (game),[30] and not *dantza* (dance), the latter being more widespread among folklorists and dance groups in the Basque Country. The dance consists of a series of crosses and clashes of swords between the eight members of the dance group. It is a short dance, and due to its simplicity, many folklorists believe that it is possibly a remnant of another dance or that it is incomplete, a part having been lost.[31] The approximate duration is twenty seconds.

04 *Banangoa. Banango* means "one-by-one dance." The taborer begins to play, beating a few bars on the tabor. When he begins to play the melody on the *txistua*, the dancers put down their swords at the side of their sticks. At the end of the first repetition, in exactly the same way as in the *zortzinangoa*, at the end of the last bar, the dancers begin to dance. First, the eight dancers dance together, as in the *zortzinangoa*, then they come to the front of the group, one by one, to dance alone. Aldekoa understood that the meaning of the dance is to show off the individual abilities of each dancer in front of the public. After each dancer has danced at the front of the group, all eight of them dance together again, as in the *zortzinangoa*, each ending the dance in their original positions. The approximate duration is three minutes and ten seconds.

05 *Binangoa. Binangoa* means "two-by-two dance." This is similar in structure to the *banangoa*. The taborer begins to play alone, the whole group dances together, then the dancers come to the front, this time two by two. Once all four couples have danced, the whole group of eight dance together again. According to Aldekoa, this dance represents a

---

30. It is important to bear in mind that in some areas of the Basque Country, *jokoa* can mean a "game," but incorporating some degree of competitive interaction, as opposed to *jolasa* (play), which is noncompetitive and usually associated with children. See Joseba Zulaika, *Basque Violence: Metaphor and Sacrament* (Reno: University of Nevada Press, 1988), 169–70 and 172–81. In parts of Bizkaia, the word *olgeta* (play) is used (from the verb *olgau*, meaning to play or have fun) instead of *jolasa*, so here, the notion of *jokoan*, literally "at play," is regarded as competitive (and can mean playing a sport, cards, and even gambling), whereas *olgetan*, also literally meaning "at play," is purely playful (meaning children's playing or joking around).

31. For example, José Luis Etxebarria, *Danzas de Vizcaya: Bizkai'ko Dantzak* (Bilbao: La Editorial Vizcaína, 1969), 36. For the English folklorist Rodney Gallop, the sword dances were the most interesting dances of the southern Basque Country, and in his opinion, the best of these were to be seen in Berriz and Errenteria (Gipuzkoa). Rodney Gallop, *A Book of the Basques* (1930; Reno: University of Nevada Press, 1970), 185.

rivalry between the two dancers to see which of them dances the best. The approximate duration is two minutes.

06 *Ezpata joko nagusia.* The dancers are unarmed. Two beats of the tabor signal the order for them to pick up their swords and dance the *ezpata joko nagusia*, the "main game of the swords." Asked about what the dance represents, Aldekoa replied: "The meaning of the dance . . . well I don't know. Before gunpowder was invented, men fought with swords, and it seems that it's a war dance inspired by those times. A sword dance or war dance, where the dancers imitate the fighting, crossing their swords, I suppose."[32]

The melody of the first part, written in 5/8 time, termed by some the *eskasak* or *seiak*, also appears as the opening piece of the eighth dance of the *dantzari-dantza*, *makil jokoa* (game of sticks). After the 5/8, the *txistularia* plays a kind of contredanse in 2/4 time. This is the point at which the game of swords begins. At the beginning of each part of the dance, an introduction, known as the *deia* (call) is played, a kind of coda to call the dancers to attention and to mark the beginning and the end of each part of the dance. The approximate duration is two minutes.

07 *Launangoa.* Again, the taborer begins by beating a few bars on the tabor. When he begins to play the *txistua*, the dancers put their swords on the ground. The melody is played once, as an introduction, with the dancers standing in their appropriate positions. *Launangoa* means "four-by-four dance," and following the choreographic pattern established in the *zortzinangoa*, *banangoa*, and *binangoa*, the dancers this time dance in fours. There is a part of this dance, however, where the dancers dance two by two. This has been interpreted as an error. On August 10, 1960, San Lorenzo's Day, a corrected version of the dance was presented by Alejandro Aldekoa and his group at the fiestas in Mendibil, following a suggestion made to Aldekoa by José Luis Etxebarria.[33] With time, however, Aldekoa went back to the original version.

Another characteristic peculiar to the *launangoa* is that to enable the dancers to end the dance in their original positions, the eight dancers together have to dance not once, as at the end of the *banangoa* or *binangoa*, but twice. The approximate duration is two minutes and forty seconds.

08 *Makil jokoa.* Two beats of the tabor give the order for the dancers to pick up their sticks. The *txistularia* plays the *eskasak*, the same melody he plays at the beginning of the *ezpata joko nagusia*, but this time the choreography is different. After the initial *deia*, the dancers, one by one, salute the authorities and the public in front of them, sticks in hand and head bowed. They then begin to dance the corresponding steps until they reach the game of sticks. Similar in rhythm to the game of swords, the *makil jokoa* is also a type of contredanse in 2/4 time, but divided in two by a *deia* in the middle. During the first part of

32. Alejandro Aldekoa, interview by the author, April 12, 1996.

33. Etxebarria, *Danzas de Vizcaya*, 92.

the dance, the banging together of the sticks predominates, with the dancers moving only to exchange positions, almost walking instead of dancing. In the second part, however, the rhythm of the music and dance becomes livelier. The dancers follow the same steps as in the first part, this time dancing instead of walking. The approximate duration is one minute and forty-five seconds.

09 *Txontxongilloa.* The last dance of the *dantzari-dantza* begins with two beats of the tabor, giving the order for the dancers to put down their sticks and pick up their swords. All the dancers carry their swords on their right shoulders, except for the two who are responsible for lifting up the first dancer. After the melody has been played once, as a means of introduction, the dance begins. At one point in the dance, the first dancer dances alone at the head of the group. When he has finished, the two dancers behind him hoist him up, horizontal and motionless, above their heads. It is the culminating moment of the dance suite, always provoking great applause from the audience. While the first dancer is held in the air, his partner (who is holding his feet) continues to follow the rhythm of the dance, making it appear that the supposedly dead figure of the first dancer is also dancing. They then lower the first dancer to the ground, and the whole group of eight dancers dances together until they are all in their original positions once again. Here the dance ends. They remain in their positions until the taborer beats the tabor twice, the order for them to pick up their sticks. Once in formation, and to the sound of a *biribilketa*, or march, they leave the square. Sometimes they raise their swords to acknowledge the applause from the public.

Rodney Gallop, who conducted research on Basque culture in the early twentieth century, describes the culmination of this dance thus:

> The performance works up to a tensely dramatic climax in the last figure, the *Chonchanguillo* [*sic*], at the end of which two dancers suddenly hoist their captain into the air and hold him like the stiffened corpse of a sacrificial victim, horizontal and motionless above their heads. The *Chonchanguillo* is done only in Berriz and Yurreta [Iurreta], each of which claims to have originated it. The Berriz men hoist two dancers and have done so for at least fifty years, but the tradition remains that originally only one was hoisted.[34]

This last dance of the *dantzari-dantza* has its own story, and it is worth repeating here because of the interest it aroused among folklorists such as Gallop and the repercussions their judgments and opinions had among the dancers of Berriz and their dance repertoire. In his songbook written in the 1920s, the noted Basque linguist and religious folklorist Resurrección María Azkue published the following:

> Another case of the imitation of events through dance is worth recording. There was in Berriz around the fifteenth century? [*sic*] a tyrannical feudal lord who devastated the Shire of Durango. When he fell into the hands of the men from Yurreta [Iurreta], he was impaled. This gave the motive for a new dance to be introduced in many towns of the

34. Gallop, *A Book of the Basques*, 188.

> area. It consisted of lifting up one of the dancers onto the shoulders of two of his partners. This dance was also introduced into the repertoire of Berriz, until they realized what it represented. It was then duly eliminated.[35]

This story became so popular that, as he says, the dancers of Berriz stopped dancing the *txontxongilloa*, ashamed of having a dance from Iurreta in their repertoire. In 1969, Jose Luis Etxebarria wrote:

> This last dance, the *Txontxongilo* [*sic*], is not recognized by the older people of Berritz [*sic*] as being a component of the *Dantzari Dantza*, but a later addition. This can be explained as, according to the distinguished don [*sic*] Resurrección María de Azkue, there was in Berritz around the fifteenth century? a little Attila who terrorized the Shire of Durango, and who, on falling into the hands of the men from Iurreta, was impaled, giving rise to the introduction of a new dance in the towns of the area, especially in Iurreta.
>
> This dance was also later adopted by the dancers of Berritz, who abolished it from their repertoire on learning its significance. The dance was forgotten, but was revived, some thirty-five or forty years ago, to become a permanent part of the *Dantzari Dantza.*
>
> I must also add, in order to give a small idea of what this dance means to the people of Berritz, that they have never known how to dance it in the same way as in Iurreta, where, of course and with reason, they boast about the fact that they can dance it better than anyone, that is, until the year 1965, when Alejandro de Aldecoa [*sic*] introduced it into his group in Berritz.[36]

The truth is that I do not know when they stopped dancing the *txontxongilloa* in Berriz, if that ever was the case. The chronology provided by Etxebarria does not throw much more light on the subject. Aldekoa once more appears on the scene, reintroducing forgotten traditions at the hands of Etxebarria, but the *txistularia* remembered having seen the *txontxongilloa* danced before the war in a different manner: "in Berriz, two dancers were lifted, instead of one," confirming Gallop's description above.[37]

Some years ago, Aldekoa and his group danced this version of the *txontxongilloa* exactly as he remembered having seen it as a boy. Some people in Berriz thought it was a folkloric reinvention, the idea of the dance master of Berriz, who wanted to demonstrate

---

35. Resurrección María Azkue, *Cancionero popular vasco* (1922; Bilbao: Euskaltzaindia, 1990), 265. We do not know the historic foundation of Azkue's legend, which gave rise to a series of changes and modifications in the dances of Berriz. The truth is that the credibility of some of his judgments and observations of dance leave a lot to be desired. For example, when he refers to the origin of the game of swords, he states: "It has not yet been a hundred years since dancing with the stick in hand was introduced into the illustrious *ezpata-dantza* in Berriz, having taken it from the dances that Iztueta organized and reorganized in Zaldibia." Ibid., 264.

36. Etxebarria, *Danzas de Vizcaya*, 11–12.

37. See also. Violet Alford's description, also observed in part in Berriz: "the real thrill is reserved for the last figure. This goes by the astounding name of *Txonkórrinka* [*sic*]. No need for hilt-and-point figures, no need for a lock round a man's neck. If ever there was a dead man, a victim-chief, you see him here. There is a sudden getting together of the company, and up in the air, stretched at full length above the heads of his men, the Captain appears. . . . The first time of seeing it one gasps. Sometimes there are two Captains, and they kill them both and display them, two corpses laid out on air, side by side." "Ceremonial Dances of the Spanish Basques," *The Musical Quarterly* 18, no. 3 (July 1932): 481.

his knowledge of the past or introduce something new to make his group's repertoire more interesting. In a rare documentary film recorded in the 1920s, the dancers of Berriz are dancing different fragments of the *dantzari-dantza*, which would appear to prove Aldekoa to be right.[38] The dancers of Berriz did lift two dancers in the *txontxongilloa* in exactly the same way as Aldekoa described it. In spite of this fact, in the last decades of the twentieth century, the dancers of Berriz lifted only one dancer in the *txontxongilloa*, except for one year, when Aldekoa's group, remembering the old style of the dance in a display, lifted two dancers. The approximate duration is one minute and thirty seconds.

Pontxie

Once the *dantzari-dantza* has ended, the group leaves the stage/square to the sound of a *biribilketa*. Before they begin to dance the *soka dantza*, the dancers have rest of five or ten minutes, when the bailiff invites them to drink the famous punch, *pontxie*.[39] It is an intimate and important part of the ceremony. The dancers comment on how the dance has gone, and the authorities approach them to see how they are or to give their own comments on the dance and to ask about the *soka dantza*, which the dancers are about to dance. Everyone makes the most of the moment to comment on the dance, the dancers, the mistakes they made, and so forth.

The Soka Dantza, Aurreskua, *and* Erregelak

After the interval, the dancers form a chain, ready to dance in a circle around the *donien-aretxa*, which is the central part of the square. The chain always dances in an counterclockwise direction. The number of dancers in the *soka dantza* is variable, but on this occasion, San Pedro's and Santa Isabel's Day, it is always eight, since the chain is formed by the dancers who have previously danced the *dantzari-dantza*. At the front of the chain is the *aurreskularia*, who is supposed to be the best dancer in the group, although the reasons for his selection may vary, depending on multiple factors such as tiredness, injury, and age. The occasion may also be used to allow a dancer who is about to retire, or, on the contrary, a young dancer in need of confidence, to dance the *aurreskua*. Once they are all in formation, holding hands, the taborer begins to play.

Some elements of the *soka dantza* have been lost. The so-called *desafioa* (challenge) used to be the first and last number of the *soka dantza*. The *aurreskularia*, or first dancer, and the *atzeskularia*, the last, leave the chain to dance face-to-face, simulating a kind of challenge to determine which of the two dances the best. They end with a mutual greeting by taking off their berets. While the choreography for this number has been lost, some choreographers and dance groups have reconstructed or reinvented the dance,

---

38. These images are included in the DVD, track 30.

39. The punch is a mixture of white wine (or any liquor), water, lemon, sugar, eggs, and sometimes a little cinnamon or mint.

following the indications they can remember from having seen it danced in the past,[40] using the habitual style and steps common to the rest of the dances of Berriz. Whatever the case may be, it has not been handed down to us through tradition, and it is not danced today in any of the towns or villages in the County of Durango. The taborer, as a reminder of what the dance once was in its day, plays the first bars of the *desafioa* as a kind of *deia* before the *aurreskua* begins, the first dance of the *soka dantza* today.

Abarketak (espadrilles), the first word of the lyrics to the song that accompanied the dance, is another part of the *soka dantza* that has been lost from the repertoire in Berriz. It was danced after the *desafioa*. Some dance groups, after a process of reconstruction similar to that of the *desafioa*, continue to the *abarketak* today. The dancers dance at the front of the chain one by one, always "pulling" in a counterclockwise direction. The number ends when all the members of the group have danced.

10 *Aurreskua*. This is where the *soka dantza* begins today in Berriz. After the first bars of the *desafioa* have been played (the choreography for which has been lost) on the *txistua* as a form of *deia* (and as a means of remembering the lost dance), the *txistularia* begins to play the melody of the *aurreskua*. The *aurreskularia*, the first dancer, begins to dance, offering his left hand to his partner, who will hold him firmly to help and act as a support while he dances.[41] It is the hardest and most complicated dance of the whole repertoire, with irregular choreographical and musical phrases and with no less than twenty-four *artaziak* or *puntapioak*, steps in which the leg is raised as high as possible. The approximate duration is two minutes.

11 *Atzeskua*. Once the *aurreskua* has ended, the *txistularia* continues to beat time on the tabor. The chain has to turn around so that the *atzeskularia* comes to the front position. This maneuver is done in many different ways, depending on the place, the occasion, or the dance group. Originally, the *aurreskularia* and his partner would raise their hands to form an arch under which the *atzeskularia* would pass first, followed by the rest of the dancers in the chain. The dancers, now facing outward from the circle, would let go of each other's hands, turn around on the spot, and form the chain again, this time with the *atzeskua* at the front. On most occasions nowadays, however (at least in the recordings I have seen of Aldekoa's group), they do not form the arch. The dancers let go of each other's hands, make a half turn, and form the chain again for the *atzeskularia* "to pull" until he reaches the front position. According to some people, the arch was made in the past to represent a kind of system of inspection and selection, in case there were elements in the chain not worthy of being there and that, consequently, would have to be

---

40. Aldekoa commented that when he was a boy, he saw adults dance the *desafioa* during the fiestas. The melody was similar to the one used today, but, according to him, it was not as structured, allowing for more improvisation.

41. On some occasions, given the difficulty of the dance, the second dancer sings the steps for the *aurreskularia* or motions to the *txistularia* to change the speed at which he is playing. In the case of Aldekoa, this was never necessary, because he knew perfectly well how to play to make each dancer feel comfortable while he was dancing.

thrown out. According to others, the arch represents a symbol of cohesion in the chain, the knot tied at the end.

Once at the front of the chain, the *atzeskularia*, like the *aurreskularia* before him, dances around the square. The *atzeskua* is shorter than the *aurreskua* and requires less of an effort to dance. When the *atzeskua* has ended, the chain inverts itself again, the *atzeskularia* forming the arch for the *aurreskularia* to pass under, with the dancers thus returning to their original positions. The approximate duration is one minute and twenty seconds.

12 *Andra soiñua.* The *txistularia* beats time on the tabor while the second dancer (the *aurreskularia*'s partner) and the seventh (the *atzeskularia*'s partner) leave the chain. They are the ones in charge of asking the authorities, berets in hand, the name of the woman chosen for the *aurreskularia.* Later, they will do exactly the same for the woman chosen for the *atzeskularia.* On San Pedro's Day, the women have to be married, and if at all possible, to have been married within the last year. There was a time when the town hall would send written notification to all the women married that year, asking them to be present in the town square so that they could be invited into the chain.[42] Once the two dancers have received the order from the authorities, they begin to walk around the outside of the chain, looking for the woman. On finding her, they kindly and respectfully ask her to join the chain. At this point, the taborer begins to play the *andra soiñua* (women's melody). Escorted by the two dancers, she is led around the outside of the chain to the side of the square where the authorities are standing. When the chain is in position, forming a half moon facing the authorities, the two dancers, and the chosen woman, the *txistularia* stops playing the *andra soiñua* with a cadence and immediately, without pausing, starts to play the *deia* of the *banango zaharra.* The *aurreskularia* and the *atzeskularia* leave the chain to stand in front of the chosen woman, where they dance the *banango zaharra.* This is of variable duration.

13 *Banango zaharra.* For many years, the normal *banango* was danced in the fiestas, but Aldekoa reintroduced the *banango zaharra* (the old *banango*), just as it was danced before the war. The *aurreskularia* and the *atzeskularia* dance in honor of the chosen woman. At the end of the dance, on hearing the beat of the *deia* opening and closing each number, the *atzeskularia* returns to his position in the chain, leaving the *aurreskularia* alone, in front of the woman, his guest of honor. The *aurreskularia* offers her his right hand and, taking hold of her left, pulls her toward him and bangs their hips together. This delightful gesture was at one time regarded as being mischievous and erotic. The *aurreskularia* leads the woman to his position in the chain, where she will remain at his side for the rest of the dance. The chain turns around again to allow the *atzeskularia* to return to the front position, all the while to the beat of the tabor. The approximate duration is thirty seconds.

14 *Andra soiñua.* The second and seventh dancers leave the chain again and approach the authorities, this time to ask for the name of the woman chosen for the *atzeskularia.*

---

42. Rosa Mari Ostolaza, the mayor of Berriz, told me that she received the written notification from the town hall the year she was married.

The taborer continues to play. The exact same process is repeated as for the *aurreskularia.* Once the chosen woman is found, the taborer begins to play the *andra soiñua* until the woman is in her place and the chain in position. The taborer then repeats the call of the *banango zaharra.* This is of variable duration.

15 *Banango zaharra.* Again they dance the *banango zaharra*, this time in front of the woman chosen for the *atzeskularia.* The dancer now stands on the right, in the same position as the *aurreskularia* before him. Once the dance has ended, it is now the turn of the *atzeskularia* to offer his hand to the woman, pull her to him, bang their hips together, and then lead her to the chain. Thereafter, once again the chain inverts itself, bringing the *aurreskularia* back to the front. The approximate duration is thirty seconds.

16 *Zortziko, seiak,* or *kunplitzekoa.* The *txistularia* begins to play a *zortzikoa*, a piece of music in 5/8 time, although Aldekoa invariably played the piece he learned from Hipólito and Serafín Amezua. The dancers who had been responsible for finding the women in the previous parts of the dance leave the chain once again and this time, without the permission of the authorities, choose women they please and lead them two by two to the chain, always walking around the outside. In the meantime, the *aurreskularia* dances "free style," improvising the first part of the *aurreskua* or any of its variations, while he directs and pulls on the chain, holding the hand of his female partner. When all the women are in the chain, the taborer ends by playing the *deia*, and the *aurreskularia* stops dancing to begin again almost immediately when each dancer with his respective female partner dances the *jota* and the *arin-arina.* This is of variable duration.

17 and **18** *Fandangoa* or *jota* and *arin-arina* or *porrusalda.* According to some scholars, the *soka dantza* ends with the previous number, the *zortzikoa*, and the *solture* dances that follow are merely an addition. According to others, they are part of the dance, and, at least in Berriz, the *jota*, the *arin-arina*, and the *biribilketa* at the end are obligatory dances in any representation of the *soka dantza.* The *jota* and the *arin-arina* were always danced with a partner, and what is more, in the part that was sung (a popular folk song), the couple danced holding on to each other. This part was known as the *balseoa.* Following a puritan tendency imposed by conservative and religious Basque nationalism at the beginning of the twentieth century, the dancers of today dance in a circle or ring. The girls form a semicircle, and the boys face them, with the exception of the *aurreskularia* and the *atzeskularia*, who form a separate quartet and dance with their respective partners in the form of a cross. In a circular layout, it is impossible to dance in couples, not only because of the distance between partners, but also because the circle obliges all its members to move in the same direction, causing the men and women to dance crosswise.[43] Once the

---

43. In the *jota* and the *arin-arina*, standing face-to-face, dancing as a couple, the man and woman have to move the same way, as if reflected in a mirror. If the man moves to his left, the woman moves to her right and vice versa. For the whole group to be able to dance in this way, here are the alternative choreographical solutions I have seen: men and women dancing in two parallel lines, facing each other, as suggested by Etxebarria, *Danzas de Vizcaya. Bizkai'ko Dantzak*, 147; men and women dancing in two concentric circles, the women on the inside facing out and the men on the outside facing in,

jota and the *arin-arina* have ended, the taborer begins to play the *biribilketa*. At this point, as with the two previous pieces, he freely selects from his repertoire.[44] This is of variable duration.

19 *Biribilketa* or *martxa* or *bidekoa*. During the *biribilketa*, the chain performs a series of almost obligatory choreographic designs:

- Arches and knots at both ends of the chain. First the *aurreskularia* passes under the arch made by the *atzeskularia* and his partner, then vice versa.
- A double arch, both ends of the chain passing under the central couple.
- A spiral that closes and, once reaching the center, opens up again.
- A ring turning in one direction and then the other.

Whether or not all these designs or their variations are performed depends on the duration of the *biribilketa*, which can be shortened for a variety of reasons, such as the physical condition of the dancers and the heat or rain. At the end, the *aurreskularia* leads the chain out of the square, waving his beret high in the air and spinning it round on his index finger.

The exit. The dancers collect their tools and the flag and stand in the same formation as when they entered the square. To the sound of the *agintariena*, or more frequently, another *biribilketa*, the *txistularia* leads the return procession from the square back to the town hall. The dancers follow the taborer, with the authorities bringing up the rear, that is, if they decide to make the return procession. Sometimes the authorities remain in the square, talking to the townsfolk. And so concludes the ritual, a ritual that is performed at midday and again in the evening on both San Pedro's Day and on Santa Isabel's Day, as well as during the rehearsal on June 28.

Lunch and Supper

The lunch and supper offered to the dancers after each performance was formerly a part payment for their services and a time for socializing and relaxing. Today, eating out is a relatively normal and frequent occasion for some, but in those days, it was regarded as a first-class social event. As noted previously, in the 1960s, Aldekoa proposed a reduction in the municipal expenditure by canceling these "banquets," celebrating only one supper at the end of all the fiestas paid for by the dance group itself.

As we can see, then, there is a complex and ritual dimension to these dance suites in Berriz. Moreover, and crucial to the present study, clearly Aldekoa understood both the complexity and the importance of ritual in these suites, without shying away from suggesting amendments to what had gone before.

---

so that each couple is opposite one another (this is how the Andra Mari dance group of Galdakao performs the dances); and dancing as a couple, alone, as in any other dance or *erromeria*.

44. In the main fiestas of Berriz, Aldekoa always played the same pieces of music he learned from the Amezuas.

CHAPTER FOUR

The Dance Event

Ethnomusicologists, like other scholars and researchers, resort to taxonomies, keys, paradigms, and typographies to compare and establish relations between different concepts and ideas. That is, they classify behavior, facts, actions, and objects. The observer frequently imposes his or her own criteria and preconceptions, manipulating the facts in accordance with a preconceived plan in the interest of the investigation at hand. The observer may ignore the way in which the studied culture itself classifies its ideas, which is many times an accurate reflection of its way of thinking. In other cases, the researcher tries to classify all that is irrelevant or unclassifiable within the studied culture. Each culture has its own way of organizing its reality or its situation into various classes in accordance with determined semantic fields, which refer to numerous and peculiar characteristics of the things signified.

The relationship between the classifiers and the classified is not a one-way street. In Berriz, as we have seen, the terms in which those who have studied music and dance in the Basque Country have attempted to classify these phenomena have, in turn, been adopted by and applied by Basque musicians and dancers in discussing their own culture and its practices. In the case of Aldekoa, his principal means of acquiring cultural knowledge and the terminology of folklore was through the journal *Txistulari* (and to a lesser extent, *Dantzariak*), his participation in dance competitions, and frequent visits from folklorists. The result was an understanding and a classificatory system of the dance that was a mixture of what might be considered strictly emic, rooted in the indigenous culture of Berriz, and etic, imported from without—a mixture that, whether we like it or not, formed a part of Aldekoa's way of thinking.

The Classification of Dances

Table 2 and table 3 show, in a simplified way, some of the characteristics or classes that result from a system where different classification criteria interact, based on dichotomies that are not always equally applicable to all elements. The establishment of each initial typology is the result of the interaction of different types of characteristics at different levels—a paradigm.[1] A similar type of paradigmatic division, with its logical variations and adaptations for the repertoires of local dance, operates in many areas of the Basque Country.

<table>
<tr><td></td><td colspan="2">Serious or ritual</td><td colspan="4">Recreational</td><td></td></tr>
<tr><td></td><td>Only men</td><td>Men with women taking part</td><td colspan="4">Mixed</td><td></td></tr>
<tr><td></td><td></td><td></td><td></td><td>Without holding each other</td><td>Holding each other</td><td></td><td></td></tr>
<tr><td>Basque folklore traditional autochthonous</td><td>dantzari -dantza</td><td>soka dantza or erregelak</td><td>biribilketa or martxa or bidekoa</td><td>solture or trikitia</td><td></td><td></td><td>The rest of Basque dances</td></tr>
<tr><td>Foreign or Spanish</td><td></td><td></td><td></td><td></td><td>loture or balseoa or agarreure</td><td>rocka*</td><td></td></tr>
<tr><td></td><td colspan="5">Old</td><td>Modern</td><td>Old</td></tr>
<tr><td></td><td colspan="4">Aldekoa's usual repertoire</td><td>Aldekoa's hidden repertoire</td><td colspan="2">Ignored by Aldekoa</td></tr>
</table>

Table 2: Classification of dances in Berriz

* Aldekoa used the term *rocka* (rock) to refer not only to rock and roll music, but to all kinds of new, modern, commercial music.

Dantzari-dantza	***Soka dantza***	***Solture***	***Loture***	***Rocka***
Basque	Basque	Basque	Spanish (especially the paso doble)	-----------
traditional	traditional	traditional	not traditional	not traditional
local autochthonous	local autochthonous	local autochthonous	foreign	foreign
-----------	-----------	not sinful	sinful (for priests)	-----------
folklore	folklore	folklore	not folklore	not folklore
-----------	-----------	without holding each other	holding each other	-----------
ancient, old	ancient, old	ancient, old	ancient, old	modern
ritual	ritual	recreational	recreational	recreational
male	women take part	mixed	mixed	mixed
group	group	couples	couples	individual

Table 3: Classification of dances in Berriz

1. Margaret J. Kartomi, *On Concepts and Classifications of Musical Instruments* (Chicago: University of Chicago Press, 1990), 20.

Euskalduna-Erdalduna

For Aldekoa, one of the fundamental and most clearly defined criteria of classification is the dichotomy *euskalduna-erdalduna.* In Basque, the term *erdara* is used to refer to any language other than Basque: in the northern part of the country, this is usually French, and in the south, Spanish. An *erdalduna* is anyone who speaks a language other than Basque. It is therefore a division between the ethnic group and the "foreign" group, emphasized with words like "us" and "them," "ours" and "theirs."

In dance, this dichotomy has been reformulated with new terms acquired from folkloric research and the academic world in general, although the basic meaning for the native remains unchanged. Thus, the opposition *euskalduna-erdalduna,* as far as music and dance are concerned, shares the same semantic field with other dichotomies such as "traditional-nontraditional" or "autochthonous-nonautochthonous." The result of this is that *euskalduna* is, in practice, synonymous with some imported terms of folklore terminology: "traditional," "autochthonous," "folklore," "pure," and "old," for example. These terms denote characteristics associated with anything *euskalduna.* What are not so clearly defined are the opposites of "traditional," "folklore," and "autochthonous." The most prudent approach is to speak of "nontraditional," "nonfolklore," and "nonautochthonous." Aldekoa preferred to use the term "folklore," rather than the adjectives "folk" or "folkloric," probably because "folk" is used ever increasingly to refer to another, more commercial type of music. Moreover, the notion of "folkloric" in Spanish implies a series of pejorative connotations that are becoming ever more widespread. On the first level of classification, we can therefore see two clearly defined blocks. On the one hand, "ours": everything *euskalduna,* "folklore," that also happens to be autochthonous and traditional and that includes the *dantzari-dantza, soka dantza* or *erregelak, trikitia, biribilketa,* and all other folk/traditional dances of the Basque Country, even though they are not included in the repertoire of Berriz. On the other hand, we find all other kinds of dance classified under the term *erdalduna*: "not ours," "foreign."

Solture-Loture

Another dichotomy that continues to be relevant because of its social importance is that of *solture-loture. Solture* means to dance without holding on to one's partner, and *loture* means to dance closely, holding one's partner. *Trikitia* is used as synonymous of *solture,* and *balseoa* or *agarreure* are terms used with the same meaning as *loture.* Although all dances fit in some way or another into either of these two groups, for Aldekoa, *solture* referred to the *fandangoa* or *jota* and the *arin-arina,* and *loture* referred to dances for couples such as the tango, schottische, or paso doble. In this sense, and in opposition to *loture,* the *dantzari-dantza* and the *soka dantza* could be classified as *solture,* but perhaps because of their ritual character as opposed to the recreational of the *jota* and *arin-arina,* they are classified in a different group.

If any dance in the Basque Country has changed its meaning, function, and choreographic style, that dance has to be the *solture* or *trikitia.* What had been considered beforehand by priests as "the prohibited world of the Devil," even though it constituted the most important means of courtship open to our forebears, has now been converted into a "pure," "clean" dance, a symbol of chastity and nobleness—the latter being a characteristic trait said to be "natural" to all Basques—all as a consequence of the repression of both the Catholic Church and the civil authorities, on the one hand, and the later influence of Basque nationalist ideology created by Sabino Arana at the end of the nineteenth century, on the other. The *fandangoa* and the *jota* are not Basque in origin.[2] However, they became new symbols of Basque identity in the twentieth century and, as such, a part of the new nationalist ritual choreography.[3]

In this process, a very important role has been played by the creation of choreographic folk dance groups and events such as dance competitions in the changing of style and meaning of dance. In official dance competitions, physical contact between the couple has disappeared, taking with it any playful or erotic suggestions. They are danced on tiptoe, in an upright, straight position demonstrating, more than anything else, the dancer's athletic abilities. Finally, the dancers ignore the musical and rhythmic structure of the *jota*, resulting in a dance that, for some of us who learned the *jota* from our parents or who do not belong to the world of academic Basque dancing and its competitions, is very difficult to understand, although nonetheless spectacular.[4]

As a consequence, there exists an association of *solture* with *euskalduna* (due to the supposedly pure and chaste nature of the dances) and of *loture* with *erdalduna,* due to the belief and conviction that it was the foreigners who brought such "sinful" dances to the Basque Country. More recently, this way of thinking and of classifying dances has been disrupted, due in the main part to dwindling social pressure on the part of the Catholic Church against *loture* dances and the appearance of progressive sectors in Basque nationalism that no longer believe in equating Basqueness with chastity. Moreover, the latest

2. At the beginning of the twentieth century, several purists, such as Francisco Gascue, were against these dances: "Long before I was born, Father Larramendi, in his *General Description of Gipuzkoa*, had categorically stated that the Basque *fandangoa* is a variation of the *jota*; that is to say, something exotic. I take this to be so, because it explains the unpleasant dissonance on hearing it played on the tabor. It constitutes a stain of color that is out of tune with our calm and noble melodies. Its setting is in a different place." Francisco Gascue, "Origen de la música popular vasca," *Revista Internacional de Estudios Vascos* (1913): 72–73, quoted in José Antonio Arana, *Música vasca* (1976; Bilbao: Caja de Ahorros Vizcaína, 1987), 325.

3. The process of assimilation and indigenization of anything "foreign" has been so successfully accomplished that the majority of people in the Basque Country are offended when someone suggests that the *jota*, *fandangoa*, tabor, or accordion are not originally Basque.

4. It would be interesting to undertake a comparative study of the effects of academic folk dance united with nationalism in different countries—Ireland and the Basque Country, for example—since at first sight, they seem to have followed parallel evolution processes in both dance and music. By way of introduction to the links between folklore in general and nationalism in these two cases, see Martin Williams, "Ancient Mythology and Revolutionary Ideology in Ireland, 1878–1916," *The Historical Journal* 26, no. 2 (June 1983): 307–28, and Cameron Watson, "Folklore and Basque Nationalism: Language, Myth, Reality," *Nations and Nationalism* 2, no. 1 (1996): 17–34. More specifically, on the connection between Basque dance and national identity, see Lisa Corcostegui, "To the Beat of a Different Drum: Basque Dance and Identity in the Homeland and in the Diaspora," Ph.D. diss., University of Nevada, Reno, 2005, esp. chaps. 3 and 7. On Irish dance and national identity, see Helen Brennan, "Reinventing Tradition: The Boundaries of Irish Dance," *History Ireland* 2, no. 2 (Summer 1994): 22–24 and *The Story of Irish Dance* (Dingle, County Kerry: Brandon, 1999).

research on the history of Basque dances and customs has led some groups to restore and arrange many *loture* dances that had almost been forgotten. This was the case of the *balseoa*, danced during the sung parts of the *jota* and the *arin-arina*,[5] and the idea that *loture* is equivalent to foreign is increasingly called into question.

The Taborer's Repertoire

As far as the taborer is concerned, his usual repertoire is made up of ritual and *solture* dances. These dances are considered to be traditional and *euskalduna*. In Aldekoa's lifetime, social and religious pressure on dance was such that he would only play paso dobles and other types of *loture* dances on very limited occasions and at private parties among friends. Although he knew the repertoire perfectly well, he would play only "in secret." This is what I term Aldekoa's secret or hidden repertoire.

Game or Dance?

We find other cases where scholars have forgotten to ask the basic question of what can be considered music and who can be considered a musician. They seem to consider that any activity that includes music and movement is automatically "dance."

Within the *dantzari-dantza* dance suite, the parts in which "tools" (swords and sticks) are used require a rather special denomination and classification. On more than one occasion, Aldekoa insisted that these parts are known in Berriz as games (*jokoa*), and not as dances (*dantza*). He was referring to the *ezpata joko txikia*, *makil jokoa*, and *ezpata joko nagusia*: "How can you call it the *makil dantza* [dance of the sticks]? Our parents never used that term, they always called it the *makil jokoa* [game of sticks]. Its origin is said to be from a form of game they used to play to practice fighting, and it's exactly that, a game not a dance."[6]

This classificatory issue is also applicable to the *biribilketa*. This is danced by forming a chain or rope (*soka*) and has a status of its own in what can be considered dance, or popular entertainments, or games. Because of its simplicity and popularity—everyone is capable of forming a chain and marching to the sound of music—the *biribilketa* should not be considered a dance in the true meaning of the word. It is said that someone dances a *jota* or a paso doble, but not a *biribilketa*. It is more appropriate to use the term *soka bat egin* or *biribilketa bat egin* (that is, to "make" a chain or a *biribilketa*) than *biribilketa bat dantzatu* (to dance a *biribilketa*). Its similarity to children's games, where singing and dancing play an important role, is also evident, thereby implying a connotation of *jolasa* or *olgeta*. Having said that, it could also be argued that, due to its simplicity, it is the best "dance" to initiate children into this activity. For these reasons, the *biribilketa* has a specific status as

---

5. The *jota* usually has three sections: *puntapioa*, *hara-honakoa*, and *kanteue* (the sung part), where the verses are sung.

6. Alejandro Aldekoa, interview by the author, April 12, 1996. Recall, though, the competitive connotation of *jokoa* (game), as contrasted with the more playful notion of *jolasa* or *olgeta* (play) noted in chapter 3, note 30.

Figure 36. Dancing *ezpata joko nagusia* during the 1998 rehearsal, Germán Aldekoa playing the *txistua*. Photo by Jordi Urioz.

a "game-amusement-dance." In addition, for the taborers, the *biribilketa* is synonymous with *pasakallea* (*passacaglia* in Italian),[7] which means to walk through the streets playing music. It does not imply dancing. In dance groups today, the *biribilketa* is used for processions and in some entrances or exits from the stage or square.

---

7. Another name for the *biribilketa* is *bidekoa*, which could be translated as "of the way" or "of the route."

Gender

Gender differentiation in the classification of dances is clearly defined. Ritual dance is for men. It is masculine. Although women do take part in the *soka dantza* (they are the guests of honor, invited to form part of the chain and to dance the *jota*, the *arin-arina*, and the *biribilketa*), it is the men who lead and who are the protagonists of this type of dance. Ritual dance is therefore not considered "mixed" in the true sense of the word. Women do take an active part in what can be classed as recreational dance. What is more, the character of the mixed dance and its main function is that of courtship. It is interesting, however, to stress the fact that today, *solture* dances (*trikitia*) are mainly associated with women, that is, they have become more "feminine."[8] This attitude could be included in today's tendency in the Basque Country to consider dance in general as something feminine. This criterion, however, excludes ritual dance, where "virility" is still unquestionable, especially in areas where these dances are traditionally maintained.

Ritual-Serious-Sacred

The limits of what is and what is not ritual dance are clearly defined, although the interpretation of the ritual and its function are difficult to specify, even for the dancers themselves. As in many other facets of community life, to analyze and put into words what takes place around the ritual of dance is complicated and sometimes difficult to understand. In general, from a local point of view, ritual dance has a more serious character. Choreography and participation are "closed." Such dances are the *dantzari-dantza* and the *soka dantza*. For example, a dancer who is in mourning for the death of a family member may dance the *dantzari-dantza*, because, as Aldekoa said, "dance is more sacred than all of that." He continued: "For example, if the father of one of the dancers has recently died, the dance has nothing to do with his state of mourning. Dance is above all that—it's more sacred. It's not like dancing a *jota* at the *erromeria*. The *dantzari-dantza* isn't a dance for living it up or having a good time."[9]

The Significance of Dance in Berriz

In ethnomusicology, the analysis of the uses and functions of music has been one of the methodological approaches to the study of the relationship of music to social life. In the model proposed by Alan Merriam, "use" refers to "the ways in which music is employed in human society," while "function concerns the reasons for its employment and particularly the broader purpose which it serves."[10] Uses are expressed as part of folk evaluation,

---

8. Frequently, at a wedding or a party, it is the women who spontaneously get up to dance on hearing the start of a *jota*. Most young men and boys do not know how to dance the *jota*, or even if they do, they prefer to be passive observers. Dance classes, frequently organized by the Andra Mari group, have no more than a token male representation.

9. Alejandro Aldekoa, interview by the author, April 23, 1996.

10. Alan Merriam, *The Anthropology of Music* (Evanston, IL: Northwestern University Press, 1964), 210.

while functions are expressed through analytical evaluation. Bruno Nettl's approach, meanwhile, presents uses and functions as "the opposite ends of a continuum that moves from the absolutely down-to-earth and factual to the most vitally interpretative and thus perhaps unprovable."[11] Having described in chapter 3 how music and dance are used and performed in Berriz in a kind of "down-to-earth" description, I will now move through a more abstract domain, attempting to explain different ideas about the meaning of dance in Berriz for the native Basque people there: the significance of dance in Berriz. In undertaking such a task, more than likely influenced by my condition as a native researcher, my own approach will be the result of a mixture of folk and analytical evaluation, and emic and etic points of view—that is, a result of my local knowledge acquired through fieldwork, my own experience as a member of the Basque community, and my status as researcher.

Despite many changes in modern society, the ritual continues to have meaning as ritual, at least for the indigenous Basque population of Berriz. This is shown by the disputes over who has the right to participate in the dance and to be selected to dance in the town square. This has provoked one of the most important conflicts and confrontations seen in Berriz this century.[12] If the ritual of dancing in the town square of Berriz during the main fiestas is still so important and relevant for today's young dancers, who have been performing in public with the Iremiñe dance group since they were children, imagine what it must have meant in Aldekoa's days, when he learned the dances from his father and started to study and work as the *txistularia.*

Dance, Music, Movement, Rhythm

In general, the traditional dancer (of a traditionally oral repertoire) carries music and movement within himself as two aspects of the same reality. For him, dance is at the same time music and movement, heart-felt music, irradiated and expanded into all his being. Movement that is worthy of being called "dance" possesses a purely musical quality, just as music for dance has an intrinsic motor quality. The same life inhabits the ear that perceives the music as in the body, converted into a silent, sensitive instrument.[13]

When dance music maintains the principal function for which it was originally created, when the natural motor response of the individual to dance music is manifest through dance, the boundary between music and dance becomes blurred, forming a

11. Bruno Nettl, *The Study of Ethnomusicology: Twenty-Nine Issues and Concepts* (Urbana: University of Illinois Press, 1983), 157.

12. On the one side were the members of the San Lorenzo dance group (Aldekoa's group, which monopolized participation for many years), and on the other, the Iremiñe dance group, who reclaimed their right to participate. See the discussions in chapter 3.

13. J. M. Guilcher, "Aspects et problémes de la danse traditionelle," *Revue trimestrielle de la Sté. d'Ethnographie française*, quoted in Carles Mas, "La danza antigua y la pedagogia musical," *Txistulari* 157, no. 1 (1994): 17.

single entity.[14] Such is the case of the dances we are studying, the dances of Berriz, for which Aldekoa played on so many occasions. The established limits between one term and another, between music and dance, are not the usual ones of our times, when music and dance, musicians and dancers, seem to grow ever further away from each other.

A story comes to mind about a well-known researcher who, on a fieldwork trip, video camera at the ready, visited a taborer, intent on recording the dances from his repertoire, the dances of his town. The taborer, quite taken aback, could not understand how on earth he was expected to play the dances in his kitchen without the dancers—a dance with no dancing. And so, although it may seem an obvious thing to say, one of the main functions of dance music is exactly that: dance, dancing, the union of music and corporal movement through what could be generically denominated as rhythm.

Social Cohesion

In his search for the social dimensions of religious beliefs, Émile Durkheim found that the collective bedrock underpinning any religion (and hence any belief system) is reinforced through rituals and ceremonies and that the collective nature of these rites is crucial to communicating a notion of group cohesion within a defined space.[15] The *dantzari-dantza* and the *soka dantza* serve to reaffirm and represent in public the social cohesion and fusion of individuals from the indigenous community of Berriz. It is a way of marking out the local group from the others—from the Spanish settlers,[16] from the surrounding towns, and from the rest of the world. Dance is a way of marking out one's own space and identity, both at a local level (Berriz) and a national level (the Basque Country). The festive "space," the town square, is, as such, a symbol of what is one's own, something that must be defended. In Berriz, to become a dancer, one has to be a native of the town. On the few occasions when "foreign" dancers danced in the square, it was regarded as an offense and disgrace for the town and its traditions. Rivalry between the neighboring towns about dance is commonplace and has been evident since time immemorial in fiestas, *erromeriak*, festivals, competitions, and in the pride and belief that they are each the best dancers of the *dantzari-dantza.*

---

14. According to the influential work of Anya Peterson Royce, dance "encompasses many things besides the actual physical activity. It includes the music, the interaction with other participants, the refreshments, indeed, the entire ambience of the event." See Anya Peterson Royce, *The Anthropology of Dance* (Bloomington: Indiana University Press, 1977), 10.

15. Émile Durkheim, *The Elementary Forms of Religious Life*, trans. Karen E. Fields (1912; New York: Free Press, 1995). Durkheim's emphasis on symbolism as a means of group cohesion has of course influenced numerous scholars of nationalism and national identity, such as Benedict Anderson, *Imagined Communities: Reflections on the Origin and Spread of Nationalism*, rev. ed. (London: Verso, 1991) and Michael Billig, *Banal Nationalism* (London: Routledge, 1995).

16. I am aware of the partial approach of the research to these matters in a place like Berriz, where two communities, the Spanish and the Basque, share the same territory. I have not explored the point of view of Spanish people who settled in Berriz about the ritual dances and the rest of the questions related to the topics studied here. It is an interesting issue to continue with in future research.

The best young dancers of the town take part in the *dantzari-dantza*. Together, they stage and dance the ritual for the whole community. Through their performance, they renew, year after year, the ties that bind them together, showing the neighboring villages and towns that they are still there, as a group, prepared and determined to defend their town square, their town, and their collective community. It is a war dance in which the inhabitants of Berriz boast of their physical strength and abilities by performing, in formation, under their local symbols or "totems": the flag of Berriz and the *donien-atxa*, or maypole, the "oak of the saints."[17] Here, Durkheim's insistence of the importance of totemic rites and symbols for building collective identity is evident.

In their desire to be loyal to tradition and to reproduce traditional ways of dancing, some folk dance groups in the Basque Country have learned the dances of Berriz for their own performances and have even copied the flag, something that has not settled very well with the natives of Berriz and that has provoked more than one complaint: "The people don't like that. A lot of people in Berriz don't agree with it. Santos Oregi from Garai doesn't like his flag appearing all over the place, either. Flags have their history and their merits—they're not just pieces of old cloth. It's much more serious than that."[18]

The same goes for the *donien-atxa* in the *soka dantza*, an open, circular dance:

> The centre of the circle is the focus, of which the dancers are very aware. All the dance action is applied to it and choreotechnically the centrifugal force is often used, enabling the dancers to go around easily. This promotes the feeling of unity and elation to a further degree. . . . The centre of the circle is the natural point of attention, and for this reason it has been used so very often as the site of the symbol around which the dance takes place, *e.g.* a fire, killed animal, offering, altar, newlywed couple, maypole, etc.[19]

In the past, the *donien-atxa* might have had other symbolic meanings of a more magical or religious kind. The majority of researchers point to it as a symbol for invoking fertility: it is the highest tree of the surrounding area, crowned with seasonal flowers, fruits, and vegetables and placed in the center of the stage by the young bachelors of the town. Whatever the case may be, nowadays, the *donien-atxa* has been converted into a gigantic flagpole for the *ikurriña* (Basque flag), which flies alongside the flowers and gives the tree a new totemic value, no longer at the local level of the community of Berriz, but at the national level of the Basque Country.

The popular support for and devotion of the people of Berriz to their dances and their belief that these dances are theirs alone are such that, according to Aldekoa, more than one local person has shown his disapproval at other groups "from outside" coming to Berriz to learn the dances and then, later, performing them for their own benefit.

---

17. At least that is how it is perceived by the inhabitants of Berriz.

18. Alejandro Aldekoa, interview by the author, April 22, 1996.

19. Roderyck Lange, *The Nature of Dance: An Anthropological Perspective* (London: Macdonald & Evans, 1975), 84.

Figure 37. *Aurreskua* during the 1998 rehearsal. Photo by Jordi Urioz.

Aldekoa's position on the matter was less radical. He did not think it was a bad idea that other Basque dance groups should learn the Berriz dances and then transmit them to the world, provided that they made it quite clear where they were from and where, how, and with whom they had learned them: "I don't mind. I think it's a good thing that they spread our dances around the world. Our group can't go abroad, and if, for example, the Andra Mari group goes to England to take part in a competition and dance our dances, well, it's propaganda for us."[20] For him, it was a way of putting Berriz on the map. Yet in either case, it is clear that for the people of Berriz, their dances are an element of collective identity. However, in Aldekoa's way of thinking, one senses that he put a wider Basque nationalist feeling before that of his local loyalty.

Similarly, another of the principal functions of dance in Berriz is to learn and share traditions of a social group of which one is a member—the dance group, in the first instance, and then, in a wider frame, the community of Berriz, one's own town. This process alone has an important social and cohesive value. It makes the individual feel that he is an active member and an important, if not indispensable part of the chain that transmits tradition. This feeling or way of thinking is expressed by the following local

20. Alejandro Aldekoa, interview by the author, April 22, 1996.

proverb: "*Izan zirelako gara, garelako izango dira, eta izango direlako gara,*" "We are because they were, they will be because we are, and we are because they will be."

Initiation

Dance in not just a means of promoting and exemplifying social cohesion in the Basque Country, but also functions as a means of initiation into adult Basque society. For Victor Turner, rites of passage or initiation rites are by definition transitional, denoting the "detachment of the individual or group either from an earlier fixed point in the social structure, from a set of cultural conditions (a 'state'), or from both," a kind of symbolic death via an intervening "liminal" or ambiguous period that leads to a moment of reincorporation or rebirth in which the same individual or group "is in a relatively stable state once more and, by virtue of this, has rights and obligations vis-à-vis others of a clearly defined 'structural' type."[21] In an analysis of the requirements and symbolic forms of the ritual dances that relate to the phenomenon of initiation, we can point out the following:

- The requirement, established by tradition, to dance in the square: to be a *plaza mutilla,* one has to be at least seventeen years old and a bachelor.
- The warlike character of the *dantzari-dantza* with the use of arms, something that belongs almost exclusively to the world of adult males.
- The representation of the death and resurrection of the warrior-dancer in the final number of the *dantzari-dantza.*
- The character of public courtship of the *soka dantza,* which is the presentation in society of a new adult.

The process of learning the *dantzari-dantza* begins in childhood.[22] When the young boy shows sufficient maturity, knowledge, and the necessary physical aptitudes, he is gradually incorporated into the adult group.[23] At first, he acts as a substitute at rehearsals in case any of the older dancers are missing. Then, little by little, his presence and participation in the group increases until he is eventually called to dance in public. This is an important process for a young dancer.

---

21. Victor Turner, *The Ritual Process: Structure and Anti-Structure* (1969; New York: Aldine de Gruyter, 1995), 94–95.

22. Not everybody learns to dance in Berriz, and only a few selected people dance in the San Pedro's Day and Santa Isabel's Day ritual, but in the Basque community of Berriz, many children were and still are sent by their parents to learn to dance, to become dancers, and to dance in a group. Aldekoa taught dance in the San Lorenzo group for many years, and regular dance classes were held in the *ikastola,* as well as in the Iremiñe group, where more than one hundred children learn to dance nowadays. It is difficult to do a statistical study of the incidence of dance and the number of dancers in Berriz, but I think that it could reasonably be said that an important percentage of boys in the town, members of Basque native families, have learned to dance and have gone through the initiation process explained above.

23. When I mention the dance group, I refer generically to the dance groups from Berriz, nowadays Iremiñe and San Lorenzo.

First, from the moment he is included in the group of adults, the young dancer begins to share in the experiences and the world of the older dancers. He shares the work at the rehearsals, the atmosphere of the changing room, the happiness of the celebrations, the experiences, jokes, and stories about the group and previous dancers, the romances, and so on. Dance is a means of promoting relationships and social integration through attitudes of approval (most of the time) or criticism. Social and human relationships, present in everyday life in an area such as Berriz, are reproduced in the dance group. Dance is an occasion for social entertainment, and a means of learning the behavioral patterns of the group to which you belong. You have to mix with the other members of the group: the one who tries hard but never achieves his objectives, the one who has innate qualities and is better than you, even though he makes less of an effort, the arrogant one who looks down on everything you do, the supportive one who always has a kind word, the natural leader who guides the group and establishes a harmonious relationship, and the grumpy one who is never happy. For the group to work, you have to be aware of the group and of working as a group, of the necessity of discipline and of being able to accept the established hierarchy based mainly on experience. It is a learning process in which the young internalize and accept the values of the group that, all in all, represents the values of the community: respect for their elders, the behavioral rules of courtship, tradition, and everything Basque.

Second, to perform in public as the main actor of the ritual, especially on San Pedro's Day and Santa Isabel's Day, is one of the most long-awaited moments for anyone who considers himself a dancer in Berriz. To dance in the square for the first time, in front of your own public, in front of your family, friends, and the authorities, is a way of publicly confirming your membership of the adult community. The young dancer moves on from dancing in rehearsals, in the neighborhood with his friends, and in *erromeriak* to dance, especially dressed for the occasion, with real sticks and swords, with the flag of Berriz, with the official municipal taborer, and in the town square on the most important festive day of the year, in front of the whole community. Although the San Pedro's Day and Santa Isabel's Day ritual is the most important celebration for a dancer and people in general, something similar occurs when a young dancer dances for the first time with the adult group to which he belongs.

Third, emulation is another of the functions of dance, especially in solo or improvised performances such as the *banangoa* or the *aurreskua*, where individual expression and competitiveness with the rest of the group is manifest. It teaches serenity, self-control, and self-confidence. To be able to perform in front of the rest of the group and in competitions in general ultimately prepares the individual for the social life of an adult within the community.

Courtship

In many places, dance is one of the main means of beginning a relationship as a couple. In fact, Aldekoa and the woman who would later become his wife, María Arriaga, met each other at a dance (see chapter 1). In the *erromeriak* and in the fiestas, the *dantzari-dantza* has served both as an initiation rite and as the presentation in society of the young men of a marrying age:

> These "nuptial *erromeriak*," like many others that were held throughout the Basque Country, served to unite communities as a whole, and, what is more important, create theatrical styles of the popular culture, with its expressive, symbolic, and ritual complexes, allowing all who attended them the possibility of obtaining—fundamentally through aggressive, competitive codes of masculine arrogance (stick and sword dances, fights and interparish wars, feasts at the inn)—the prestige and the distribution of the women of a marrying age.[24]

The ritual of courtship in the *soka dantza* is more clearly defined as described by Aldekoa:

> After Mass came the *aurreskua*, and when it was time to bring out the girl for the *aurreskularia*, his partners would ask him who he had chosen. He would say, "Bring So-and-So," because he wanted to get to know her, start a friendship with her, or as they say in Spanish, start going out with her. Many times, the *aurreskua* was well thought out beforehand with the sole objective of finding a girl for a friend. That was how contact was made, the first words spoken, and after that came the *erromeria*, where they would dance holding on to each other. First, the *aurreskuak*, four or five times they would dance, and then off to the *erromeria*. A group from Garai would come and dance the *aurreskua* in San Lorenzo, we would go to Zaldibar, and another *aurreskua* before the *erromeria*, all with the same idea in mind, getting to dance with a girl you knew or wanted to get to know. That's how many relationships started. A lot of them ended up in marriage.[25]

Although the different ways of courting among young people today have changed, dance and dancing are still a way of starting up a relationship with someone of the opposite sex. Mixed dance groups, such as Iremiñe, for example, lead to the formation of new couples, and many people started their relationships in a dance group.[26]

Social Lubricant

During the eighteenth century, when the civil authorities began to intervene and take charge of the celebration of the ritual dances, steering their original meanings to serve their own interests, most of the changes were made that have since been handed down to current generations as tradition. The great social differences that separated the elite from the common people and the concentration of municipal power in the hands of the

---

24. José Carlos Enríquez, *Sexo, género, cultura y clase* (Bilbao: Beitia, 1995), 108–9.

25. Alejandro Aldekoa, interview by the author, April 15, 1996. Although *aurreskua* is the name of the first dance of the *soka dantza*, frequently, and in this quotation, it is used to name the whole suite of dances, as a synonym of *soka dantza*.

26. Lisa Corcostegui notes that many dancers in the mixed Oñatz group of Oñati (Gipuzkoa) refer to their group jokingly as a "marriage agency." "To the Beat of a Different Drum," 228.

privileged few provoked a fracture in the social fabric. This obliged the dominant class to make some kind of gesture in order to improve their relationship with the working classes. In this case, the *soka dantza*, as a symbol of social cohesion, was perceived as being the ideal means to restore basic equality for all Basque citizens, even though in reality this was not true. The upper classes knew how to make the most of the symbolic gesture of dancing with the common people in their own interest. It was a gesture that acted as a "social lubricant" making "the mechanism of power and exploitation turn with greater ease."[27]

Nowadays, the ritual surrounding the celebration of San Pedro's Day and Santa Isabel's Day continues to act as a social lubricant, although, as is to be expected, with different overtones. What began in the eighteenth century as the active participation of the dominant class in the ritual, dancing, and leading the chain of dancers, changed completely over time. In other words, from "merely" dancing, the role of the dominant class changed to "accompanying" the town in the ritual, then on to "presiding" over the dances, to end today with the authorities being at the "center" of the ritual. In other words, today, the ritual is danced "for" and in honor of the authorities.

Despite these changes, the ritual is still used by the authorities and townspeople as an opportunity to approach each other and improve their relationships. The town appreciates the fact that the municipal authorities uphold the tradition and share in the community spirit by accompanying the common people in the ritual. Meanwhile, the authorities use the ritual as a way of diffusing political propaganda, their intentions being different depending on the particular demands of the historical moment. In the postwar period, with the pro-Franco governing apparatus in power, the importance of ritual dance as a social lubricant for eliminating friction with the dominated classes, a people defeated by force and subjugated economically, politically, and culturally, was understood perfectly and accepted widely, just as it had been with the dominant class in the eighteenth century. This is the main reason why the ritual dances were allowed to continue to be celebrated after the fascist invasion. Nowadays, apart from the profitability of political propaganda, the municipal authorities use the dances of Berriz to send a message reasserting the traditional, conservative, Basque character of the PNV, the Basque nationalist political party that governs the town hall. In contrast, the community takes advantage of the situation to make contact with the ruling group, to whom they make their requests, complaints, and ideas known.

Emotion and Entertainment

The dances of Berriz are capable of entertaining and provoking emotion, not only among the people taking part, but also in the public watching the ritual. They make people and everything around them feel good. For some, the dance is full of precious, touching

---

27. Carlos Sánchez, *Del danbolin al silbo: Txistu, tamboril y danza vasca en la época de la ilustración* (Pamplona: Euskal Herriko Txistulari Elkartea, 1999), 18.

moments: when the *banderaria* throws his *txapela* into the air and waves the flag of Berriz, when the whole group begins to beat their sticks in the *makil jokoa*, or when a good *aurreskularia* leads the chain (*soka*) with authority and elegance. Everything acquires a special dimension when the dancer is someone one knows and loves, a son, boyfriend, friend, or grandson, for example, not to mention the possibility that he might be the son of a previous dancer. For most of the local Basque people, the simple fact of watching a group of young people dance the *dantzari-dantza* in the twenty-first century is in itself a source of satisfaction and pride.

Many people ask how the dancers can go on always dancing the same thing and the community can continue to support it. Do they not get bored and tired of performing or watching the same *dantzari-dantza* or the *soka dantza* year after year, in all the fiestas and in all the celebrations? Everywhere we are sold the idea that anything "new" is stimulating and valid in today's society, maybe because such a slogan does no more than inspire greater consumerism. But the fact is that repetition of the ritual and knowledge of the choreography that creates it, together with its history and environment, provide the native community with a sense of security and control—stable, permanent references that people can hold on to in this rapidly changing society. This feeling of control is positive and stimulating. On the other hand, there might also be problems of acculturation, informed by different levels of understanding of the same dances and ritual, distinguishing different, more subtle perceptive levels of sense, significance, and aesthetics. The appreciation and perception of the dance is always different when one forms part of the group or the community involved, compared with that of the spectator, who, when all is said and done, attends the ritual simply to watch a dance.

Therapy

In Aldekoa's time, when there were no movies, television, or soccer, dance was considered a leisure-time activity for young people, a kind of sport. Today, a dance rehearsal is regarded by many dancers as a perfect way of letting off steam and relaxing after a hard day's work and of forgetting, for a while, all the daily problems that modern life presents. Apart from the physical effort and attention required to dance and the serious and competitive dimension it might entail (*jokoa*), dancing can also be a game (*jolasa*/*olgeta*), because it is fun, helps you feel better, and makes you enjoy yourself. In this sense, dance today continues to have a therapeutic function, not only in the performances or the fiestas, but also during rehearsals.[28]

On the other hand, many native Basques who believe they live under French or Spanish imperialist domination, who feel "foreign" in their own country, who are forced to speak what they see as their oppressor's language and renounce their own culture,

28. I have deliberately chosen the term "therapeutic," despite the enormous profusion with which the word is used today that clouds its real meaning. In this case, either of the two main meanings of the word in the *Collins English Dictionary* are applicable: "1. of or relating to the treatment of disease; curative. 2. serving or performed to maintain health."

who have been imprisoned, persecuted, and oppressed for daring to defend their own sovereignty, find, in their music and dance, a kind of balsam against impotence, pain, fear, and stress provoked by the situation in the Basque Country. The *dantzari-dantza* and the *soka dantza* take them back to a time in the past when they were free. Local dances in general, and the ones of Berriz in particular, strengthen the group or collective feeling. It is comforting to feel supported by one's own tribe and to know what one does has been done that way for centuries. Looking to the past, the collective creates, if only for a moment, an illusion and hope for the future, as if to say: "If we have come this far, here, now, in the new millennium, and we're still dancing like our ancestors used to, so all is not lost." Some Basque people are moved to tears when they see a group of young people rehearsing or dancing, when the *banderaria* waves the flag in the air, when the group dances well, or when a dancer reminds them of his grandfather who danced before him.

The ritual of Berriz, the annual celebration around the *donien-atxa*, seems to defy time. All generations join together in the square to share and enjoy a common past, present, and future. The Spanish invasion, repression, and imperialism have changed all their lives and their country, but they are still there. The feeling of group cohesion transmitted through music and dance is especially useful and beneficial in a conflictive situation such as this.

CHAPTER FIVE

Music Theory and Performance

What is music? Who is a musician? To cite the words of Helen Myers, "In defence of my colleagues, one man's music (say, to the ethnomusicologist) may be another man's Call to Prayer (music is forbidden in Islam); in fact, the seemingly tedious review of first principles is perhaps the major contribution of ethnomusicology to music studies."[1] One of the basic principles missing from most examinations of Basque music to date has been establishing the limits of the subject of our research, the limits of what is considered music and who are to be considered musicians.[2] Of course, the direct question "What is music?" is difficult to answer clearly and concisely, and there is no general consensus, even among ethnomusicologists. As a consequence, in one of my interviews with Alejandro Aldekoa,[3] to get at what he considered to be real music and real musicians, I approached the question progressively, marking the way and defining the matter at hand with concrete questions about different instruments and activities he knew well: the songs of *bertsolariak*, the playing of *trikitilariak*, the use of *tarrañuelak* and the *panderoa*, and the playing of the *alboka*, *txalaparta*, and *dultzaina*.

Bertsolariak, improvised verse singers, improvise verses with complicated rhymes using different airs that give them the basic metric structure and the points of rhyme at the end of each musical phrase or sentence.[4] According to Aldekoa, "To be a *bertsolaria* you need to be naturally talented or skilled."

1. Helen Myers, "Ethnomusicology," in Helen Myers, ed., *Ethnomusicology, Volume 1: An Introduction*, (London: Macmillan, 1992), 15.

2. At least I do not know of any musicological or ethnomusicological study on music in the Basque Country that has raised the question of what is and what is not music for the native people, assuming, as is customary, the dictates of the classical Western musicological inheritance.

3. Alejandro Aldekoa, interview by the author, April 15, 1996. All quotes following on this page and the next are from this interview.

4. See track 21 on the DVD. For English-language treatments of *bertsolaritza*, see Gorka Aulestia, *Improvisational Poetry from the Basque Country*, trans. Lisa Corcostegui and Linda White, foreword by William A. Douglass (Reno: University of Nevada, Reno, 1995); Joxerra Garzia, Jon Sarasua, and Andoni Egaña, *The Art of Bertsolaritza: Improvised Basque Verse Singing* (Donostia: Bertsozale Elkartea; Andoain: Bertsolari Liburuak, 2001); and Samuel G. Armistead and Joseba Zulaika, eds., *Voicing the Moment: Improvised Oral Poetry and Basque Tradition* (Reno: Center for Basque Studies, University of Nevada, Reno, 2005).

> Some *bertsolariak* were not academically trained. Now you can study and there are special schools. For example [Xabier] Amuriza [winner of the Basque Bertsolari Championship in 1980 and 1982, who lives in Andikoa, Berriz] is teaching young people. But before, there were no schools, and they learned naturally like Lopategi, Lazkao Txiki, Baserri, Txirrita [all well-known *bertsolariak*] . . . and they have been the best in the world, better than the ones from the new schools. They had the skill to make *bertsoak* at any time and on any occasion, they talked and joked through *bertsoak*, but I don't consider that to be music. It is something natural and special. Of course, they were able to choose the right music for each occasion, and the same *bertsoak* could be sung with different tunes. They use the music to calculate the *bertsoak*, but the lyrics are independent. In my opinion, they are separate from musicians.

The *trikitilaria* is someone who plays a two-row diatonic accordion.[5] According to Aldekoa:

> The old *trikitilariak* played without music, like the old *txistulariak*—they played by ear. They didn't know *solfeggio*, either, which note is "doh." Etxezabal and other players I knew in my time didn't know any *solfeggio*. They had a good ear and learned the positions, the fingering, and that's how they learned to play. The music was introduced later, but there are still some players who don't know *solfeggio*. But before, no one knew *solfeggio* to play the accordion.

The *tarrañuelak* is the name for the stick clappers held in one hand and used to accompany other instruments such as the accordion, and *panderoa* is the Basque name for the tambourine.[6] Aldekoa said that "I consider the person playing these instruments to be like the *txistularia* who uses the tabor. It's another tool to mark the rhythm, and to get that, you don't need to know *solfeggio*. I wouldn't say that the *panderoa* player is a musician." The *alboka* is a double-piped hornpipe with a single horn bell and single reeds played in the Basque Country.[7] Aldekoa said:

> I don't think that the *alboka* has a scale or a musical level. I think it has just a few notes. On the one hand, it can be said that it isn't music. On the other, it can be considered music, with its limitations, but, nevertheless music. I don't know if the *alboka* has any music scores. Perhaps, but it has a short scale—it isn't chromatic. And it's difficult to play. You must blow continually. But the fingering is simple. I could say yes, it is music, or no, it isn't music.

The *txalaparta* is a kind of very basic and rudimentary xylophone consisting of one or two big wood bars usually played by two musicians.[8] Aldekoa said: "Maybe they have some scores, but I'm afraid that those who play the *txalaparta* have learned just by practicing, without any score at all. I wouldn't give them the name of musicians." The *dultzaina*

---

5. See track 22 on the DVD.

6. See track 23 on the DVD.

7. See track 23 on the DVD.

8. See track 24 on the DVD.

is a kind of shawm used in the Basque Country.[9] Aldekoa said, simply, "Yes, the *dultzaina* has music."

Little by little, he thus outlined what he considered to be music: "In order to say that you are a musician, you must know *solfeggio*. Without that, you can't say you're a musician, neither a good one nor a bad one. First you learn *solfeggio* to become a musician, and later you decide to play an instrument—the piano, the clarinet, or the *txistua*—but first you need *solfeggio* to be a true musician. Without *solfeggio*, there's no music. It's impossible."[10] For him, a musician is someone who knows *solfeggio*.[11] For Aldekoa, without *solfeggio*, and without a score, there is no music.

Oral Transmission and the Introduction of Notation and the Repertoire

If there is no music without *solfeggio* and a score, when did music, understood in this sense, come to the Basque Country? The first reports we have about literate pipe and tabor players in the Basque Country date from the eighteenth century. In the nineteenth century, the use of scores among Basque taborers was quite common, as shown by the collections of repertoires from that time found in the archives. But the authentic revolution of the score among *txistulariak* arrived with the publication of the journal *Txistulari*, beginning in 1928, edited by the Association of *Txistulariak* of the Basque Country. Through this journal, music scores for *txistua* reached all corners of the Basque Country, and reading music was converted, among the *txistulariak*, into a standard system of musical transmission and learning. From that moment on, the *txistularia*, to be "normal," to be a "real musician," had to be able to read and write music.

Until then, the repertoire had been one of the taborer's most precious belongings, more important than virtuoso technique. Each taborer jealously guarded his own repertoire, with his professional success depending to a great extent on its quality and originality. Anecdotes about taborers going to listen to their competitors to learn new pieces of music secretly, to copy them and so "steal" these pieces, give us an idea of how important the repertoire was at that time and how the system of musical transmission then worked.

In this type of process, it was inevitable that changes and adaptations of the original would be made. Each musician would make his own version from what he could remember he had heard. With the arrival of the score, this was to change radically. Oral transmission of the repertoire was much easier within the family unit, and it is in this context that we find the saga of the Amezua family, or the "Patxikoak," in Berriz,[12] taborers for

9. See track 25 on the DVD.

10. Alejandro Aldekoa, interview by the author, April 15, 1996.

11. Remember that for Aldekoa and for most Basque people, the term *solfeggio* refers not only to the singing of scales, intervals, and melodic exercises to solmization syllables, but also to the whole theory of music and especially the ability to read and perform from scores.

12. See the introduction for more information about the Amezua dynasty.

at least five generations: "Before, the *txistulariak* from around here couldn't read or write music. Their small repertoire was learned from memory. You can't have an extensive repertoire if you don't have a score. You can't keep it all up here in your head. Those who have learned the *txistua* with a score have a large repertoire. That's one of the great advantages of learning to read and write music."[13]

If we understand a taborer's repertoire to be the set of pieces of music he learns from memory, Aldekoa (whose repertoire was effectively much larger than that of his predecessor, Serafín Amezua) may have been referring to the fact that having a score made access to and the learning of new repertoires easier. However, reality seems to show that, apart from Aldekoa, for the majority of the *txistulariak*, the score has simply become a substitute for memory. Once the *txistulariak* came to be regarded as "musicians," their memorized repertoire became gradually more and more limited. Today, it is not unusual to see a *txistularia* playing from a score, even for the dances:

> One of my students from Zaldibar who has taken over from me giving classes in Atxondo has also started to play in Garai. He's a good *txistularia*. But to play for the dancers . . . the first time he played, last year I think, Sabin Egiguren was there recording on his video camera:
>
> "Good grief . . . ! What a disaster! The *txistularia* playing the *erregelak* from a score, with a music stand and all! Where have you ever seen anything like it? And to top it all, in Garai! Well, well, well . . ." said Sabin.
>
> "Well, if he can't play from memory, he'll have to play from the score," I answered.
>
> "We've never played for the dancers from a score—never, not in Garai and not in Berriz either."
>
> That was true. If you need a score and you can't dance yourself, there's nothing that can be done. The dancer needs you to play in time with him. If he dances quickly, you follow him. But now, I don't know if you can ask that much of him. He still hasn't learned them. The *erregelak* are difficult. You've got to have played them many times.[14]

As we can see, Aldekoa's opinion was somewhat contradictory. On the one hand, he made it clear that to be able to play well, one had to know how to dance, to follow the dancer and help him, which meant that you could not be looking at the score at the same time. In this respect, he himself was highly skilled. On the other hand, he showed his respect and maybe his personal appreciation of his old student, saying that he was a "good *txistularia*" capable of reading the score correctly.

Aldekoa's Scores

The transcriptions of the *dantzari-dantza* that we know of are numerous and appreciably different one from another, depending on when they were written and the author who wrote them. From among all the transcriptions that Aldekoa came across in his lifetime,

---

13. Alejandro Aldekoa, interview by the author, April 15, 1996.

14. Alejandro Aldekoa, interview by the author, April 22, 1996.

the one he used most as a reference was by Pedro de Abaitua y Aresti (1870–1919), taborer, organist, and music teacher in Berriz. Curiously, Pedro de Abaitua was blind, and the quality of the handwriting leaves no doubt as to the fact that he could not have written these scores himself. The end of the transcription reads: "Property" of Pedro Abaitua y de Aresti, leaving its authorship or the provenance of the copy unclear. It is also strange that Aldekoa should use Abaitua as a reference and model, because it is difficult to imagine how, being blind, Abaitua could have worked as a taborer for the dancers of Berriz. What is more, Abaitua was a contemporary of Hipólito Amezua (1870–1954), Serafín's father, whom Alejandro knew well as a musician.[15] Hipólito, according to Aldekoa, was an exceptional taborer and dance master, municipal taborer with a temporary contract since 1889, and heir to the Amezua family tradition. In light of this, it would seem that Abaitua must have been on the fringes of the tradition of taborers and dance masters in Berriz, and his exact relationship with the music and traditional dance of Berriz remains unknown. Once again, Abaitua's principal merit, from Aldekoa's point of view, was that he was a "musician": he could play the organ, and he was the author (so Aldekoa believed) of the oldest scores of the *dantzari-dantza* he knew.

As far as the instrumental version of the *soka dantza* is concerned,[16] one of the transcriptions used as a reference in my study of Aldekoa and the oldest I know of is that of Don Modesto Arana (Aldekoa's music teacher) in 1932, who wrote the transcription of the *aurreskua* and the *atzeskua* by listening to them being sung by Ambrosio Aldekoa, Alejandro's father. This was the score that, as a boy, Alejandro used to study and learn the

---

15. Hipólito Amezua worked as *txistularia* until his death in 1954 at the age of eighty-four. Aldekoa was thirty-four at the time.

16. As we have seen, the process of learning the dances in the past took place within the family unit or with friends, a situation in which music and instrumental musical accompaniment was generally missing. This deficiency was compensated for by the dance master singing or humming the dance tune. Even today, despite the availability of taborers and audio equipment and recordings, singing is still used in the rehearsals of many dance groups and in dance classes or courses. The advantage of this is that the dance master can begin where and when he likes, and he can control the rhythm and general character of the dance (accents, emphasis, pauses, and so on). Singing and humming is therefore an essential part of the rehearsals and dance classes. In the County of Durango, the teachers and/or apprentices of dance have adapted verses to the melody, giving the song a sense and significance and probably helping to make the music easier to memorize.

Here, I must mention the numerous popular folk songs and adapted verses specifically written for dance in which the names of the dancers or anecdotes and local stories appear. These popular folk songs, many of which are humorous and ironic, also have an evident ludic function. The music of the dances is an excuse to write new verses and a vehicle for its diffusion and popularization. Apparently, this is not the case for the *aurreskua* and the *atzeskua*, whose music is the well known theme "Ardautxoak parau gaitu dantzari" ("The Wine Has Made Us Dancers"), a theme compiled in the collection *Soiñu Zarrak* (Old Melodies) by Iztueta under the title "San Sebastián" in *Euscaldun anciña anciñaco ta are lendabicico etorquien dantza on iritci pozcarri gaitzic gabecoen soñu gogoangarriac beren itz neurtu edo versoaquin* (Donostia: Baroja, 1826), facsimile ed. in *Txistulari* 163, no. 3 (1995): 62. It seems that the *aurreskua* and the *atzeskua* were originally songs for dance, rather than a substitute for instrumental music. The tradition of singing the *erregelak* (*aurreskua* and *atzeskua*) in verse disappeared years ago, and today I do not know of anybody capable of singing the verses of "Ardautxoak parau gaitu dantzari," nor have I had access to recordings that were made in their day by J. M. Mendizabal. His transcriptions, published as "Erregelak (Bertsotan)," transcriptions, *Txistulari* 75–76, nos. 3–4 (1973): 2069–72, are the only source of information available. Curiously, the sung and instrumental versions of the Amezuas and the Aldekoas are notably different, especially as far as rhythm is concerned, if we consider the transcriptions by J. M. Mendizabal and the comments of both Aldekoa and José Luis Etxebarria, *Danzas de Vizcaya: Bizkai'ko Dantzak* (Bilbao: La Editorial Vizcaína, 1969), 17.

dances and that was later edited in the journal *Txistulari*,[17] converting it into the model for interpretation of the present-day taborers. Instead of referring to the taborers and dance masters of the Amezua family, the Aldekoa family chose to use Ambrosio's sung version written down on paper by the "musical" priest.

With Solfeggio, *the Status of the Taborer Changes*

Traditionally, the name *musikoa* (musician) was (and still is) given to those who played the clarinet, trumpet, or any other musical instrument. The *danbolinteroa* (taborer) was just that, a taborer. In some areas, this idea still prevails today. For my colleagues in the Bilbao municipal band of *txistulariak*, the term "musician" excludes *txistulariak*, and for the Bilbao city hall, it is clear that "musicians" are members of the municipal brass band and that we are the *txistulariak*. Such terminology indicates a clearly inferior standing for *txistulariak*, with "musician" status reserved for players of other instruments and associated with greater social consideration (qualifications, prizes, prestige, and fame) and work options (better salaries, better working hours, and better promotional perspectives).

Unlike my colleagues and many other *txistulariak*, Aldekoa seemed to have fully assumed his condition as a musician. "How do you introduce yourself, as a musician, or as a *txistularia*?" I asked him. He replied, "Both as a musician and a *txistularia*. But to earn money, I learned the trade of gunsmith, and apart from that, I worked on the farm. As far as culture and folklore are concerned, I learned to play the *txistua* and studied *solfeggio*—you needed it to learn the instrument—and so I'm a musician. Everyone who has studied *solfeggio* is a musician. I play the instrument from music."[18]

Once the point had been cleared up that he was a musician, as well as a *txistularia*, I asked him what his relationships with other musicians had been like. He answered: "The musicians I have met, taking into account the peculiarities of each instrument, have respected the *txistularia* as a musician. That respect has been mutual. I consider them musicians, and they consider me the same. We didn't have any problems. If you are a good player, and if they know about your quality, they will consider you a good musician, that's all."[19]

Aldekoa also believed that knowledge of *solfeggio* had changed the social status and reputation of the *txistua* and the *txistulariak*:

> In large municipalities such as Bilbao, there were *txistulariak* who had been able to read music for a long time, but here, in the small villages or towns, the *txistulariak* learned how to play without music, from father to son, by ear, copying the positioning of the fingers, they didn't know how to play the sharp notes or the chromatic scale. Since the arrival of solfeggio the *txistua* has evolved, with solfeggio the *txistua* has more value.[20]

---

17. Modesto Arana Fuldain, "Erregelak," transcription, *Txistulari* 74, no. 2 (1973): 2040–42.

18. Alejandro Aldekoa, interview by the author, April 15, 1996.

19. Ibid.

20. Ibid.

During his professional life, and especially while Serafín Amezua was municipal *txistularia*, Aldekoa consciously used these arguments to promote himself. In his opinion, he was the musician, and Serafín was not.[21] It was Aldekoa who introduced the score in Berriz. According to him, it was a great improvement for the *txistua*, but the notation of the dances presented a few problems.

Scores and the Rhythm of the Dances

The Basque taborers, and local musicians in general, detected problems in the reading and interpretation of the scores for Basque dances a long time ago, especially when the performers were not local and did not know the local customs and style. With respect to the rhythm of the dances, this had been a problem since the inception of the scores themselves in the eighteenth century. "La Música en el País Vasco," written around 1802, declared: "The *zortzikoa* is a repetitive melody of eight bars in two measure times, divided into two parts. It is played better in 6/8 time than in common time; but even then, the foreign musician will not be able to get it right and give it the characteristic expression of the Basque Country, no matter how well-written or exact the transcription may be."[22] And for Rodney Gallop (although somewhat simplistically), writing in 1930, "The most interesting aspect of Basque folk-song is probably that of rhythm," but as regards the *zortziko*, "it seems probable that 5/8 time is a mannerism which has crept into sung music within the last hundred and fifty years,"[23] during which time the scores diverged from the traditional dance rhythm, yet at the same time established a new reality (a different kind of *zortziko* rhythm).

At the same time as the *txistulariak* were acquiring more academic, technical, and musical knowledge, the problems of the notation system were becoming increasingly obvious: on the one hand, taborers could not play "exactly" the same as what was written on the score (they could not even play the same as each other), and on the other, the transcriptions were not able to reflect faithfully the reality of traditional music. This was the case with the dances of Berriz, in which we find two of the most emblematic rhythms

---

21. I have my doubts about Serafín Amezua's ability to read and write music. His granddaughter sent me a folder containing his scores: a few manuscripts, an old copy of the journal *Txistulari*, a study method of *solfeggio*, and a few other items. His daughter Elena assures me that her grandfather Hipólito "could not read music," but that her father, Serafín, could. One has to take into account that it would be unusual for Elena to admit that her father could not read music, because within her scale of values, it would be the same as admitting that her father was not a musician or that he was a bad musician, especially if he were compared with Aldekoa. From all the information I received and, above all, because of Aldekoa's certainty when he spoke on the topic, I believe that Serafín's knowledge of *solfeggio* must have been rudimentary, which, as such, was nothing out of the ordinary among *txistulariak* in those days.

22. "La Música en el País Vasco" (ca. 1802), probably by Juan Antonio Moguel, and edited, together with the rest of the so-called "Papeles de Humboldt" (Humboldt Papers) by Aita José Antonio de Donostia, *Cancionero Vasco* (San Sebastián: Eusko Ikaskuntza, 1994), 1531. On Moguel, see Juan Madariaga Orbea, *Anthology of Apologists and Detractors of the Basque Language*, trans. Frederick H. Fornoff, María Cristina Saavedra, Amaia Gabantxo, and Cameron J. Watson (Reno: Center for Basque Studies, University of Nevada, Reno, 2006), 391–401.

23. Rodney Gallop, *A Book of the Basques* (London: Macmillan, 1930; rpt. Reno: University of Nevada Press, 1970), 156–57.

Figure 38. Hand-written score of the dances of Berriz corresponding to *binangoa*, *launangoa*, and *makil jokoa*. The end of the transcription reads: "Propiedad de Pedro Abaitua y de Aresti" ("Property of Pedro Abaitua y de Aresti").

of Basque folklore, the *zortzikoa* (literally, of eight) and the *ezpata-dantza* (sword dance).[24] The five quavers of the *zortzikoa* and the compound rhythm of the *ezpata-dantza* have been the resources most widely used by the Basque Country's musicians to make their music "sound" Basque. Their identifying and distinguishing importance has been widely assumed and is used in any musical theme, radio station jingle, or television commercial where the wish is to strengthen a Basque ethnic meaning.[25] Despite its diffusion, there are few people who know the origin and the original rhythms of the dances. Even fewer know their performing style, and fewer still are able to play the dances like the Amezuas or the Aldekoas. Confirming some of these views, Violet Alford (writing in the 1930s) describes the *zortzikoa* as, "one of those 5/8 tunes so difficult for any but a Basque ear."[26] But what is it that makes the native Basque taborers' interpretation so special?

An Analysis of the Rhythms of Zortzikoa *and* Ezpata-Dantza

In the survey that follows, I hope to explain the rhythmical characteristics of the dances analyzed. Why do the dances sound strange when played by "foreign" musicians? What are the features that make a performance of these rhythmic patterns "authentic" from the local view?

For analysis, I chose two pieces from the *dantzari-dantza. Eskasak* belongs to the *zortzikoa* rhythm usually transcribed in 5/8, and *banangoa* belongs to the *ezpata-dantza* rhythm normally written in 6/8+3/4. During the dance, the *banangoa* is played eleven times. I analyzed the first rendition, the introduction. *Eskasak* is played at two different moments in the *dantzari-dantza*, at the beginning of *ezpata joko nagusia* and *makil jokoa.* I used one of these because of the time required to do the different analytical tasks. A similar analysis of all the repetitions and events of all the *dantzari-dantza* (the *zortzikoa* and *ezpata-dantza* rhythms are used in other dances) would be desirable in order to gain more accurate conclusions about these rhythms, but the size of the task is beyond the scope of this work.

My first sources were analog recordings. The one used in *eskasak* played by Serafín Amezua was a tape with quite a bad quality, a poor signal, and a lot of ambient noise (track **26** on the DVD). I found it by chance in Durango as part of Anton Mari Aldekoaotalora's personal collection, but the recording must have been made by Iñaki Irigoien, for it is his voice that is heard on the tape describing the dances, and as I found out later, this tape was missing from his own collection. (He told me the recording was made around 1970.)

---

24. There has been great controversy about these rhythms, how they should be termed, their transcription, and so on. I will mention just two interesting articles published in *Txistulari* where a general review of the issue is made: Carlos Sánchez, "En torno al zortziko," *Txistulari* 146, no. 3 (1991): 44–53, and Jose Inazio Ansorena Miner, "El zortziko: la frase de ocho compases y el cinco por ocho," *Txistulari* 141, no. 1 (1990): 7–10.

25. Even Gallop noted this as long ago as 1930: "For some reason or other the *zortziko* has come to be regarded as the only typical Basque song and has found its way into the works of [Pablo de] Sarasate, [Isaac?] Albeniz and [Gabriel] Pierné," *A Book of the Basques*, 156.

26. Violet Alford, "Ceremonial Dances of the Spanish Basques," *The Musical Quarterly* 18, no. 3 (July 1932): 476.

The *banangoa* track played by Serafín Amezua was recorded by Juan Mari Mendizabal on June 30, 1973, as stated at the beginning of the original tape (track 28 on the DVD). It was recorded on an open tape using, according to Mendizabal, a "rare and strange Italian machine." I needed the help of Alexander Iribar from the Phonetic Laboratory of the University of Deusto to convert the recording to standard DAT format. The other two recordings of *eskasak* and *banangoa* played by Aldekoa were made around 1990, and I found them in the archive of the Andra Mari dance group of Galdakao (tracks 27 *and* 29 on the DVD). Here, the quality was much better than on the other two recordings.

The next step was to digitalize the sound recordings in order to make it possible to load the tracks as sound files from the Sound Edit program. I used this software because it is relatively cheap, easy to get, and allowed me to measure the length of each sound in milliseconds, which I judged to be precise enough compared with all the previous analyses made about these rhythms.

The process of delimitation (fixing the exact starting point) of each sound took a long time. The files were expanded 100 percent in time, doubling their length and changing the speed to half that of the original version, but without altering the pitch. This allowed me to listen more accurately to some fast notes. Once the files sounded at half the speed, I isolated and measured each sound by using the screen tools. The Zoom and Label systems were especially helpful in this task. The time figures shown in the analysis correspond to the tunes sounding at half speed. To obtain the real values, it is enough to calculate half the value of the given numeric quantities.

Once I knew the length of each sound, I used this information to convert the numbers into music characters. Using the conversion table (see appendix 2) and the necessary corrections to round up or down the figures mathematically, I drew up the descriptive/phonetic transcriptions. In order to facilitate a comparison with the prescriptive/phonemic transcriptions to be made, they have been placed together. I used the conversion table shown in appendix 2 after some evaluations of the more convenient ratio in order to obtain a score "similar" to the prescriptive transcription used by the Basque taborers. The purpose of this was to get two different, but comparable transcriptions. One of the problems of this calculation process was the need to do these adjustments manually. In other words, an automatic device able to round up the different figures and adjust them to the values given for each note would have been more desirable in order to avoid any kind of human mistake.

The main musical parameter I took into account (and really, for the later analysis, the only one) was that of rhythm, so there are no indications of dynamics, articulations, and so on. My aim here is to analyze the rhythm, and the transcriptions are focused on this analysis. The *txistua* is usually transcribed in F, and I did this in all the different versions.

As a general rule, I transcribed the length of each sound as the total length from its beginning until the starting point of the next sound. Normally, it is very difficult to know when a sound is extinguished, and I think that this version shows better the rhythmical meaning or value of each sound, thinking of them as percussions, where the main point is the beginning of the sound.

In a fashion similar to the drawing up of the transcriptions in classical European notation, I processed all the time information written in milliseconds by using the statistical applications of the Microsoft Excel program in order to know what the actual tendencies of each player are and to be able to group and compare the amount of numbers, trying to make sense of them (see appendix 3). Even though a better knowledge of statistical methods would have aided me in this task, it still appears to be a very good tool to help discover and show the real trends of a musical piece. I used the graphic options of these programs to show proportions, measures, ratios, and so on in a visually understandable and clear way (see appendix 4).

An Analysis of the Eskasak

To make analysis of the rhythmic characteristics of the *eskasak* easier, I used the following division, with **a** even bars, and **b** odd bars:

After analyzing all this, I came to the following conclusions (among other thoughts). On the one hand, both taborers, Amezua and Aldekoa, play with a characteristic alternation of short even bars (**a**) and long odd bars (**b**). In percentage terms, the difference between long and short bars is more notable with Amezua (115.35 percent, which would be the equivalent to the time of a quaver) than with Aldekoa (103.87 percent). On the other, in percentage terms, the relation between **a1–a2** and **b1–b2** shows the kind of time or rhythm used. A relation of 100 percent means that both parts are equal, which could be musically transcribed as (♩ ♩) in 2/4 time. In 5/8 (♩. ♩), the relation would be 66.66, and in a ternary division such as 3/4 (𝅗𝅥 ♩), the proportion would be 50 percent. Consequently, the more the values near 100 percent, the more binary the rhythm will be (2/4), and the more they near 50 percent, the more ternary (3/4). Both taborers are situated in the 70 percent band, with a tendency to play long "more binary" bars (**b**): (Amezua **a1–a2** = 69.18 percent and **b1–b2** = 74.22 percent; Aldekoa **a1–a2** = 70.08 percent and **b1–b2** = 72.24 percent).

Within the framework of the number of samples and variables studied (it would be interesting to extend the study), considering the repetitive rhythmic cycle of two bars (**a+b**) as the main rhythmic unit (100 percent) and averaging out the values of Amezua and Aldekoa, the rhythm of the *eskasak* would be graphically represented as follows:

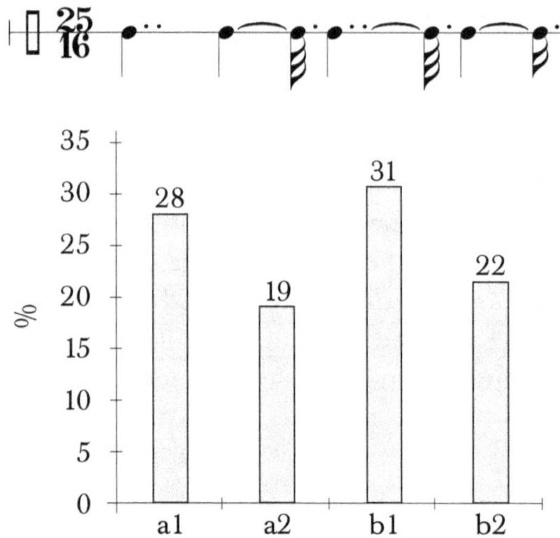

	a+b %
a1	27.946769
a2	19.405424
b1	30.56259339
b2	22.06747323

An Analysis of the Banangoa

To make the analysis of the rhythmic characteristics of the *banangoa* easier, I used the following division, **a** being odd bars in 6/8, and **b** even bars in 3/4:

Again the alternation between long and short bars appears. The bars in 6/8 (**a**) are longer than those in 3/4 (**b**), the difference now being a little higher with Aldekoa (112.08 percent) than with Amezua (111.06 percent). Both taborers play the first part of the 6/8 (**a1**) a little longer than the second (**a2**) in almost exactly the same way (Amezua **a1** = 51.61 percent, **a2** = 48.38 percent; Aldekoa **a1** = 51.68 percent and **b2** = 48.31 percent). The distribution of the three thirds of the bar in 3/4 (**b1**, **b2**, **b3**) is not the same. Amezua plays a kind of progressive *rallentando* in each bar **b** (**b1** = 31.43 percent, **b2** = 33.49 percent, and **b3** = 35.07 percent). Aldekoa lengthens or delays, especially the last part, **b3** (**b1** = 32.68 percent, **b2** = 32.37 percent, and **b3** = 34.94 percent). However, as can be seen in the graph in appendix 4, in some bars (second, eighth, tenth, twelfth, and twentieth), that is, in five out of ten, the *rallentando* played by Aldekoa is also progressive.

With the number of samples and variables studied, considering the repetitive rhythmic cycle of two bars (**a+b**) as the main rhythmic unit (100 percent) and averaging out the values of Amezua and Aldekoa, the rhythm of the *banangoa* would be graphically represented as follows:

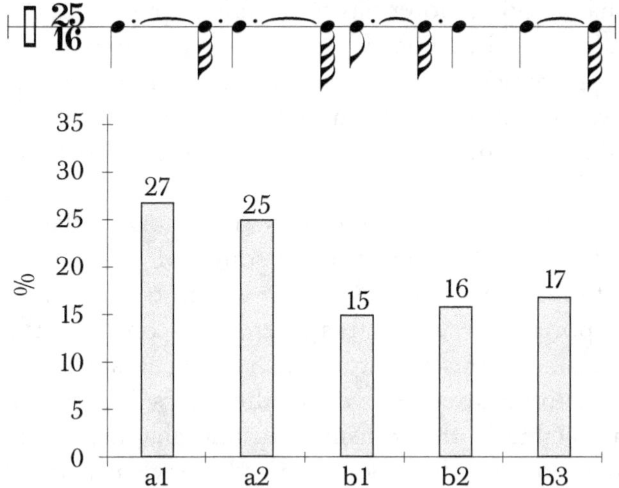

	a+b %
a1	27.190049
a2	25.4976614
b1	15.1524053
b2	15.6020517
b3	16.5578327

Interpretation of the Data

An analysis of the recordings of the *banangoa* (rhythm of the *ezpata-dantza*) and *eskasak* (rhythm of the *zortzikoa*) dances performed by Serafín Amezua and Alejandro Aldekoa shows several similar subtleties in the style of the taborers, or to put it another way, the rhythmical features both players show in the way they play. Although they came from two different generations, with Amezua practically musically illiterate and Aldekoa considering himself a musician because he had studied *solfeggio*, they have two things in common: the local dance repertoire and the influence of common musical references. It is because of this that the way each of them played, despite important differences in personal style, demonstrates common rhythmical characteristics (especially important for dance) that are learned and reproduced unconsciously, but that are nevertheless present in their music.

> By the time I was twelve, I had learned to sing all the dance music by heart, and then . . . how many thousands of times I'll have played. I could go a month without playing, or six, or more, but if I were in a good physical condition to play, I'd be able to play them again from memory with no problem whatsoever. But one thing—it's very important—when I play, I dance, marking out each step in my head.[27]

The taborers of Berriz, Amezua and Aldekoa included, learned to dance when they were very young. They listened to the music of Berriz thousands of times, they danced and played all their lives, and when they played, they danced mentally along with the dancer. That is, they established an interpretative dialogue with the dancers: the dancer directed the taborer through the choreographic movements he made with

---

27. Alejandro Aldekoa, interview by the author, April 22, 1996.

his feet. I would therefore conclude that a good taborer has to be able to put the music to the dance that he sees, in real time. To do this, he needs to know the dance perfectly and have the necessary technique to respond with his instrument to the orders he receives from outside. In a certain way, it is the choreographic structure that conditions and draws the musical rhythm, within, of course, the limits that a good taborer will take care to maintain.

This appears to be the fundamental reason why the taborers knew how to play in order to make the dancers feel comfortable while dancing to the sound of their instruments and the reason why subtle rhythmic characteristics are present in their style. It is also why there has been a notable aporia between what is written in scores and the performances of *txistulariak* versed in local customs and style. These are characteristics that are difficult to perceive, distinguish, and transcribe, even for the actors themselves. I believe there are several factors interacting in the transmission and shaping of the particular rhythmic style of these dances: the way in which the rhythm style is handed down within the community of dancers, the changes introduced by the dance master and taborer, and the rhythmical features imposed by the motional structure of the dance itself.

A particular local rhythmical style is handed down by the whole community of dancers, with the musicians being members of this group. The musicians first learn the dance music and the local rhythmic style of dancing, and it is only after learning to dance that they come to play the dances with the pipe and tabor. This explains, to some extent at least, why Aldekoa, despite being a literate pipe and tabor player, kept the main features of the local style.

The influence of the dance master also is very important. Although Aldekoa, despite being a respected leader, complained about the dancers in his group who did not follow all his dance instructions, and although what the San Lorenzo group dances does not actually reflect the ideal model of dance described by Aldekoa, the influence of the dance master nonetheless affects the rhythm of the dance. Aldekoa introduced several changes related to rhythmical style. As a rule, but especially in *eskasak*, he was generally more regular than Amezua. This is demonstrated by the standard deviation in each of the variables measured (see Appendix 3). We might therefore say that Amezua played more "freely."

Also, being an important sounding reference for the dancers and the dance, the tabor patterns used regularly by Aldekoa were more complex than those of Amezua (see footnote 36 in this chapter).

***Zortzikoa* rhythm**	
Amezua	5/8
Aldekoa	5/8 5/8 5/8
***Ezpata-dantza* rhythm**	
Amezua	6/8 3/4
Aldekoa	6/8 3/4

As far as I know from the comments of those who danced with both Amezua and Aldekoa, the latter did change the tempo of certain dances. And thanks to the recording of Serafín Amezua playing in Garai around 1970, we know that Aldekoa not only changed the tempo but also the rhythm of at least one dance: the dance titled "Gernikako Arbola" was played by the Amezuas in 6/8+3/4 (the rhythm of the *ezpata-dantza*),

but in 5/8 (the rhythm of *zortzikoa*) by Aldekoa.

Finally, there are certain steps that, due to their kinetic features, can be danced only at a certain speed or tempo, necessarily conditioning the structure of the rhythm to that of the movement. In this process, we assume that the *txistularia* knows the dance and is able to follow the dancer's movements, or as Aldekoa termed them, the *puntoak* (points):[28] "The *puntoak* are the notes you play or mark with your feet in conjunction with the music, to mark the rhythm with your feet. In the same bar you can add more or fewer *puntoak* or notes, as if it were an instrument. The *puntoak* are like the notes of the instrument."[29]

A detailed analysis of the influence of the dance's structure on the rhythm would require the use of refined video and audio analysis equipment and a test of different

28. I have seen many performances of the *dantzari-dantza* where the music and the dance, that is, the musician and the dancers, play without any coordination.

29. Alejandro Aldekoa, interview by the author, April 15, 1996.

dancers and taborers to check the rhythmical boundaries or the temporal limits of certain steps. Whatever the case, in order to illustrate this point briefly, based on my own experience as a dance apprentice and *txistularia* playing for dance, I am going to refer to the most decisive movements that clearly shape the rhythm and determine the structure of the rhythm in the *banangoa* (the rhythm of the *ezpata-dantza*). These movements are described and related to the music through a rhythmical transcription of the steps. For a better understanding or more detailed analysis of the dance, please refer to the accompanying DVD.

The *banangoa* is played eleven times, and the first statement is played as a kind of introduction while the eight dancers stand in their positions waiting for the last bars to start to dance.

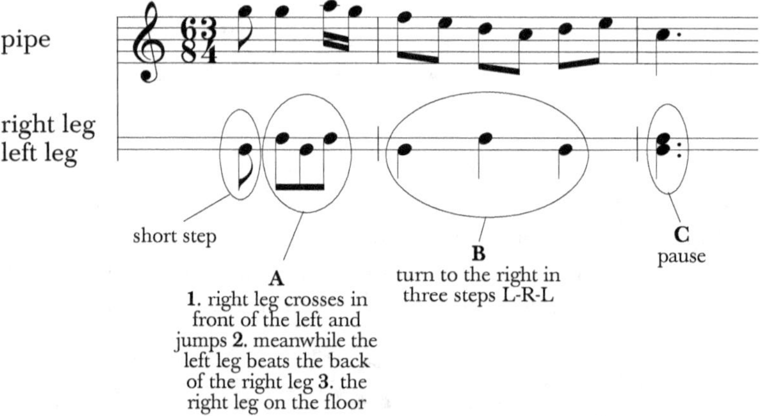

The same sequence of steps (A-B-B) is used when a dancer begins to dance while he goes from the back to the front of the group to perform his solo part, at the end of each of the sections as described below, and at the last coda when the dance finishes.

After this introduction, the first part of the *banangoa* is danced as follows:

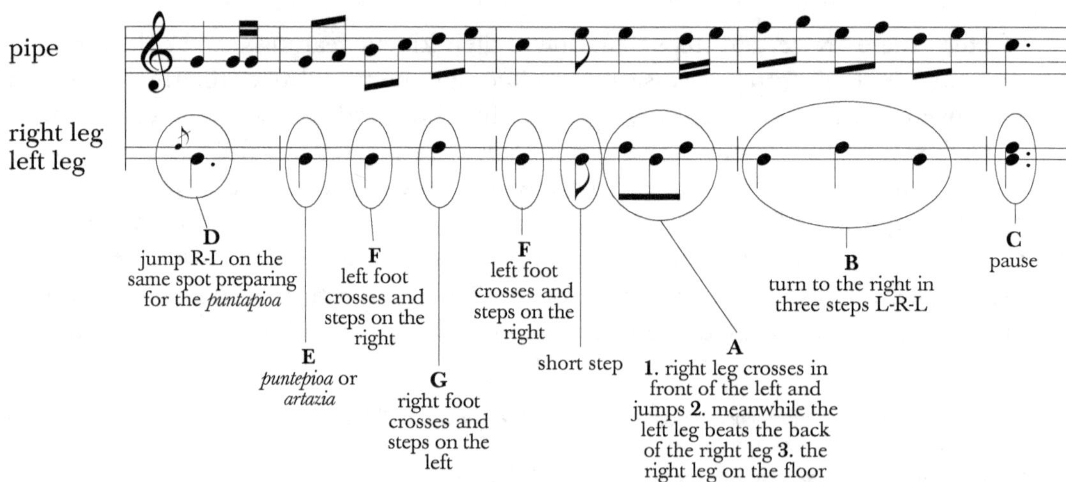

This section is repeated with the same music and the same steps. Afterward, the next section starts. It is basically the same sequence of steps, but now after the *puntapioa* (E), instead of steps F and G, the dancer performs two *grabilletak* (I, J):

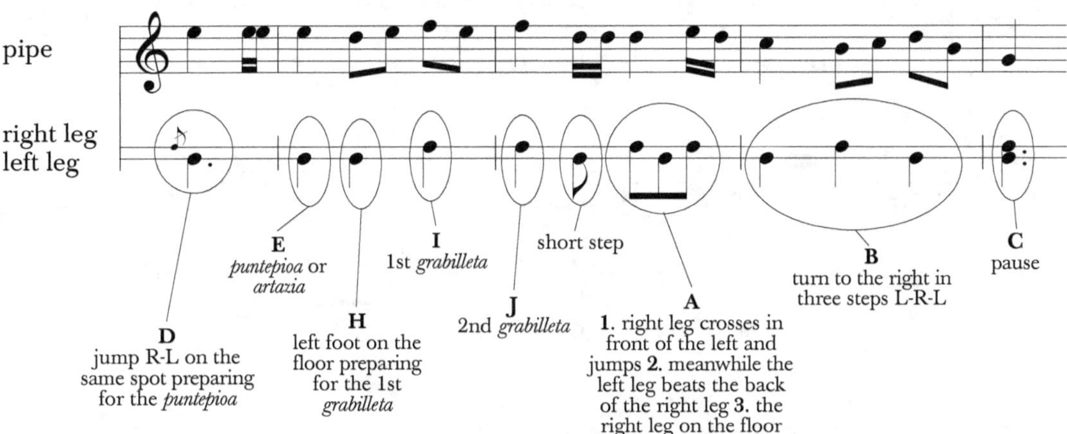

For the next four bars, this sequence of steps is repeated with a different melody.

Put together, the general diagram of the steps in the *banangoa* would be:

Note that **(a1)** is longer than **(a2)**: as we have seen in the analysis, Alejandro Aldekoa and Serafín Amezua played the first part of the 6/8 (**a1**) a little longer than the second (**a2**). The first part (**a1**) coincides with three different steps:

- The pause (C) after the turn (B) (bars 1, 5, 9, 13, 17, and 20).

- Step F, which is a step on the floor (bars 3 and 7).
- Step J, which is the end of the second *grabilleta* (bars 11, 15, and 18).

During the second part (**a2**) the following steps are danced:

- Step D, a short jump changing from the right leg to the left, which is risen to perform the step called *puntapioa* (bars 1, 5, 9, 13, and 17).
- Step A, basically a hop on the right foot (bars 3, 7, 11, 15, and 18).

The kind of steps danced in (**a2**) are movements in the air, while the movements in (**a1**) are on the floor. In the case of the *grabilleta* (J), if the dancer is going to mark it by raising his knee and drawing a high, wide circle with his foot, as the dancers from Berriz usually do (see chapter 3), the performance of the step requires a certain time as well, more than the jumps or hops performed in (**a2**). This explains why (**a1**) is longer.

Note also that **(b1)** is shorter than **(b2)** and **(b3)**: in the 3/4 bars, Alejandro Aldekoa and Serafín Amezua tend to play the first parts shorter, playing a kind of *rallentando*. The first third, the beat (**b1**) coincides with the following steps:

- The highest point of the *puntapioa* or *artazia* (E) and the left leg going down (bars 2, 6, 1, and 14).
- The first step of the turn B (bars 4, 8, 12, 16, and 19).

The steps danced in (**b2**) are:

- Step F, the left leg on the floor coming from the explosive movement *puntapioa* (E) (bars 2 and 6).
- Step H, on the floor preparing the *grabilleta* (bars 10 and 14).
- The second step of the turn B (bars 4, 8, 12, 16, and 19).

The steps danced in (**b3**) are:

- Step G on the floor coming from F, another step on the floor (bars 2 and 6).
- Step I, the first *grabilleta* (bars 10 and 14).
- The third step of the turn B (bars 4, 8, 12, 16, and 19).

There are basically two movements shaping the particular rhythm of the 3/4 bar. On the one hand, there is the *puntapioa*, which is the most energetic and aerial step of the dances from Berriz. One can be in the air for only a short instant, and that explains the trend to play the first beat (**b1**) shorter. At the other extreme, (**b3**) needs to be played slower, because the *grabilleta* requires a longer time if the dancer is going to mark it properly—high and wide, as Aldekoa insisted it should be done. The kind of movements performed in (**b2**) could be classified as transitional steps insofar as the length required to perform them is concerned.

To conclude, one might say that there are certain steps that clearly shape the rhythm, while the influence of others is not so noticeable. In the 6/8 bars, C is the place for a pause in (**a1**), as opposed to D and A, which are jumps or hops preparing the *puntapioa* (E) or the turn (B). In the 3/4 bars, the *puntapioa* is the energetic movement that forces the first part to be shorter, and the *grabilleta* danced in the third part is the step requiring a longer time to be performed.

I should point out, moreover, that each dancer has his own style: they have different bodies, different training, and different preferences. For example, it is commonly noted that tall dancers have to do wider and longer movements. As a result, the music goes slower for them, but I found so many exceptions (tall, strong, energetic, and fast dancers) that it is difficult to accept this principle as a rule. A detailed study of the motional features of the dances, their relation to biomechanical matters, and to the structure of the music, as well as the cognitive processes involved, remains to be done.

The Tabor: The Old Drumming Style

Unfortunately, we know little about how the old taborers played the tabor. In the case of Berriz, we have only a few recordings of the last of the Amezuas, Serafín, and it appears, according to all the testimonies that we have, that he was not a brilliant taborer, especially if he is compared with his father Hipólito or his successor, Aldekoa. The recordings seem to demonstrate this.[30]

The earliest information about the beats of the tabor of the old taborers is to be found in Thoinot Arbeau's *Orchésographie* (1589). Arbeau points to the importance of simple rhythms and emphasizes the importance of stressing the first beat of each bar to help the dancer distinguish between them. The simple rhythmic patterns he proposes remain constant throughout the whole book. The *Orchésographie* has been used by many early music ensembles to "reconstruct" the old style of rhythmic accompaniment of the taborers.

At the beginning of the nineteenth century, two books were published containing interesting information about the tabor: the *Gipuzkoako dantza gogoangarrien kondaira edo historia* (An Account or History of the Most Celebrated Dances of Gipuzkoa, 1824), by Juan Ignacio de Iztueta, and a notebook of the melodies that the same author published along with the musician Pedro Albéniz as a complement to the text *Euscaldun anciña anciñaco ta are lendabicico etorquien dantza on iritci pozcarri gaitzic gabecoen soñu gogoangarriac beren itz neurtu edo versoaquin* (Ancient Basque and Even the First People's Dances and their Faultless Pleasant Celebrated Melodies with their Measured Words or Verses, 1826). According to Iztueta, in a comment made long ago, but that still holds true today: "Years ago, I realized that those taborer musicians were gradually forgetting the known beats of the tabor, and for that reason the dancers were making mistakes."[31]

---

30. These recordings were made when Serafín was old, and his lack of energy is noticeable during his performance. Premature conclusions should therefore not be made about them.

31. Juan Ignacio de Iztueta, *Gipuzkoako dantza gogoangarrien kondaira edo historia* (1824; Donostia: Euskal Editoreen Elkartea, 1990), 115. According to Juan Madariaga Orbea, Iztueta's "fundamental preoccupation centered on the

Iztueta continues by pointing out that the musician Pedro Albéniz, apart from transcribing the melodies for the pipe, also transcribed the beats of the tabor used by the old taborers that Iztueta himself had sung to him. Albéniz thought them to be more appropriate to accompany dance than the beats of the contemporary taborers of that time. Unfortunately, these transcriptions have disappeared, so once again, we can only speculate.

Jose Inazio Ansorena has studied Iztueta's work at length, revising his notebook of melodies and compiling a new critical, revised edition of the transcriptions. This revision incorporates one of the fundamental concepts on which the musical system of the old taborers was based: "The melody—whose fundamental objective is to serve the dance—is not totally focused on all the detail of measurements, values, adornments, etc., as we understand today. It is made up of a few general guidelines—the points or beats, a few basic designs—that the performer is free to vary to his own liking in each performance."

This means that, if the melodic guideline is, for example:

the taborer can play in any of the following ways:

or many other variations.[32]

A similar approach could be expected for percussion: if the interpretation of the melody is free and open to improvisation and adornment, why should the rhythmic accompaniment of the tabor not be the same? But instead, Ansorena Miner says of the tabor, "the rhythmic formulae of these nonmusician taborers would be fairly repetitive and simple."[33] However, in his work on eighteenth-century taborers, Carlos Sánchez

decadence of traditional dances, because new musicians were influenced by foreign sounds and rhythms and the Basque Country's own themes were danced badly and less and less frequently." Furthermore, Madariaga considers Iztueta to be "the first Basque folklorist" because of the work he carried out on music and dance. See Madariaga, *Anthology of Apologists and Detractors of the Basque Language*, 510.

32. See Jose Inazio Ansorena Miner, "Iztueta eta Albéniz-en musika bilduma," *Txistulari* 163, no. 3 (1995): 33.

33. Ibid., 38.

criticizes Ansorena's study, observing that "he dispatches this question in little more than four words."[34] Instead, Sánchez defends a more elaborate performance of the tabor:

> In my opinion, it is not ridiculous to assume that the old taborers used the tabor, from which they get their name, in a more active way, including polyrhythms similar to those used by taborers who play the *gaita* [three-holed pipe] and *tambor* [tabor] today (instruments of the same family as our *txistua* and *danbolina*) in Salamanca, Zamora, León, or the north of Cáceres. If this, to a great extent, is not so, I do not understand why they were known as "taborers," given that the role of the tabor was so small. Nor why the new performers whom Iztueta mentions did what they could to be known by another name.[35]

In my opinion, such reductionist interpretations—based on the opposition between a simple or elaborate style—are not very illuminating. The performing style of the tabor is influenced by a variety of factors, among which I would stress the following.

The function of the tabor as an accompaniment to dance is fundamental at the time of developing a performing style. Indeed, it is one of the main determining factors. Dance, however, is variable in its forms, depending on its use or meaning and the customs of each place and time. Amezua and Aldekoa beat the rhythm of some dances differently, and we know that the dancers who danced with both of them noticed the change.[36] Whatever the case, each group of dancers inevitably ends up adapting to their *txistularia*'s style of playing the tabor in the same way that he has to be able to adapt to the customs of the repertoire and the dancers.

---

34. Carlos Sánchez, *Del danbolin al silbo: Txistu, tamboril y danza vasca en la época de la ilustración* (Pamplona: Euskal Herriko Txistulari Elkartea, 1999), 142. In his critique, Sánchez perhaps forgets Ansorena's subsequent and interesting ideas that underline the importance of the tabor in accompanying dance and marking the choreographical-musical phrases, as well as pointing out the formulae that have been handed down to us by tradition. Moreover, Ansorena is open to further analysis, making it clear that his is only one of many possible interpretations. Basing his investigation on his own theoretical work and with instruments especially made for the task, Ansorena recreated what, in his opinion, could have been the tuning of the old *txistuak* and made a historical type of recording of the dances in question, a reconstruction of the old style. However, the treatment given to the *txistua* and the tabor in the recording is unbalanced. While the *txistua* flows freely and adorned, the part of the tabor is simple, uncomplicated, and of an exaggerated metric regularity. I believe that this recording influenced the judgments and criticisms of Sánchez and others just as much as, if not more than, Ansorena's actual theoretical analysis.

35. Sánchez, *Del danbolin al silbo*, 143.

36. The pattern played on the tabor is important for the dancers. I remember one occasion when the Andra Mari dance group invited Rafael Albizuri, nicknamed "Otsue," "The Wolf," and Roberto Maiztegi to dance the *erregelak* so that the group could record them. Mikel Zamalloa, the group's *txistularia*, was playing that day. He is an experienced player and knows the repertoire well because he has been a dancer himself. When Otsue began to dance the *aurreskua*, Zamalloa played the first part with the following pattern on the tabor:

Otsue stopped and said that the tabor was wrong, that this was not the beat. The problem was solved when the pattern that Aldekoa usually beat was played on the tabor:

It is not possible to establish a unified stylistic tendency either in time or in space, since the elaboration and ornamentation of the rhythmic patterns ultimately depend on the technique of the taborer, and this, as one would expect, varies from one generation to the next and from one place to another. During the twentieth century, for example, Berriz witnessed the mastery of both Hipólito Amezua and Alejandro Aldekoa, as well as an intervening period of decline with Serafín Amezua.

The Tabor: Rhythmic Patterns or Movement Patterns

Txistulariak, like many other drum players, use basically two different beats: the single beat and the drumroll. When playing, they use two basic techniques to play on the drum, that is, two ways to move and control the stick and the beats: moving the wrist and moving the fingers. The skilled taborers I know combine both techniques, both kinds of movement, in order to achieve more complex patterns. Basically, fingers are used to control the balance of the stick, especially during the drumroll. Then the movement of the wrist is used when playing single beats and to fill the gaps between different drumrolls or a drumroll and the following single beat.

The pattern used by each taborer depends not only on the score, when the music is written down, or on the models and references he tries to imitate, such as his teacher or local taborer. Ultimately it depends directly on his command of the technique required to play each combination of beats. For example, the beat of the *biribilketa* rhythm, in its simplest form, has no drumrolls, but instead what Aldekoa called the *bikotxa* (twin), a pattern that coincides with the beat of the rhythm that the dancers keep with their feet:

This is the pattern employed by Serafín Amezua, whose technique, judging from the few records I have and the comments of people to whom I have spoken, did not allow him to play the drumroll. When the pattern is embellished, as Alejandro Aldekoa played it (except when an *atabala* accompanied him), it is played with a drumroll. In this case, one can hear, among other things difficult to transcribe, the following rhythmic patterns:

Patterns **a** and **b** are easier because there is a gap between the two beats of the drumroll and the following one.

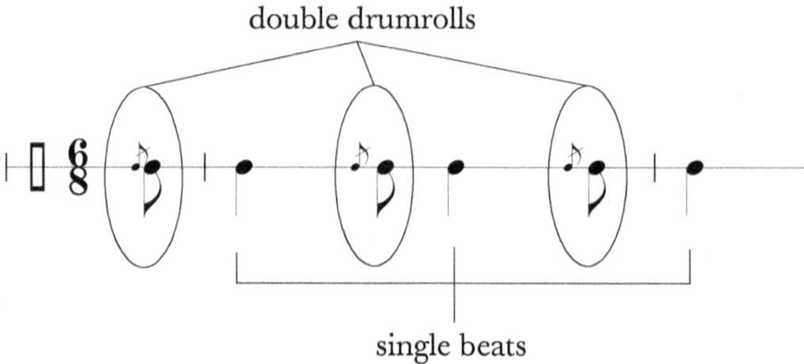

Patterns **c**, **d**, and **e** require a more complex technique, a good control of the movement of the stick with the fingers during the drumroll, and a quick movement of the wrist to connect the drumroll to the following single beat. The gaps between the first beat of the drumroll, the second one, and the following beat must be the same.

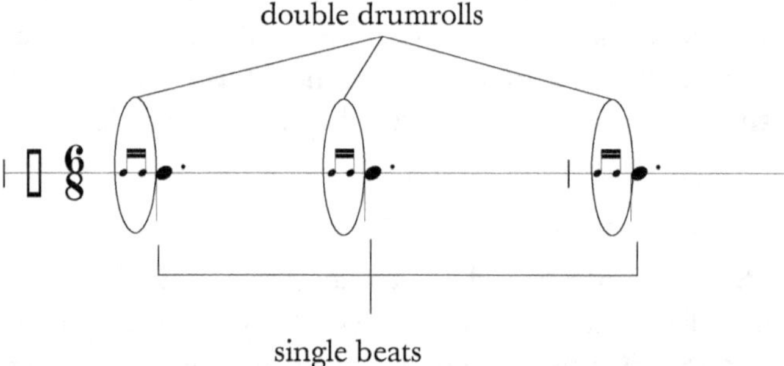

Pattern **f** is the most difficult, because the gap between the three beats must be equally spaced, demanding a very good control of the drumroll to separate the two beats adequately and of the movement of the wrist to get the rest of the beats in time.

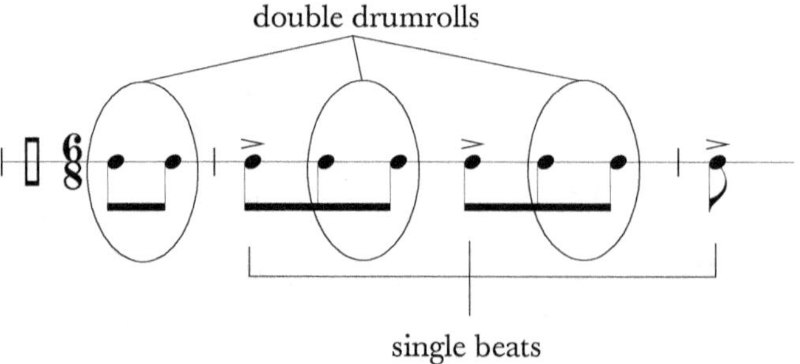

Aldekoa played something that could be transcribed between the **c** and **d** patterns, although the second beat of the drumroll was a bit longer, or in other words, the single beat played by the wrist was played later. The following example comes from the *banangoa* analyzed previously. It is the third bar of the version played by Aldekoa. Although it is not a *biribilketa*, the example illustrates the way he played this kind of pattern and the technical difficulty involved in playing a "perfect" drag (♫♩) with one hand. The spectrum and the descriptive transcription below show the longer gap between the two beats of the drumroll and the following beat:

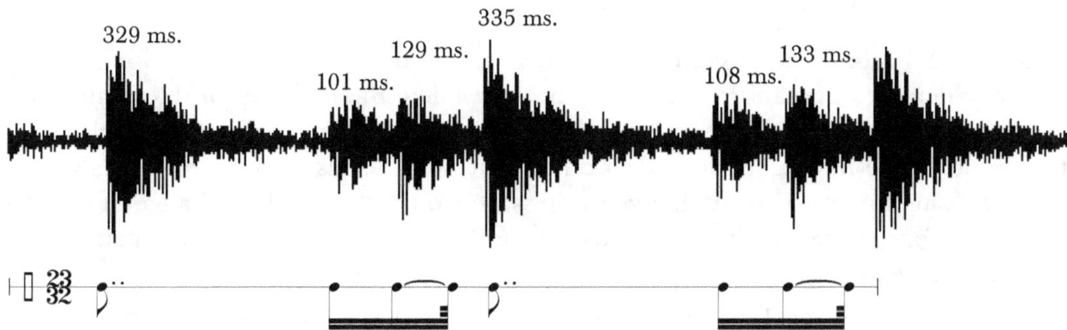

Among many of the *txistulariak* I know, there is a syllabic code to talk about the rhythms they play. The single beat is called *ta*, and when it has a rhythmical accent, *tan*. The double drumroll is called *tara*, and when the rhythmical accent is on the second beat, *taran*. Following this code, a triple drumroll would be *tarara*. Consequently, when I asked the *txistulariak* about how they played the *biribilketa* on the tabor, most of them answered the same: *tara-tan*, *tara-tan*, a double drumroll plus a single beat. Yet when it was time to play, I heard any of the above-mentioned patterns, **a** to **f**, although all of them were perceived as equal, with the same sense or meaning: *tara-tan*.

I would conclude, then, that for these *txistulariak*, at a cognitive level, the actual sounding utterance is not as important as the kind of movement employed when playing. Therefore, the pattern *tara-tan* does not imply a specific rhythm, as we analytically perceive and classify rhythms. Instead, it means above all "a drumroll plus a single beat," a combination of two different movements of the body. This is firm evidence for musicians thinking in movements as well as in sounds, as suggested by the research of John Baily.[37] Of course, there are certain limits, and the rhythm must serve to accompany the dance. A useful analogy for understanding the relations between these patterns comes from phonetics. An allophone is one of several similar speech sounds that belongs to the same phoneme. A phoneme is an abstract unit of speech sound that can distinguish

37. See John Baily, "Music Structure and Human Movement," in *Musical Structure and Cognition*, ed. Peter Howell, Ian Cross, and Robert West (London: Academic Press, 1985), 237–58, and "Some Cognitive Aspects of Motor Planning in Musical Performance," *Psychologica Belgica* 31, no. 2 (1991): 147–62.

words: change the phoneme, and you've changed to a different word. So it could be said that these patterns work as allophones or contextual variants of the same phoneme. Only recently, after a process of acculturation chiefly through conservatory education, have modern *txistulariak* developed their analytical listening, musicality, and technique. This has allowed them both to discern at least the main variants of this pattern and to have the necessary skills to play the different variants, using them as individual, different patterns with different meanings—in other words, using the allophones as new phonemes.

The Tabor: A Dynamic Resource

Apart from beating the rhythm, the tabor has another important function: adding dynamic depth to the taborer's music. The *txistua*, like the majority of duct flutes, has a limited dynamic range. The change of air pressure necessary to adjust the volume of the sound would have a sudden effect on the harmonic levels—that is, the notes would change, going up or down. A change in pressure would also imply a change of tension and pitch. For this reason, the tabor is used to add the expressive effects of dynamics and volume, crescendos, and diminuendos.

So important is this function that Aldekoa declared that a *txistularia* without a tabor is not a real *txistularia* and that the two together are essential to the dance. "The tabor is obligatory to play a *fandangoa*, a *zortzikoa*, or anything else. Even to play a *biribilketa*. The tabor is necessary and obligatory."

> Compared with when I was young, today there are a lot of *txistulariak*, but none of them are outstanding. For example, in the San José concert celebrated this year in Zaldibar, where I usually conduct, there were about sixty of them. They didn't play half of the notes, because they didn't know how. There were also quite a lot of twenty-year-old girls who took part, but the majority of them didn't even know how to play a *biribilketa* with the tabor [the rhythm of the *biribilketa* is the easiest and simplest to play]. And this is what I say, to be a complete *txistularia*, you have to be able to play the *txistua* and the tabor, whatever the music may be, from a *kontrapasa* to a *fandangoa*, which is more complicated. Some fifteen or so years ago, a competition was held in Donostia, and there was a certain amount of controversy, because some *txistulariak* turned up without the tabor, and as one of the journalists from the journal *Txistulari* said, to take part in the competition, you have to have a tabor—a complete *txistularia* has to play the tabor.
>
> Anyway, you can't play the dances without a tabor—it can't be done. I wouldn't do it even if they paid me. On more than one occasion, away from home, people have offered me a *txistua* to play something for them.
>
> "Have you got a tabor?"
>
> "No."
>
> "Well I won't play then. Nothing."[38]

38. Alejandro Aldekoa, interview by the author, April 9, 1996.

However, Aldekoa played the tabor in a much simpler, less adorned way when he was accompanied by the *atabala*, and he preferred to play with a good *atabalaleroa* who knew the dance repertoire well, to playing alone.

> When I started to play the tabor, the first thing I learned was the *biribilketa*, playing *bikotxa* [the twin]:
>
> 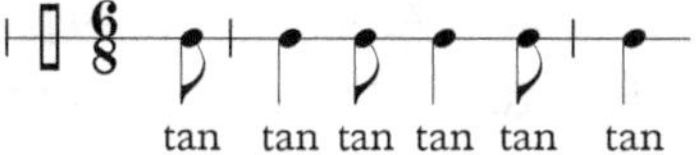
>
>
> My teacher taught me that with the *atabala* at your side, it wasn't necessary for the tabor to play the drumroll,
>
> 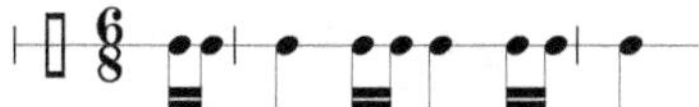
>
> that was done by the *atabala*. That's why, when I play with an *atabala*, I just play *tan-tan, tan-tan*. When I play without the *atabala,* I play the drumroll, even when there are three or four *txistulariak*, but no *atabala*, like in Zaldibar in a procession through the streets with my students. When I play the *dantzari-dantza*, I feel more comfortable if there's an *atabala*—if the *atabalaleroa* plays well, that is, not just with anybody, because the *dantzari-dantza* has special different beats. For example, in the *ezpata joko nagusia*, you have to play a drumroll at the same time as the tabor when the dancers bang their swords together, but in some groups, they continue to play without stopping. Here, in Berriz, in the old *txistulariak*'s way, we play the tabor and the *atabala* only when the dancers cross their swords—the rest is done in silence. The same goes for the *makil jokoa*—only when they bang their sticks together.[39]

While Aldekoa conceived the pipe and tabor as one and the same instrument and could not imagine a taborer without a tabor, today, things are different. Many *txistulariak* (I would say the majority) use the tabor very little, foregoing the dynamic resources of the instrument, and if they do, they play it badly. We might conclude that today, the majority of the performers of the pipe and tabor in the Basque Country are more *txistulariak* (pipers) than *danbolinteroak* (taborers).[40]

---

39. Alejandro Aldekoa, interview by the author, April 12, 1996.

40. A similar process of promoting the flute to the detriment of the drum has been experienced in other areas where, as in the Basque Country, the pipe and tabor have had greater contact with classical music and academic education. In Catalonia, for example, the conservatory-educated, learned taborers and the *coblas* (an orchestral group of wind instruments, typical there) use the instrument in a very simple, almost exclusively symbolic way. In a similar and significant way, they have given the name of *flabiolaire* (from the name of the flute *flabiol*) to the musician, leaving out completely any mention of the percussion instrument. Paradoxically, the style and level of execution of the drum used by the *flabiolaire* in the Catalan oral tradition is one of the richest and most varied I have known. Here I would stress the importance of Josep Verdaguer, "en Rovirettes," one of the best taborers I have ever seen, and an authentic virtuoso of percussion whom I had the honor and fortune to meet, listen to, and play with, thanks to my good friends Jordi Urioz and Lidia de Mena.

The *Txistua*: Intervals and Modes

Another result of a process of acculturation that began in the eighteenth century, when Western classical music was established as the prevailing musical system, imposing itself on all others, involves the imposition of the concepts of classical tonality, its scales, and the distinction between the major and minor modes. Prior to that, the musical system of the old, traditional taborers, was not grounded in classical major or minor tonalities. Nor was it based, as some have suggested, on the old medieval or ancient Greek modes, but instead on something as apparently simple as the sounds and intervals that the *txistua* itself was capable of emitting, using what we might describe as its proper or natural positions. The range of sounds that traditional *txistulariak* used, with their own particular tuning, which is not reflected in standard notation, spans the following notes:

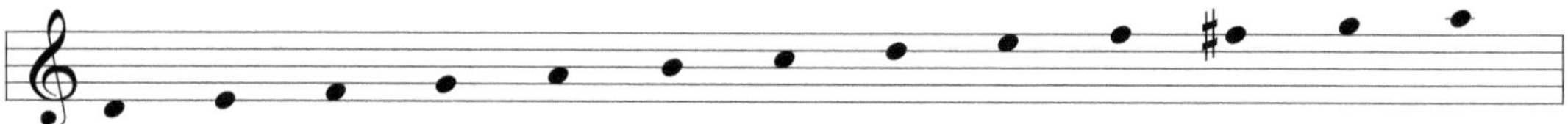

In Berriz, Aldekoa, due to his academic training, was responsible for the introduction of concepts of classical tonality and modes. Within the dance repertoire of Berriz, one of the examples that best illustrates this process of transformation from one system to the other is the case of the *andra soiñua* (women's melody). Serafín Amezua played the melody without any alterations, following the old, traditional range, whereas Aldekoa's version, most certainly learned from one of the many transcriptions of the theme, was in C minor. It is difficult to guess which the original version is. The most probable likelihood is that traditional taborers adapted the theme in C minor from musically educated taborers to their own execution technique.[41] Yet it is also possible that a musician who was unaware of the peculiar tuning characteristics of the instrument transcribed the *andra soiñua* in C minor.[42]

In the old *txistulariak*'s musical system, we thus find ourselves faced with a different way of perceiving and experiencing the sounds and intervals of the scale or range of sounds: a unique system of tuning in which the range of intervals precedes over its amplitude or mode. This system has been used in the practice of some taborers from Salamanca and Extremadura, where the tabor and its music survive to a certain extent on the fringes of classical-academic music, thanks to oral transmission. At a 1997 tabor conference in Iruñea (Pamplona), for example, I recall how Oscar Duarte, on learning a new theme when we played and danced together, could begin from any note and then

41. The structure and style of the melody seems to denote its relatively recent and classical origin, which probably means that it was incorporated by the traditional taborers.

42. The interval between C and E, which is the one that most clearly defines the difference between one mode and another, is 338.88 cents in Serafín Amezua's *txistua*, nearer the 300 cents of the minor third than the 400 of the major third on the chromatic scale. The cent is a unit of pitch based on the equal-tempered octave. One equal-tempered semitone is equal to 100 cents. An octave is then 1,200 cents.

build the rest of the melody up from there, respecting the progression of the intervals, but not the mode—that is, without a change in the framework and tonality to which modern-day *txistulariak* and other academic musicians are accustomed. For example, the well-known theme "Jota de los Toros":

could be performed in any of the following ways:

Using the same distinction that a linguist would use between phonemes and allophones to contribute to the explanation of the phenomenon, in this case, the phoneme would define the intervallic distances that outline the melodic succession of the theme, independently of its major or minor mode, in such a way that the different proposed versions would be perceived with the same meaning.[43] The allophones, or contextual variants of each phoneme, result from the major or minor amplitude of the intervals that invariably fluctuate between the major and the minor modes, these being of an ambivalent character or difficult to qualify. It is the melodic contour that counts, rather than interval size.

The *Txistua*: Rhythm and Dance

The functioning of the particular system of the traditional taborers is defined and conditioned by another, deeper level of significance, beyond intervallic and modal distinctions of the melodic design and even beyond the melody itself. Here, I am referring to the rhythm. The rhythm is what connects and synchronizes the resonant message (music) with the corporal choreographic movement (dance). In the context of the *dantzari-dantza* and the *soka dantza*, the melody, independent of its tonality or mode, would

43. I use the term "meaning" instead of the more linguistically accurate "minimal contrast" or "minimal opposition," considering that such a distinction might exceed the purpose and size of this work and that the aim of the analysis is not linguistic, but musical.

have a secondary role. Even today, what really counts for the majority of the dancers is the rhythm.[44] Within this framework, the melody could be considered as a contextual variant,[45] while the rhythm acquires a relevant diacritical value for the dance, whose sequence of movements, or spatial discourse, is what defines, in the end, the meaning and significance of the traditional taborer's music. The choreographic function is what equips the rhythm with a more relevant meaning and significance than that of the melody.

The *Txistua*: Tuning

When I saw some photographs of the Amezua family, the *txistua* they played caught my attention, due to the type of rings that adorned the instrument, because they were wider than usual and had grooves engraved on them. Aldekoa used to praise the sound of Hipólito Amezua's *txistua*, and the recordings of Serafín Amezua clearly show an instrument with a somewhat idiosyncratic tuning. I was extremely curious about that instrument. For me, it was the equivalent of what a violin used by Paganini might represent for a violinist. On this topic, my first visit to Ereña, the Amezua family *baserria*, where Elena Amezua, Serafín's only daughter, and Florencio Berrojalbiz, her husband, live, was frustrating to say the least. All my attempts to find out more about the Patxiku *txistua* came to nothing. "There's nothing here. They took it all away, the instruments, the scores. . . . We don't know anything. If you want to know anything, go see Alejandro," I was told by Elena Amezua.

Two years later, I tried again, and finally managed to convince them that it was worth talking about this issue. This time, the doors opened. Elena and Floren chatted with me in the kitchen of their home for a while, we looked at an album of old photographs, and we spoke of the old times. When I asked about her father's *txistua*, they told me it was in the storeroom, and we continued chatting about one thing and another. I had great difficulty following the conversation once I knew that the *txistua* I had given up for lost was in that house. After a while, Floren brought me the *txistua*, two *danbolinak*, and an *atabala*. Shyly, I asked if I could play it, and the answer I received was very disconcerting: "They're for you. If you want them, you can take them. We don't need them, and we're sure that you'll use them and look after them better than us." I was excited. Although it took me some time to get the *txistua* to sound, I played the *erregelak*. "You play just the same as my father," said Elena.

44. On more than one occasion, Jon Zamalloa (a *txistularia*) has put to the test the capacity of the dancers of the Andra Mari group to discriminate between pieces of music by playing, for example, the *binangoa* instead of the *launangoa*. The rhythmic structure of both dances is the same (the same number of bars, beginning in anacrusis, the same rhythm of the tabor). Most of the time, the dancers, apart from dancing with no problem whatsoever, never even noticed the melodic change. On other occasions, I have played the *andra soiñua* theme in the same way as Serafín Amezua, in C major instead of in C minor, with my friend and master Jon Zamalloa being the only one who noticed the change in the mode used.

45. In fact, there are many known variants of the melodies of the *dantzari-dantza* and the *soka dantza*, variants in which we find differences ranging from a simple note or musical motif to the structure and order of the musical phrases, changes of mode, and even the entire melody.

To my surprise, the Patxiku *txistua* was not so hard to play, nor was it as loud and powerful as Aldekoa had described it. But without a doubt, what most attracted my attention was its tuning, in which the "irregularities" of certain intervals, something very common in old *txistuak*,[46] were very prominent. The peculiar tuning of the instrument led me to carry out a comparative study of the three *txistuak* that Alejandro Aldekoa used in his working life and Serafín Amezua's *txistua* to see to what point the tuning of the instruments could have influenced the musical system used by the old taborers. To analyze the tuning of the pipes, I contacted Alexander Iribar, phonetic laboratory technician of the Faculty of Philosophy and Arts at the University of Deusto, and an excellent musician and taborer.

I obtained the following acoustic data in the Phonetic Laboratory of the Faculty of Philosophy and Arts at the University of Deusto using the digital sonograph KAY DSP 5500. Sonographic or spectrographic analysis was undertaken using a Hamming window weighting with an input range of 4 KHz, and a 125 Hz bandwidth filter. This kind of analysis allows one to obtain clear and defined representations of each sound's first harmonics, where the fundamental frequency (F_0) and its bandwidth can be observed, as well as the frequency fluctuations during the length of each sound measured in milliseconds. The input range of each sound was adjusted for each note in order to get the most accurate results. In certain cases, I carried out other kinds of complementary analysis, such as a spectrographic examination using narrower input ranges, FFT, LPC, and the automatic calculation of pitch, in order to verify the obtained data through the previously described analytical method.

The analyzed material was previously recorded on a DAT Fuji tape using two Shure SM57 microphones and a Sony DAT TCD-D10 PRO. In order to get comparable results, the following procedures were observed:

- The four *txistuak* were played by the same expert *txistularia*, the author, Sabin Bikandi.
- Similar warming-up exercises were used for each instrument (about five minutes of playing).
- The recording was made using the same microphone setup and distance from each instrument.

---

46. Despite research and the efforts of *txistua* makers, some of these irregularities have still not been corrected today, not even in the most modern instruments. At the moment, it seems practically impossible to tune the *txistua* in all its note range without recurring to the use of correction positions on the part of the performer. To be able to understand the tuning of the instrument, its evolution has to be placed within a wider framework and compared with that of other similar instruments in Europe. Almost all the old *txistuak*, and the majority of the old three-holed flutes I know of, have three equal holes, all the same distance apart (approximately) and all producing similar "irregularities" in their tuning. In the eighteenth century, when taborers began to perform classical music on the pipe and tabor, the third interval, D–F, that is, the interval resulting between the position ●●●○ and ●○○○, was understood and interpreted in different ways. In some regions—for example, in England or Provence—the particular interval was defined as third major, while in the Basque Country, it became defined as third minor. In this way, the succession of tones (T) and semitones (S) in the present *txistua* is T-S-T, whereas in other flutes it is T-T-S or T-T-T.

- The same sequence of notes and scales was recorded with each *txistua*, trying to get different dynamics from *piano* to *forte* in order to get the average pitch of each note, which would be an ideal mezzo forte.

The names I have given to the instruments refer to the owner of the instrument, the maker or just the origin. The analyzed *txistuak* were:

- "Patxiku," *txistua* of the Amezua family. It belonged to Hipólito Amezua and Serafín Amezua.
- "Lizaso," Aldekoa's first *txistua*, made by Guillermo Lizaso in Errenteria (Gipuzkoa) in 1932.
- "Landaluze," Aldekoa's second *txistua*, made by Joaquín Landaluze in Bilbao in the 1960s.
- "Bergara," Aldekoa's third *txistua*, made in Bergara. I do not know the name of the maker or when it was bought, but Aldekoa appeared with it during the last two or three decades of his life.

Results of the Analysis

Table 4. Intervallic distance in cents

Interval	Patxiku	Lizaso	Landaluze	Bergara
	199.212	203.91	161.161	184.566
	161.579	129.672	147.428	149.015
	163.445	185.97	184.169	185.97
	179.253	182.404	195.064	182.404
	188.071	191.038	175.294	178.07
	146.389	136.584	123.712	161.451
(II) *	156.476	181.209	202.583	158.524
	182.988	191.929	213.171	169.311
(II)	182.404	173.78	157.263	174.813
	155.891	163.06	146.674	164.026

* The "second position D":

has been analyzed as well. Its fingering is oooo, and although it was not a note Alejandro played regularly, it belongs to the natural range of the instrument.

Table 4. Intervallic distance in cents				
Interval	Patxiku	Lizaso	Landaluze	Bergara
	165.004	131.075	126.219	140.828
	233.577	214.683	231.174	220.135
	213.598	235.677	243.528	227.789
	145.025	152.068	138.573	148.482
	155.14	151.836	171.402	165.723

Table 5. Intervallic distance in cents				
Interval	Patxiku	Lizaso	Landaluze	Bergara
	367.324	373.442	370.358	360.474
	696.701	701.955	707.241	691.235
	1231.19	1231.77	1223.66	1223.88
	327.031	368.373	379.233	368.373
	661.49	695.995	678.239	707.894
	1165.37	1182.06	1164.3	1182.06
	513.712	510.026	494.07	521.924
	852.592	865.015	853.915	855.262
	338.88	354.989	359.845	333.337
	717.482	721.741	729.592	701.955
	360.791	333.582	308.589	333.582
	334.459	327.622	299.006	339.521
	320.895	294.135	272.893	304.855
	508.569	519.551	492.759	519.551
 (II)	460.935	508.832	501.589	498.045
	534.493	529.812	516.421	532.644

Table 6. Statistics (all measurements in cents)				
	Patxiku	Lizaso	Landaluze	Bergara
Total range (D–A)	1910.57	1903.15	1887.822	1909.15
Mean interval	173.688	173.014	171.620	173.559
Mean tone	179.699	188.228	186.307	182.232
Mean semitone	157.687	132.443	132.453	150.431
Standard deviation	20.740	33.663	36.457	23.033
Diff. tone/equitempered tone	20.3	11.772	13.7	17.767
Diff. semitone/equitempered semitone	57.687	32.443	32.453	50.431
Diff. tone/semitone	22.012	55.785	53.854	31.801

Analyzing the information from the measurements carried out in the laboratory, we see that the four *txistuak* share certain basic tuning characteristics that could be defined as similar, although there are certain noticeable changes designed to improve the tuning of the instrument. For example, the interval D–F:

In the Patxiku *txistua*, this is 361 cents and appears to be corrected in Aldekoa's first *txistua*, the one from Lizaso (333 cents), and even more so in the second, the one from Landaluze (308 cents), which nears the ideal 300 cents of the third minor. However, the last of Aldekoa's *txistuak*, the one from Bergara, returns to the third of 333 cents. The tuning of the theoretically third major C–E also suffers a similar process of coming and going:

In the Patxiku *txistua*, the third (339 cents) is nearer to the third minor (300 cents) than to the 400 cents of the third major. In Aldekoa's first *txistua*, the interval measures 355 cents, in the second 360, and in the third, returns to the 333 cents.

Whatever the case, a tendency toward a "neutral" tuning of the intervals of the whole scale can be seen in all of them, although this is more pronounced and obvious in the Amezua *txistua*. Generally, the major seconds are narrow and the minors wide, without the existence of a clearly differentiated distribution of tones and semitones, as would be expected in a diatonic scale. The oldest *txistua*, the Patxiku, demonstrates the greatest equality between the grades of the range. The difference between the averages of what, in theory, are the full tones of the scale and the semitones is only 22 cents.

This tendency toward an equal tuning of the steps of the scale supports my interpretation of the way the old taborers played. The ideal system of tuning, where all the grades of the scale are the same, would result from a division of the octave of 1,200 cents into seven equal intervals of 171.42857143 cents each. In this way, any melodic design would sound in proportion independent of the grade of the scale in which it had been started. That is, all the intervals would be the same.

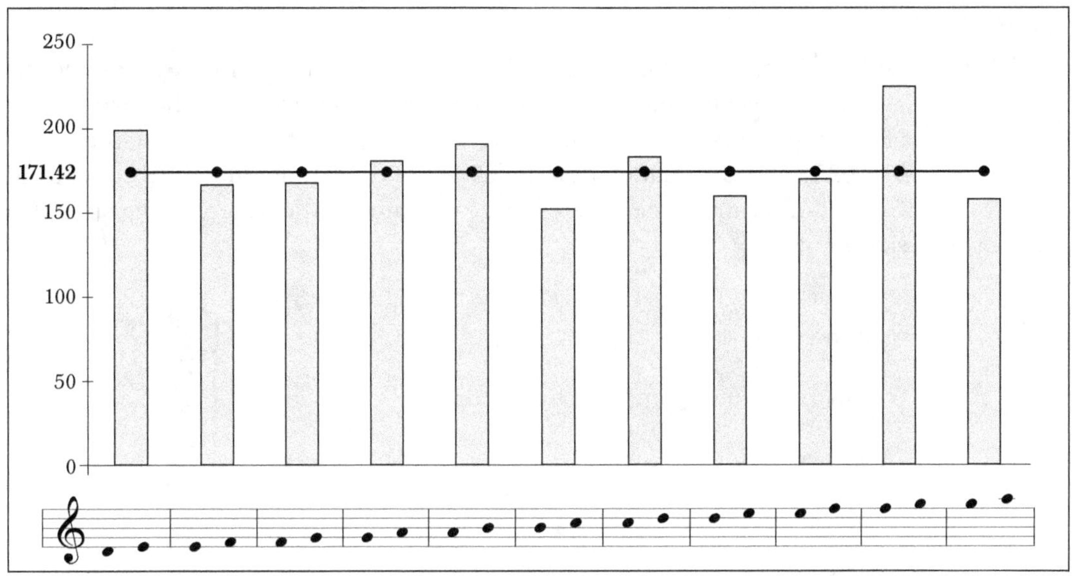

Figure 39. Patxiku's *Txistua*: Intervals in cents compared with the tone of 171.42 cents of the scale of seven equal tones.

The old taborers thus clearly perceived and classified musical sounds in a different way, basing their playing on the general perception of the melodic contour without paying much attention to the modal distinctions of its intervals. With dance as the main function of the music, the melody was considered less relevant than the rhythm, which was necessary to coordinate both music and choreography. The fact that the old three-holed flutes had their own system of tuning, designed on a scale of approximately equal intervals and suppressing or lessening the difference between tones and semitones, also contributed to this peculiar mode of perception.

The *Txistua*: The Chromatic Tabor Pipe

One of the specific and distinctive characteristics of the *txistua* with respect to other three-holed flutes is the ring used to hold the instrument with the ring finger, which allows the partial covering of the lower end of the tube with the little finger, converting the *txistua* into the only completely chromatic three-holed flute.[47] But it seems that this way of hold-

47. According to Jeremy Montagu, the Basque *txistua* "is the world's only fully chromatic tabor pipe (achieved by covering the distal end more or less with the little finger to flatten the pitch)." Jeremy Montagu, "The Pipe and Tabor Is Alive and Well and Living in Euskadi," *FoMRHI Quarterly* 89 (1997): 17.

ing the *txistua* was already known and used in ancient times: "The mouth piece is held in the player's mouth and the lower end rests between the little finger and the third finger, besides which, in order that it should not slip through the player's hand, there is a little cord [*effguillette*] at the end of the flute through which the third finger is passed to support and hold it."[48]

There must have been some knowledge of chromaticism in the Middle Ages and the Renaissance, as well, especially among educated taborers. If we examine the instructions given and the fingering tables for different wind instruments in Marin Mersenne's *Harmonie Universelle* (1635), the chromatic possibilities of the three-holed flute are equal to or greater than those of other instruments, such as, for example, the flageolet, the six-holed flute, or the recorder itself.[49]

Figure 40. "Three-holed Flute with Range and Tablature"
(From Marin Mersenne, *Harmonie Universelle: The Books on Instruments*).

In any case, despite the fact that four centuries ago people were familiar with the three-holed flute with a ring or equivalent ways of holding it and, to some extent, familiar with chromaticism, its use did not depend so much on the instrument, but rather on the developed technique employed by its performers to respond to the requirements of the repertoire. In this way, in the Basque Country, and more concretely in the case we are

48. Thoinot Arbeau [pseud. Jehan Tabourot], *Orchésographie* (1589; Langres: Dominique Guéniot, 1988), 22.

49. Marin Mersenne, *Harmonie Universelle: The Books on Instruments*, trans. Roger E. Chapman (1635; The Hague: Martinus Nijhoff, 1964), 300, 302, 305, 308.

studying, in Berriz, the same instrument has been used diatonically and chromatically,[50] with Alejandro Aldekoa as the main protagonist in the introduction of the chromatic potential of the instrument: Aldekoa introduced the chromatic two octave scale into Berriz. Aldekoa was conscious of the change between his way of playing and that of his predecessors: "The Amezuas didn't know how to play sharps or flats. For example, in Garai, they played the dance 'Gernikako Arbola'":

"And the melody, when it rises, asks for an F-sharp, and they never played it. I've always played it, though":[51]

"On the other hand, they did play the F-sharp an octave above":

"And of course, they couldn't play the *andra soiñua* in C minor—they played it in C major":

As we have seen, Aldekoa's predecessors, the Patxikus, performed all their repertoire using the system of the old taborers. With Aldekoa's rise to prominence in Berriz, the extension or note range of the instrument was increased, adding more notes to the bass and treble register, reaching a full two-octave scale. Aldekoa also introduced the use of altered notes, that is, the full chromatic scale:

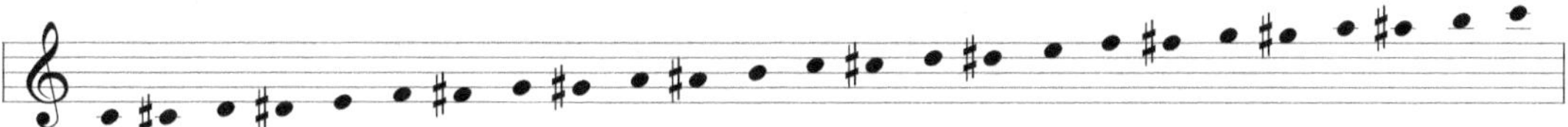

The extension of the ambitus of the *txistua* and the change in the habitual register of the *txistulariak* happened approximately a century ago, when the noise level in the environment of the *txistua*, especially in urban, industrialized areas, increased considerably,

50. In this context, I use the term "diatonic" only to express the absence of modified notes.

51. The introduction of chromaticism was not the only change introduced into the dance piece "Gernikako Arbola." Serafín Amezua did not play the dance in 5/8, but in 6/8+3/4.

thus demanding a greater volume of sound from the instrument. Competition from other instruments (especially the accordion) also contributed to the change, as did an ideological transformation in the conception of the ideal sound qualities of the *txistua* that, influenced by Basque nationalism, went from being soft and sweet to warlike, shrill, and bittersweet, as I've noted before. As we have seen when discussing the Amezua family's old *txistua*, Alejandro Aldekoa shared this view, idealizing the old *txistua* for its "loud and powerful" sound, when, in fact, it was not nearly as powerful as he made out.

While the old taborers played almost exclusively in the register D–A,

the new ones rarely went any lower than the A, and their favorite octave is from middle C to C-sharp,

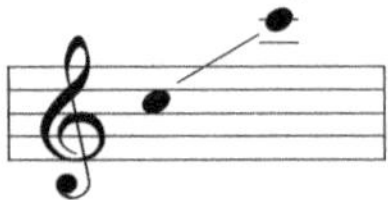

a much stronger tone, but, at the same time, much harder to obtain with exactitude and refinement.

Chromaticism and Fingering

The positions of the notes on the *txistua* repeat themselves. Thanks to the harmonic system, with the same fingering, different sounds and different notes can be obtained from the same positions, causing significant problems for beginners. Aldekoa complained that his modern students were not taught to intone and sing the notes correctly by their *solfeggio* teachers, leading to many problems when they had to distinguish between notes emitted from the same positions: "they don't care if it's a B or an E, a D or an A."

Fingering has evolved with chromaticism and the need for finer tuning. In this context, I will only point out the fingering and the range of sounds used by Aldekoa.[52] Here is a general table showing the fingering used by Aldekoa in the chromatic scale:

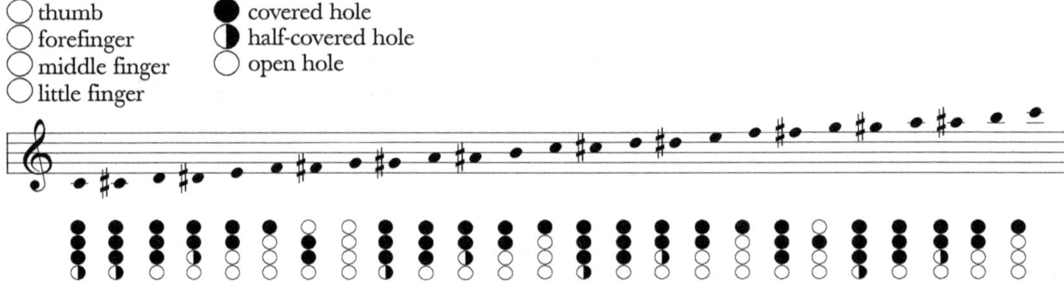

52. For information on fingering and other technical problems of the modern, academic *txistua*, see Jose Inazio Ansorena Miner, *Txistu Gozoa: Txistu Ikasbidea-Método de Txistu. Lehenengo maila. Primer Curso* (1985; Donostia: Erviti, 1995).

For the low register:

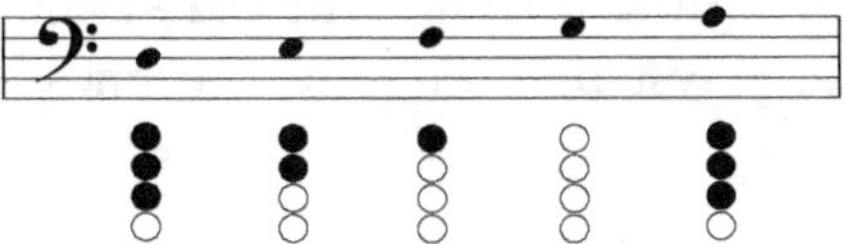

Chromaticism and Tuning

"The low C didn't come out as it should. The C-sharp did, but when you played the natural C, you had to be very careful—cover the hole well and blow very gently."[53] For Aldekoa, as for many other *txistulariak* of his time, the low C was always a problematic note to play, due to its tuning and tone. Similar problems appeared in other positions and with other notes, but with the difference that Aldekoa was not apparently aware of them. In fact, the majority of the chromatic notes on Aldekoa's scale were out of tune with reference to the ideal chromatic scale and compared with the levels reached by contemporary *txistulariak.* There are several reasons for this. His instruments presented certain irregularities for a fine tuning of the basic diatonic scale of the *txistua.* To this I should add imperfect fingering and technique (or at least they were not good enough to correct the tuning problems of the instrument) and a standard of performance lower than that expected today.

However, the principal reason why the chromatic notes on Aldekoa's scale were out of tune with reference to the ideal chromatic scale was that educated *txistulariak* such as Aldekoa had adapted the scale to the peculiarities and limitations of their instrument and their technique, creating once again a closed system, especially as far as the tuning of sounds and their perception were concerned. Aldekoa perceived many notes to be in tune that a Western musician with a moderately trained ear would class as out of tune. Only when the *txistua* entered conservatories and had to be tuned alongside other instruments did our closed system begin to open up.

I, too, began to play the *txistua* in the same system as Aldekoa, and I remember that when I first entered the conservatory, the tuning of some notes with their new fingering, in theory much more in tune, sounded strange, odd, and definitely out of tune, accustomed as I was to my old instrument and my old system of tuning. As definite proof of the change in my way of listening and of perceiving, I remember how I used to enjoy listening to some old recordings of the *txistua* that now, after my long journey through a process of academic training, I find almost unbearable. They are, in general, out of tune.[54] Having said this, it is not my intention to underline or praise the level of perceptive sophistication that we are now reaching, nor is it my intention to establish any value

53. Alejandro Aldekoa, interview by the author, April 12, 1996.

54. I might mention the case of the Toccata and Fugue in D (BWV 565) by Johann Sebastian Bach, which the Ansola brothers dared to adapt and record a version of for the band of *txistulariak.* Although it now sounds strange to say so, I used to enjoy listening to that recording.

judgment on any of the systems. I am only trying to point out the different stages that taborers such as Aldekoa have passed through in their professional life: the old system that preceded him, his own system, and the conservatory system of more recent times.

A *Txistularia*'s Sound

Apart from introducing chromaticism in Berriz and emphasizing the score, Aldekoa also developed a personal style that differentiated him from his predecessors. Sound and the quality of sound were important to him. The qualities of the instrument were also important, but as he himself pointed out, the same instrument in the hands of a beginner sounds completely different than when it is in the hands of a professional musician. According to him, a *txistularia* has to "fill" each note with sound and bring out all the possibilities of the instrument. As an example, he cited his own teacher, León Laspiur, whose personal sound was unmistakable. After the Civil War and many years of musical inactivity, Laspiur was invited to play in the festive celebrations of Eibar by certain cultural societies. The inhabitants of Eibar came out on to their balconies, recognizing the sound of their old *txistularia*: "That's Laspiur." The same thing happened to Aldekoa himself. His brilliant sound and personal style made him unmistakable, not only among taborers and dancers accustomed to his music but also to most people in Berriz.

Articulation

The basic articulation that Aldekoa used to produce sound from the *txistua* was what he called *mingaiñeko pikaue* (tongue stroke). In other words, articulation—the movement of the tongue—is similar to that used when pronouncing the consonant [t].

The ligature, the legato, is easy to produce in the *txistua* between notes that belong to the same harmonic level, whereas in other intervals, some kind of articulation has to be used to help bind the notes together, or at least to produce the effect of legato. Aldekoa knew how to produce these ligatures by "dragging" the notes and using an articulation similar to a [d] to achieve the effect of the legato. But, as a general rule, he preferred to play all the notes detached, separating them, producing short, crisp, disconnected notes. According to him, the Amezuas used to bind passages together because they did not have the necessary technique to play them by articulating each note separately. In the dance repertoire of Berriz, however, Aldekoa did sometimes play certain passages in legato, in memory of the old Patxiku style, for example:

In a fashion similar to most players of wind instruments, when *txistulariak* need an element of speed in the articulation, they resort to the combination of the normal [t] strokes with the [k], using various combinations according to the rhythmic patterns of the passage to be performed. Generally, when the passage is binary, the pattern followed is *ta-ka / ta-ka*, and when it is ternary *ta-ka-ta / ta-ka-ta* or *ta-ta-ka / ta-ta-ka*. This is known among *txistulariak* as the *eztarriko pikaue* (throat stroke), and for Aldekoa, it was what distinguished good from the run-of-the-mill *txistulariak*. As I've noted before, he used the term "perform" to refer to the *eztarriko pikaue*, so for example, when he said, "so-and-so can't perform," he meant that he did not know how to use the binary or ternary tonguing. Or "so-and-so was a good performer" meant that, apart from being a good *txistularia*, he could also use the *eztarriko pikaue* well. The *eztarriko pikaue* was one of Aldekoa's main improvements to *txistua* technique, compared with the simpler playing of his predecessors, such as Serafín Amezua.

Ornaments and Vibrato

For Aldekoa, one of the main characteristics of the Amezua family style was the ornaments or adornments they used, especially trills and semitrills. Aldekoa used them only in certain passages of the *dantzari-dantza* in which, by playing in the old style, he imitated the Patxikus:[55]

In the rest of the repertoire, except where the score demanded, Aldekoa hardly ever used trills and semitrills to adorn the melodies.

A prominent feature of Aldekoa's style was the use of vibrato: "I play with vibrato. In the fast passages, you hardly have time to use it, but in the rest, you do. I use the vibrato in C and in F, and also in B and E. Before, the old ones, the Amezuas, they didn't know how to make the notes vibrate. They used trills and mordents, but not vibrato."[56] To achieve the effect of vibrato, he used his fingers, controlling both the frequency of the vibrato and its range by moving them up and down over the holes. To the list of notes he mentions, we can also add G, both high and low. The only notes without vibrato being D–A, in which the three holes are covered, so the vibrato can be played only with the little finger.

This type of vibrato, very common among traditional taborers, was regarded as a sign of good taste and virtuoso technique, but has now been practically prohibited by the academic style of the conservatory and has been replaced by a vibrato achieved by

---

55. In this musical example, I have transcribed the way Aldekoa used to sing the music, humming syllables with the same vowels of the corresponding notes do-re-mi-fa-sol-la-si, something very common among Basque musicians.

56. Alejandro Aldekoa, interview by the author, April 12, 1996.

modulating the column of air using the muscles of the diaphragm or the throat. Apart from its ornamental function, the vibrato can contribute, on occasions, to covering up tuning defects, since the overall perception of the pitch of a note changes when a note is played with vibrato. However, the original style of the vibrato was very personal. It haled form the peculiar sound of each instrumentalist.

Conclusion

The reasons, ideas, theories, and facts that describe and explain (however partially) Alejandro Aldekoa's interaction with his social, political, and cultural environment form a complicated web in which the same processes overlap repeatedly. Any analytical description of this complicated map inevitably requires the development of parallel discursive lines that often cross and juxtapose, as we have seen throughout this work.

As a consequence of the influence of Enlightenment ideas on both the ruling classes and the population in the Basque Country, the social status of the *txistularia* underwent a transformation, with the pipe and tabor player coming to be seen as a professional musician and serving as a representative and agent of the municipal authorities. In the twentieth century, and in some ways counter to this trend, yet in other ways consonant with it, with the rise of modern Basque nationalism, the *txistua* and Basque music and dance generally were appropriated and disseminated as symbols of Basque national identity, especially poised against the encroachments of Spanish political authority and culture. The need to give traditional culture universality for the diffusion of Basque music and dance consequently led to the "academicization" of *txistularia*-musicians and choreographic groups of Basque dance. But this effort at dissemination also resulted in the dilution of traditional and local music and dance, which, by way of reaction, led to the rise in an interest in identifying and conserving "pure" traditional forms. As a consequence, the role of *txistularia* and dance master occupied by Aldekoa also became one of cultural conservator. But Aldekoa was no reactionary. At the same time, he recognized that his role as conservator of the rural folk traditions also entailed transmitting them to the new, academically trained musicians who would follow.

This transgenerational orientation on the part of Aldekoa also cuts in many important ways across the dichotomy of autochthonous rural folklore versus the professionalized urban revival of traditional forms into which analysts of the phenomenon too easily fall. In fact, Alejandro Aldekoa, while acting as a conservator of traditional folk music and dance, also both passively reflected and actively advanced the "urbanization" and modernization of the role of *txistulariak* underway since at least the nineteenth century. His insistence on the introduction of a mode of musical perception based on *solfeggio* and the score is a major element in this transformation, which, in turn, had consequences for the playing of the music itself (the decline of percussion and a focus on melody and the flute) and for the quality of the music played.

More generally, these developments have amounted to a fundamental change in the way the music of the *txistularia* is perceived and understood, as well as performed. Aldekoa's liminal position in that change, as both a product and conservator of traditional ways of learning and playing music while at the same time a proponent of the idea that real musicians know *solfeggio* and work from scores, and that professional training is useful and desirable, puts into question any absolute distinction between traditional and "artistic" music and musicians.

Finally, what is to be said about the current state of the *txistularia* and of traditional dance and music in the Basque Country? One consequence of the mutually imbricated developments that we have been mapping here is the demotion of the *txistua* as *the* paradigmatic Basque instrument in the post-Franco democratic era with the fracturing of the nationalist movement. And more broadly, the holistic unity of dance and music, their mutual implication and involvement that Aldekoa understood so thoroughly, has been lost, with each becoming isolated and lacking a common language.

At the center of these developments in the modern history of dance and music in the Basque Country stood Alejandro Aldekoa. In 1993, the town of Berriz paid homage to him, celebrating different social events: a book was published, *Alejandro Berrizko txistularia zahar berria* (Alejandro the Old and New *Txistularia* of Berriz), an LP/cassette was recorded on which he played the *dantzari-dantza* and the *soka dantza*, and a large dance festival/party was held that brought together his family and friends with dancers, musicians, choreographers, and folklorists from all over the Basque Country. Later, on June 2, 1996, only days before his death, the Association of *Txistulariak* of the Basque Country awarded him the gold medal, its highest distinction. The social recognition of the *txistularia* Alejandro Aldekoa, of his person and his work, was more than evident in this award. He had redefined the status of the "humble" *txistularia.*

The Enlightenment

The eighteenth century was a decisive era for the pipe and tabor in the Basque Country. During this time some of the instruments' main characteristics that have in one way or another been influential to this day began to be outlined. It was also during this era when an important change in the role and social consideration of taborers began to take place: They began to be considered as musicians, because they could read music and adopted the foreign repertoires in fashion among the dominant classes. The first wage-paying positions for taborers were created at this time, and they appeared beside the authorities in solemn public acts, gradually becoming institutional representatives. Their situation changed from being one of disregard and persecution as low-ranking people to being responsible for upholding good, moral conduct in dances. In other words, the work of the taborer became professional and dignified, and thanks to their knowledge of music theory or *solfeggio,* they acquired a new status as "musicians."

This process was not homogeneous, nor did it extend throughout the whole of the Basque Country. Alongside these learned *txistulariak,* many traditional *txistulariak* continued to be active. The latter were not musically learned, such as the Amezua dynasty in Berriz. However, the musically literate taborers became the role model to follow and altogether contributed to a substantial improvement in the social prestige of the taborer.

Nationalism

From the beginning of the twentieth century, music and folk dance acquired an important value as a marker of ethnic identity in Basque nationalist ideology. And because of its supposed ancient and distinct characteristics, the *txistua* became a symbol of Basque nationalism. The dances of the County of Durango, under the name *ezpata-dantza*, became a symbol of everything Basque, the quintessential Basque dance, and a strong political tool for diffusing nationalist ideology throughout most of the *batzokia* centers and schools in the Basque Country. To achieve maximum acceptance and diffusion of the traditional dances and music, it was necessary to "universalize" them. In other words, it was a question of improving their reputation, prestige, and image, as well as the mechanisms of transmission and teaching of what had been, until then, the music and customs of illiterate village people.

In this context, important developments included the creation of the Association of *Txistulariak* of the Basque Country and the publication of the repertoire in the journal *Txistulari*, along with the publication of the first study methods, making access to and distribution of this repertoire easier and thus facilitating the "universalization" of local dance and music in the Basque Country as a whole. It also included the creation of choreographic folk dance groups, willing to take the special features of Basque dance to a wider stage and convert it into a choreographic show of "universal" value, and the creation of Basque dance and music academies, such as the Academy of *Txistua* and Dance, founded in 1928 in Donostia, with the sponsorship of the city hall and under the technical direction of the Society of Basque Studies. Likewise, it included the organization of competitions and championships to promote Basque dance and music.

In many ways, Aldekoa's professional career in Berriz was no more than a local manifestation of wider processes taking place in the rest of the Basque Country: He learned to read music with Don Modesto Arana and to play the *txistua* with León Laspiur. In time, he became the first municipal taborer "musician," as well as a teacher of *txistua* in several localities of the County of Durango. The first group of *ezpatadantzariak* in Berriz was created in 1933, around the town's *batzokia*. It was directed by Ambrosio Aldekoa, Alejandro's father, and Alejandro himself was a *txistularia* in the group. Furthermore, in 1952, Aldekoa founded the San Lorenzo dance group, and for many years, apart from being the official *txistularia* in the majority of the dance competitions in the area of Durango, he was also one of the main promoters of those events.

The Traditional Taborer and Dance Master as Conservator

In the Basque Country, the inevitable movement away from traditional sources of style and form as a consequence of the decontextualization of dance and traditional music and their massive diffusion (the Association of *Txistulariak* had thirty-five hundred members by the 1960s) increasingly began to worry many Basque folklorists. In the late 1960s and throughout the 1970s, several leaders and ideologists of Basque dance founded a movement for a return to traditional, autochthonous sources, a revived interest in dance in its "purest" and "most original" form.[1] From this time on, scholars, folklorists, and choreographers from all over the Basque Country began to visit Aldekoa, and gradually, he came to be recognized as the "great master" of the old tradition of the County of Durango's dances, the *dantzari-dantza* and the *soka dantza*.[2] In the 1970s, apart from being the innovative, virtuoso, technical *txistularia* he was, he also gradually assumed the role of guardian of the old customs he had learned from his elders, especially from his father: "I always tried to keep the dances exactly as my father had taught them to me, without making any changes or alterations."[3]

Another determining factor in this changing attitude was the fact that by the 1970s, the quantity and the musical and technical level of the *txistulariak* had considerably improved, and Aldekoa was not the only qualified *txistularia* musician in the area any more. A new generation was ready to take over, and the introduction of the *txistua* in conservatories must have been an important turning point for him and for many other *txistulariak*. In the period when the *txistua* was enjoying a new-found official academic status, Aldekoa, at the age of sixty and with his prestige and professional career well consolidated, remained deliberately at the margins of the new direction that the *txistua* was now taking. Yet unlike other veteran *txistulariak*, his attitude toward the "conservatory

1. The following paragraph, taken from the prologue written by Lucile Armstrong for the book by Juan Antonio Urbeltz, *Dantzak* (Bilbao: Jakin, 1978), perfectly expresses the spirit that guided some dance groups, Aldekoa's included, during the 1970s. Urbeltz was and continues to be one of the most important and controversial ideologists of Basque folklore. He visited Aldekoa on numerous occasions, and Aldekoa was proud of his friendship with him and for having been his teacher insofar as the dances of Berriz were concerned. According to Armstrong: "The importance of preserving popular dance in its traditional form is . . . understandable, because only in this way can we faithfully come any nearer to our past. If we modify it in the slightest way, it would no longer hold any significance and be transformed into a simple means of physical exercise whose only aim would be to keep ourselves fit. There are some who have the bad habit of rebuilding dances, taking a bit from here and a bit from there, mixing country dances with those of fishermen or ritual dances and presenting them together in the form of 'Popular Dances of Wales' or 'Dances of Portugal.' . . . It would be better if they left the subject alone, if they did not try to look for publicity at the expense of these 'shows' or 'beautiful' dances. It is an aberrant custom and extremely harmful to a country's culture." Lucile Armstrong, "Hitzaurrea/Prefacio," in Urbeltz, *Dantzak*, 24.

2. Aldekoa understood tradition in a rather curious way. He criticized his predecessor, Serafín Amezua, for not having been able to teach and maintain the tradition of the dances. Yet he also criticized some folklorists, choreographers, and dance masters of urban dance groups such as Sabin Egiguren (Bilbao) and Kepa Artetxe (Galdakao) for their fixation on detail and for being excessively meticulous about tradition. Aldekoa laughed when he talked about those who had been his students (Sabin Egiguren, for example) who now dared to criticize his group and give lessons on the "authenticity" of dance to their master.

3. Alejandro Aldekoa, interview by the author, April 9, 1996.

txistua" was not critical. In fact, I believe he was fairly consistent in his ideas about music and the need for an adequate musical training for the *txistulariak*. He was proud that some of his students went to conservatories to continue with the work that he had started. Yet whatever the case may have been, faced with this fresh panorama in which the new *txistulariak* were "better musicians" than he was, Aldekoa understood how to redefine his control within the world of the *txistua* and dances of the County of Durango. The new generation of conservatory teachers may have had a superior academic education—they knew *solfeggio*, harmony, new techniques, and fingering—but they lacked something very important: knowledge of the trade of taborer-dance master. Aldekoa appreciated very well his advantage in this respect and used it to maintain his reputation and position of leadership and authority.

Rural versus Urban

From the eighteenth century on, there was an increasing demand for pipe and tabor musicians to fill the post of municipal taborer created in most Basque towns. Positions in the more important towns and cities were obviously the most coveted, and required a higher grade of professional dedication.[4] The technical and musical level required for these posts in the competitive exams held to select from among the various candidates was notably higher than the average. In general, posts in important municipalities were taken by taborers who were better prepared both musically and technically. In the competitive exams, there were exercises in sight reading, harmony, and the composition of new pieces of music. In many other municipalities, however, especially in rural areas, the post was taken by taborers who could not read music or who could do so only with some difficulty. This may have been due to the lack of a sufficiently attractive salary, to the tradition of passing down the position of *txistularia* to members of the same family, or to a lack of taborer-musicians available to fill the position. This division led some Basque folklorists to classify the *txistulariak* of the Basque Country into urban and rural musicians.

The rural-urban dichotomy is a very convenient tool for the researcher, because apart from having a certain ethnographic basis, it also defines different surroundings and spaces, different ways of life, and different cultures. However, this dichotomy is an excessive simplification of reality. In order to be able to formulate the archetypal characteristics of the urban *txistularia*, I observed the municipal *txistulariak* of the provincial capitals, Bilbao, Donostia, Iruñea, and Gasteiz. Meanwhile, at the other end of the scale, I placed rural *txistulariak*, such as those of the Amezua family in Berriz or the Elizalde family from the Baztan Valley in Navarre, and analyzed them all in the historical context of the twentieth century,[5] Alejandro Aldekoa's basic lifespan.

4. Often, though, the precariousness of the salary obliged taborers to look for other, complementary work.

5. I am conscious of the fact that the twentieth century, as can be seen in this work, was an unsettled period and perhaps far too long to be able to define precisely all the different phases there are. However, regarding the rural-urban

Table 7. Main Contrasts between Urban and Rural *Txistulariak*	
Rural Taborer	**Urban Taborer**
Part-time employment, less economic dependence on the post.	Full-time employment or with a higher salary.
Musically illiterate, basically oral transmission of music.	Musically literate, use of the score.
Native Basque without an excessive nationalist consciousness.	Conscious active Basque nationalist.
Folklore, tradition that remains alive in its context.	Folklorism, tradition that one tries to perpetuate or recuperate. Revival.
The condition of taborer is inherited through the family tradition (ascribed musicianship).	The condition of taborer is achieved through education and public promotion examinations (achieved musicianship).
Local type of tradition, closed. Traditional autochthonous repertoire.	Greater contact with music from other cultures and of other styles. Contemporary, educated, and classical repertoire.
Main performance: Dance and dancing.	Main performance: Dance music, concerts, and ceremonial municipal duties.
Low social rank.	Considerable social prestige. Medium social rank.
Relations with the town hall limited to certain ritual celebrations. Dance and ritual master. No excessive symbolic value per se.	Herald of the local authorities. Important representative functions. Symbol of the municipality.

Table 7 summarizes the main contrasts between rural and urban *txistulariak*, certain qualifications are in order.

The rural-urban contrast is complicated in the Basque Country. There was extensive industrial development in the twentieth century, and the *baserria* and industry came to share a large part of the territory. Is Berriz an urban or rural enclave? The answer is not straightforward, because although it remained a small town with an important rural hinterland, Berriz also witnessed industrial and urban development, with the building of factories, expansion of its urban nucleus, and a changing demographic structure as a result of the immigration of Spanish people. On the other hand, the salary of *txistulariak* does not necessarily depend on the size or the demographic or economic importance of the municipality, but also is the result of other factors of a more political and provisional nature. In the case of Berriz, for example, the money destined for the expenses generated

---

txistularia dichotomy, there are two basic characteristics that give a certain coherence to the chosen era: the emergence and growth of Basque nationalism and the important processes of industrialization and modernization in the Basque Country.

by the dances and the taborer varied considerably, depending on the epoch, and as a result, the professional situation of the taborer changed accordingly.

The assumption that an urban *txistularia* is necessarily educated and musically literate, as opposed to the musically illiterate rural *txistularia* also needs to be qualified. Although generally, the *txistularia* posts in the most important cities have been filled through tests or competitive public promotion examinations, in the post–Civil War period, when some municipal bands were reestablished, many *txistulariak* took charge of these positions without having taken any examination at all. Some began to work in a semivoluntary way to improve, little by little, their professional situation, while others acceded to the positions thanks to their personal contacts or influence. Consequently, the technical and musical level of some of these professional taborers left a lot to be desired, compared with that of many taborers considered rural, such as Alejandro Aldekoa.

Industrialization, immigration, and the loss of Basque culture was much more accentuated in the industrial, urban areas than in the rural districts, where, around the *baserria*, traditional culture and the autochthonous language, Euskara, survived until well into the twentieth century. In urban areas such as Bilbao, with a high level of immigration and fewer Basque speakers as a percentage of the overall population, the *txistua* developed strong Basque nationalist symbolic connotations.[6] For many *txistulariak* of Bilbao, to be a *txistularia* is their way of being Basque patriots. Symbols also affect the way they dress, with the *txapela*, the Basque beret, for example, being an essential part of the *txistularia*'s clothing. By contrast, in rural areas of the Basque Country, people experience or live their Basqueness in a very different way. One is considered Basque without having to wear the *txapela*, and one is a *txistularia* for reasons of family, tradition, or profession. Nevertheless, the Basque national problem affects the whole country, and nationalist consciousness is widespread. Aldekoa criticized the lack of nationalist awareness among some of the *baserritarrak* and their lack of consciousness or awareness of just how important folklore is. In general, though, we could say that his relationship with his instrument and music was not based on their symbolic and emblematic Basque character. Aldekoa did not need to be a *txistularia* to be Basque, simply because he was Basque. He wore a *txapela*, as his father had done before him, because, as for nearly all Basque men of his generation, it was a fundamental part of their dress, without which they felt "naked."

As mentioned, one becomes a professional, urban taborer through education or training and passing competitive examinations (that is, via achieved status), whereas in smaller towns, the transmission of the post—perhaps due to its semiprofessional and semiofficial character—has been carried out in various ways, although mainly through family ties (that is, via ascribed status). Berriz and the Amezua family are a good example of this. But if we examine the best known *txistularia* families in the Basque Country, we find that actually most of them have urban *txistularia* profiles. Here I would cite the Ansorena,

---

6. I should point out that since the implementation of democracy in the late 1970s, Bilbao has been governed in the main by Basque nationalist mayors.

Ansola, Onraita, Garai, Arzuaga, Bergaretxe, Basurko, Elola, Azkarate, Laskurain, and Martinez de Lecea families. Family transmission of the trade thus does not depend so much on the condition of being a rural or urban taborer, but rather on social, political, and cultural factors.

To continue with the family trade or business was very frequent and common in the past, not only among musicians, but in general among many professions. This custom has all but disappeared today, due to changes in family structures and relationships, in economic systems, and in access to education. The *txistularia* tradition in the Amezua family ended with Serafín, the last ascribed pipe and tabor musician in Berriz before Alejandro Aldekoa, and Aldekoa achieved his musicianship and his post of municipal *txistularia* through a rather long and complicated process: learning the dances, learning the instrument, and creating his own dance group. Aldekoa's sons, Jon and Germán, learned the trade from their father. After Alejandro's death, the town hall announced the holding of competitive public examinations to cover his now vacant position. Neither of Aldekoa's two sons took the examination, and in the end, the town hall, ignoring all current legal regulations, cancelled the examinations and reached an agreement with Germán so that he would become taborer of Berriz on a temporary contract. Despite the irregularity and the illegal nature of the step taken by the town hall, nobody protested. The family inheritance of the trade of taborer in Berriz continues.

Urban taborers, preceding and accompanying the mayor on all kinds of official occasions, acted as the herald of the municipal authorities and still do. This function has converted the *txistularia* into a symbol of the municipality. In cities such as Bilbao, the band's presence is bound to the most important moments of the city. Its image has been frequently used as a representation of the city. The formal dress of the Bilbao *txistulariak* is typical and distinctive: the image of the *txistularia* in a red frock jacket, blue vest, white shirt and tie, and a two-cornered hat is synonymous with Bilbao. It is also quaint, like the guards outside Buckingham Palace, connoting historical stability and rootedness. This is not the case in villages or towns such as Berriz. There, the *txistularia* does not have a defined image expressed by traditional dress. In this environment, the individual person and musician is the key symbol—in our case here, Alejandro Aldekoa.

If we generally accept the existence of the specific characteristics differentiating rural from urban taborers, in the case of Berriz, Aldekoa's influence as the "urbanizing" agent of the *txistua* and dance in his immediate surroundings seems to be more than evident.[7] Indeed, on taking over from Serafín Amezua, the last rural taborer of Berriz, Aldekoa introduced precisely those characteristics that we would associate with those of an urban taborer: professional consciousness, *solfeggio*, execution technique, education, the achieved condition of musician, and a better social image and prestige. In certain

7. The system of choreographic dance groups that Aldekoa introduced into Berriz was also an initially urban phenomenon, in the same way as the more traditionalist tendency that emerged in the 1960s, led by groups such as Argia (Donostia) or Andra Mari (Galdakao). Moreover, these were groups that had originally consulted Aldekoa about traditional dances and that he, in turn, also followed in the innovations they introduced.

ways, the "urbanizing" of the role of *txistularia* promoted by Alejandro Aldekoa was in tune with the process of urbanization and industrialization taking place in Berriz itself, as well as a consequence of this transformation.

Scores and Acculturation: From Taborers to Pipers

The score and *solfeggio*, the things that for Aldekoa defined music and musicians, have been one of the main agencies of musical acculturation of Basque pipe and tabor players. This process of acculturation gradually defined what the *txistua* is today in the Basque Country, and Alejandro Aldekoa was one of its principal leaders and promoters in the Durango area.

According to Juan Ignacio de Iztueta, writing in the early nineteenth century, local Basque musicians "believe themselves to be so important that they do not want to be called by the name of *danbolina* [taborer], but first *silbo* [pipe], second, major musician and similar."[8] Already at that time, the learned taborers began to identify themselves more with the flute than with the drum, wanting to differentiate themselves as "musicians" from the traditional taborers. Gradually, the title of *txistularia* became popular, and nowadays it is completely standardized. Behind all the different titles, we find two very different ways of understanding the instrument and its functions.

Percussion's lack of prestige is not a problem exclusive to the pipe and tabor. In general, within contemporary Western culture and even in classical music, melody and melodic instruments are considered more musical and enjoy a higher status and importance than percussion and percussion instruments.

The learned or educated taborers gradually began to forget one of their main functions, accompanying dance, and instead began to dedicate themselves to playing concerts. The tabor is one of the basic instruments for dance, whereas for the refined aesthetics of chamber music, it is rather rough and unrefined, especially when played in a group. In concerts by large groups of *txistulariak*, of which Aldekoa was a conductor on so many occasions, the *danbolina* was not played at all. If one adds to this the fact that many *txistulariak* play in public only at these kinds of events, it makes the use of the *danbolina* practically nonexistent.

The written score brought with it an increasing predilection for the melody, to the detriment of the drum. Similar processes have taken place in other regions where the pipe and tabor tradition is musically literate, such as Catalonia and Provence. In such cases, the best taborers (tabor/drum players) form part of oral traditions, but once the "culture of the score" had been established, the *danbolina*, and percussion in general, was marginalized. I believe this was because of two main reasons: the difficulty of transcribing some of the rhythmic patterns of the tabor and the difficulty of reading a two-staff system vertically.

---

8. Juan Ignacio de Iztueta, *Gipuzkoako dantza gogoangarrien kondaira edo historia* (1824; Donostia: Euskal Editoreen Elkartea, 1990), 129.

Also, one of the consequences of the spectacular increase in the number of *txistulariak* in the 1960s and 1970s promoted mainly by the association and conservatories/music schools was a decline in the performers' quality. In short, many *txistulariak* had enough trouble trying to make the pipe sound, without needing the added difficulty of the drum.

Despite being a musically literate *txistularia* (a "musician"), Aldekoa always made it clear that to be a complete *txistularia*, one had to play with the *danbolina*—that the *danbolina* is necessary and obligatory. I also believe he was conscious of his masterly playing of the drum, both technically (due to the difficulty of the patterns he used on some occasions) and through his control of the tempo (something in which he was a real master). This, together with his profound knowledge of the dances, served to distance him from many of the new conservatory *txistulariak* who were incapable of handling the drum as he did.

The Science of Music and Musical Perception

The musical literacy of the *txistularia* that has developed during the past few decades in conservatories and music academies has brought important changes insofar as musical perception is concerned, providing a new way of recognizing and classifying musical events.

Equal-temperament tuning has been imposed as the obligatory reference model, along with all the musical language associated with the Western classical scale: modality and tonality. The development of new prototypes of *txistua* with finer tuning has also played an important role in the process. Indeed, one of the immediate consequences of this, for which Alejandro Aldekoa was in part responsible, was the disappearance of the "system of the old taborers."

As regards the rhythms of the *danbolina*, what for traditional taborers were contextual variants or allophones of the basic dance rhythms we are beginning to perceive as distinct and as played with a different sense or meaning, constituting new phonemes. Furthermore, much of the wealth, variety, and freedom of the traditional interpretive style based on dance and choreographic movement has been lost. This is the case of the singular subtleties that characterize some rhythms of the dances of Berriz and that Aldekoa, despite being "a musician," knew how to maintain.

Art Musician or Traditional Musician?

For some researchers, the concepts of traditional music and artistic music are completely mutually exclusive, a distinction they apply, in the same way, to musicians. As a musician, one is either an artistic musician or a traditional musician. In such a distinction, the dividing line is clear and well-defined, marked by the use of *solfeggio* and the score.

As we know, Alejandro Aldekoa considered himself a "musician" because he knew how to read music. He believed that the score is a kind of god, the absolute truth in music. Yet he first learned to dance and sing, and although he used the score often, a large part of his repertoire and style when playing the dances had been learned orally (and aurally) within the local tradition of Berriz. Many taborers of the Basque Country have learned in a similar way, that is, through a combination of tradition and score. Indeed, I think that among us, instead of an absolute dichotomy between the artistic musician or and the traditional musician, one might speak of a perfectly defined continuum between the purest artistic musician (the "product of the laboratory," limited to playing the score without ever listening to other taborers or other musicians in his environment) and the purest traditional musician (I do not know if there are still any active examples). In this continuum, the two sources of knowledge (art and tradition) are not mutually exclusive. That is, one can be a qualified, competent, and professional artistic musician and at the same time a very good traditional musician. Curiously, nowadays, the same taborers are at the forefront of some of the most ambitious projects at both extremes of the continuum.

Compared with his predecessor, Serafín Amezua, one would place Aldekoa much nearer to artistic music on this continuum, but from a local point of view, he was also clearly a traditional musician, and this for many reasons. For example, the use of a score among taborers is now established and has become part of "tradition." (In this context, tradition is understood as the body of customs, thoughts, and practices belonging to a particular country, people, family, or institution over a relatively long period of time.) Moreover, the importance given by local people to oral transmission as a definitional feature of the term "tradition" is very limited and/or not very relevant. Finally, despite the fact that he was a "musician," Aldekoa's role as a dance master and his mastery of "dancing while he was playing" was acquired and learned through the purest tradition of word of mouth, something that is certainly not taught in conservatories.

One thus might say that although Alejandro Aldekoa was a literate musician who used *solfeggio* as a fully operational model and who considered himself a musician,[9] with the same level and status of any other artistic musician. From a local point of view, he was a traditional musician and the guardian of old folk customs, as well.

The Post-Franco Politicization of Basque Instruments

At least as far as the popularity and social establishment of the instrument were concerned, the 1960s and 1970s, the last decades of Franco's dictatorship, were the golden years of the *txistua* and the Association of *Txistulariak*. The *txistua* was seen as the Basque instrument par excellence, the instrument of all the Basques, and the symbol of union among different groups of Basque nationalists. With the arrival of the so-called "democratic transition" after Franco's death in 1975 and the disappearance of the common enemy, Franco, however, the newly legalized Basque nationalist political parties began to distance themselves from one another.

---

9. See John Baily, "Anthropological and Psychological Approaches to the Study of Music Theory and Musical Cognition," *Yearbook for Traditional Music* 20 (1988): 114–24.

In the face of this new political context, the *txistua* gradually began to lose its privileged position and came to be considered by new generations as conservative, old-fashioned, out-of-date, boring, and too closely connected with the Catholic Church. This was perhaps due to its proximity to power, to the authorities, to the system, or maybe because the *txistulariak* were civil servants or embodied the traditionalist Basque nationalist and religious ideals encouraged by Sabino Arana, the founder of Basque nationalism. Therefore, in a process that is too long to describe in detail here, these new generations began to conceive of a new map of Basque music and its instruments. As a result, today, the *txistua* is regarded widely as a conservative, right-wing Basque instrument, as associated with the traditionalist nationalism of the PNV, and *txistulariak* are associated commonly with the *kaiku*, the traditional Basque jacket, and the *txapela*, the beret.[10] By contrast, the diatonic accordion known as the *trikitrixa* is now regarded as a modern, progressive, fashionable Basque instrument. And the most "revolutionary," "Red," and left-wing Basque nationalist instrument is the *txalaparta*, the primitive xylophone consisting in one or two big wooden bars usually played by two musicians. The *alboka* and the *dultzaina*, the double-piped hornpipe and shawm, meanwhile, are just regarded as Basque, without any other particular political dimension.

In this process of the political and social relocation of musical instruments, the history, careers, and functions of some instruments have been invented, creating a new image and ideology to fit the desired political and/or commercial objectives. Nobody seems to care anymore that the music they play comes from the repertoire of the *txistulariak*. Nobody seems to care that the rhythms they themselves identify as "Basque" and use so much come from the dances of the repertoire of *txistulariak* such as Serafín Amezua or Alejandro Aldekoa. What is more, the majority of *dultzaina* players, *alboka* players, *txalaparta* players, and others began their musical careers playing the *txistua*. They were and are *txistulariak*. Yet the *txistua* is not fashionable anymore, although this does have its advantages: what is not in fashion cannot go out of fashion.

Dance and Music: Two Worlds Today?

In the context of the dances of Berriz analyzed here, dance and music form a single entity. It could be said that the music is understood, learned, and felt through the dancing body. It is the organic activity of dancing that shapes the way dancers and dance musicians internalize, feel, and understand the music/dance, with no borders between music and choreography, something difficult to understand for many contemporary musicians and dancers whose approach to the event is only partial. The importance of the body's action, of each body, and of the motional/musical potentiality of each dancer's body determines to a great extent the structure of the music, at least when dancers and musicians share this holistic conception of dance and music and when the musician is a dance master like

10. The wearing of the *kaiku* and the *txapela* is often spoken of in a pejorative way, as a criticism of the overly folkloric dress of some *txistulariak*.

Alejandro Aldekoa, someone able to "follow the dancer." This idea, the movement of the body dancing and conducting the musical event, has led to whole new research lines for the future—a new approach to the analysis and understanding of the music and dances of Berriz and the Basque Country in general.

On the other hand, the current situation regarding dance groups reveals a different reality. During my research, through my privileged position as an apprentice dancer and musician, I had the opportunity to share rehearsals, performances, courses, tours, meetings, and problems with my colleagues in the Andra Mari dance group from Galdakao. My contacts with other dancers and musicians, especially those from Berriz and the Durango area, were frequent and of great use. As a result, I came to understand quite well the problems that dance groups encounter today. Among all the problems I observed, I would underline one in particular: the separation of dancers from musicians, a separation between the world of dance and the world of music.

Even the most agile of dancers and those who are dedicated to teaching do not know the difference between a binary and a ternary rhythm, not only as an analytical-abstract concept, but also during the performance of the dance. The truth is that it is amazing how some dancers have a capacity to impose their own conception of the rhythm on the music to which, in theory, at least, they are listening.

The panorama for musicians is no more encouraging. It seems that only a privileged few are capable of understanding the rhythmic structure of the dances for which they are playing, of "hearing the dance steps." I often heard that to be a good dance musician, one had to know how to dance, but now I know that this is not enough. Even those who are dancers and musicians (in the Andra Mari dance group there are a few, and I know of many more) are not capable of connecting the two sides of the coin, music and dance, united through what we generically call "rhythm."

After my contact and experience with Alejandro Aldekoa and his son Germán (another master taborer), I took it for granted that all dancers, or at least those who work as dance masters, would be able to sing the steps the way Alejandro could, that they would be capable of singing the movements in a way that the rhythmic pattern described by the choreography would be made clear, describing the rhythm of the movements. Nothing was further from the truth. Today, only a few taborers (among them, Germán Aldekoa and Jon Zamalloa) are able to "transcribe" the dance steps rhythmically.

All of this leads me to the belief that taborers such as Alejandro Aldekoa worked as dance masters not only because they acted as transmitters between different generations of dancers, with the younger ones taking over from their elders, but also because of their knowledge of both music and dance, and a factor that gave them a superior understanding of the choreographic structures, a higher level of knowledge and understanding of the dance that other members of the community could not reach. The dance master–taborer was a specialist in that he knew as much about the science of dance as he did about the science of music.

Social Status

One of Aldekoa's most important contributions was unquestionably the change he brought about in the local image of the taborer. His predecessor, Serafín Amezua, was, to use a local term, a *gixajoa* (a poor, unhappy man, shy and not very energetic). Basically, everyone has fond memories of him, and he was a good person, but from the numerous opinions and commentaries I heard, I would conclude that his lack of drive or inspiration led people to think of him as being excessively humble and without a great deal of social standing in the local community. This is because he was not a musician (he could not read music), and he was unfortunate to have been born between two taborers who eclipsed his career: on the one hand, his father, who remained in active service until his death in 1954, and on the other, Aldekoa, who shortly afterward robbed him of his post. Moreover, he did not know how to face up to the dance crisis of the post–Civil War period, due, it seems, to his lack of leadership abilities. Yet there were still other reasons why he did not enjoy an especially prominent social status. His job as a cattle dealer (traditionally seen as a kind of wheeler-dealer and therefore untrustworthy in rural Basque society) and slaughterman did nothing to help his social image, and he also had a drinking problem. People knew about the problem, although it was not so surprising in those days, when he had to go from *baserria* to *baserria* playing the *albonada* and was invited inside for a drink at each visit.

By contrast, Aldekoa was very careful about his image. He did not drink, or if he did, he drank moderately. (I did not hear any comments to the contrary.) He stopped playing the *albonada* in Berriz, almost certainly because to go around from house to house playing for a little money and food was to lower himself too much, at least among the inhabitants of Berriz, his neighbors, since he maintained the tradition of the *albonada* in Zaldibar while he could. Furthermore, Aldekoa put an end to all types of payment that were not of a strictly commercial or professional kind—that is, no more lunches, suppers, or banquets, just the agreed-on price or fee and nothing more. Aldekoa was a musician and acted and worked as such, even as a teacher of *txistua* in several centers. As a dance master, he managed to reestablish ritual dances that were dying out. As director and manager of the San Lorenzo dance group, he consolidated a group that functions successfully to this day. Finally, all the important folklorists went to Aldekoa to learn from him. In short, Alejandro managed to create an image of a professional *txistularia* as a serious, good musician and expert dance master, and he became one of the best-known, most appreciated, and most loved characters in Berriz.

Appendix 1: Notes on the Dances and Their Transcription

The transcriptions of the ritual dances from Berriz included at the end of chapter 3 as part of my ethnographic work have a clear illustrative purpose. That is, the notations are intended as a complement to the text in conjunction with the images and sound of the DVD. Indeed, this is why I have tried to make them easily intelligible, leaving a more detailed analysis of the music for chapter 5.

Moreover, although the existing notations of the *dantzari-dantza* and *soka dantza* (there are several transcriptions of the music of these dances issued in the Basque Country) could be used to illustrate the essential features of the ritual, in this case, I tried to reflect on the scores the way Alejandro Aldekoa, the central figure of the research, understood the dances, including the music and the steps. As far as I am aware, this is one of the first attempts to codify rhythmically the basic steps of these dances.[1] Within this framework, the transcriptions have a clear prescriptive purpose, since they try to reflect "the blueprint of how a specific piece of music shall be made to sound."[2] Furthermore, echoing Bruno Nettl, this labor "has as its aim, the direction of a performer, and the adequacy of prescriptive notation is judged by the adequacy of the performance, or by the degree to which a performer perceives, through the notation, the composer's wishes."[3] For that reason, the transcription has been a long and demanding process requiring different tasks.

- A study of the scores that Alejandro Aldekoa used, as well as other transcriptions of these dances issued in the Basque Country.
- An analysis of all the available audio and video recordings of Alejandro Aldekoa.
- Learning the dances in order to understand the whole process of dancing and what is relevant for the dancers, discovering both the basic structure of the dances and the local and personal styles and performing variations.
- Testing the adequacy of the transcriptions, "the degree to which a performer perceives, through notation," and Alejandro Aldekoa's wishes by reviewing the notations with the assistance of his sons, Germán and Jon Aldekoa, and Kepa Artetxe from Galdakao, and comparing the scores with the writings of José Luis Etxebarria in his seminal *Danzas de Vizcaya. Bizkai'ko Dantzak.*

---

1. As I explain later, I am aware of the limitations of the transcriptions of the steps I have done.

2. Charles Seeger, *Studies in Musicology 1935–1975* (Berkeley: University of California Press, 1977), 168.

3. Bruno Nettl, *Theory and Method in Ethnomusicology* (London: The Free Press of Glencoe, 1964), 99. In this case, the "wishes" are those of Alejandro Aldekoa, the local taborer and dance master.

Following the principle of prescriptive or phonemic transcription, the notations of the pipe and tabor parts played by Alejandro Aldekoa have been written omitting contextual variations (improvisations, mistakes, ornaments, tempo, and rhythm changes), which are very common in this music due to the interaction between the music player and the dancer. Related to that interaction, the rhythmic features that make the performance of the dances authentic from the local point of view—in other words, what is *not* written in the common standard notation or what we might term "the local style," especially that of Aldekoa—are analyzed in depth in chapter 5.

The *txistua* has been transcribed in F and by assuming the standard diatonic tuning of the instrument. A detailed analysis of the pitches of the *txistuak* from Berriz, mainly those used by Aldekoa, can also be found in chapter 5.

Equally, the rhythmic transcription of the steps notates the basic pattern of the movements in their ideal performance as I learned and understand them. There are several variations and ornaments that have been left out for practical purposes.

The dance notation shows only the temporal location or rhythm of the main choreographic movements or steps that the *txistularia* needs to know in order to "follow the dancer." The movement of the body while dancing is rather complex, so I have transcribed only the most prominent or noticeable movements. For example, in the step called *artazia* or *puntapioa* (✂), I have transcribed only the movement of the left leg, the one that is raised, transcribing the moment when the leg is fully raised, even though at the same time the right leg moves, as well, so that while jumping up, the dancer's whole body is in the air for a moment. As I have commented previously, a fully detailed description of the dance, with all its steps and variations, requires space way beyond the limits of this present work.

There are a few key steps or movements that have been graphically notated to be used as a reference to make the comprehension of the transcription easier and to follow the dances on the video. These are the movements and the symbols used:

- ✂ *artazia* (scissors) or *puntapioa*, raising of the left leg by kicking it in the air.
- ❍ *grabilleta*, drawing a circle with the foot in the air by raising the knee.
- ✓ beating the left shinbone with the right heel.
- ▼ moving the foot indicated (left or right) across the other foot, as though treading on it.
- ➢ the beginning of a complete turn.
- ❏ a repose or rest point, normally at the end of a complete turn.
- ◆ stepping forward, crossing the left foot behind the right one.
- ➶ in the step known as *penduloa* (pendulum), raising one leg to the front, but keeping the other on the ground.
- ➷ in the step known as *penduloa*, raising one leg to the rear, but keeping the other on the ground.

Apart from these symbols, there are a few movements that, because of their punctual use, have been marked using a brief text note on the transcription, such as the moment when the dancers kneel down and the *banderaria* throws the *txapela* in the *agintariena*, or when the dancers simulate mock attacks and parries with the swords in the *ezpata joko nagusia.*

Ordering the Steps: Main Patterns of Movement

For the beginner or the musician with no training in dance, it is not easy to arrange the vast number of steps and movements performed in carrying out these dances. This is not an exhaustive choreographic classification or description, but rather an attempt to put the steps of the dances in order, to discern certain patterns of movement, and to make the comprehension of the dances and their rhythmic transcription easier.

The Zortzikoa *(5/8) Rhythm:* Eskasak, Aurreskua, Atzeskua, *and* Kunplitzekoa

All these dances share similar steps, rhythm, and a kind of common choreographic style. *Eskasak* is the name of the first part of *ezpata joko nagusia* and *makil jokoa*, the difference between the two dances being that during the beginning of *makil jokoa*, after the initial *deia*, the dancers walk in front of the authorities for a while, retaking the dance some bars later. On the other hand, the *aurreskua*, *atzeskua*, and *kunplitzekoa* are dances of the *soka dantza*, danced by a soloist dancer using basically the same steps.

The sequences of movements have been classified and named according to the following chart:

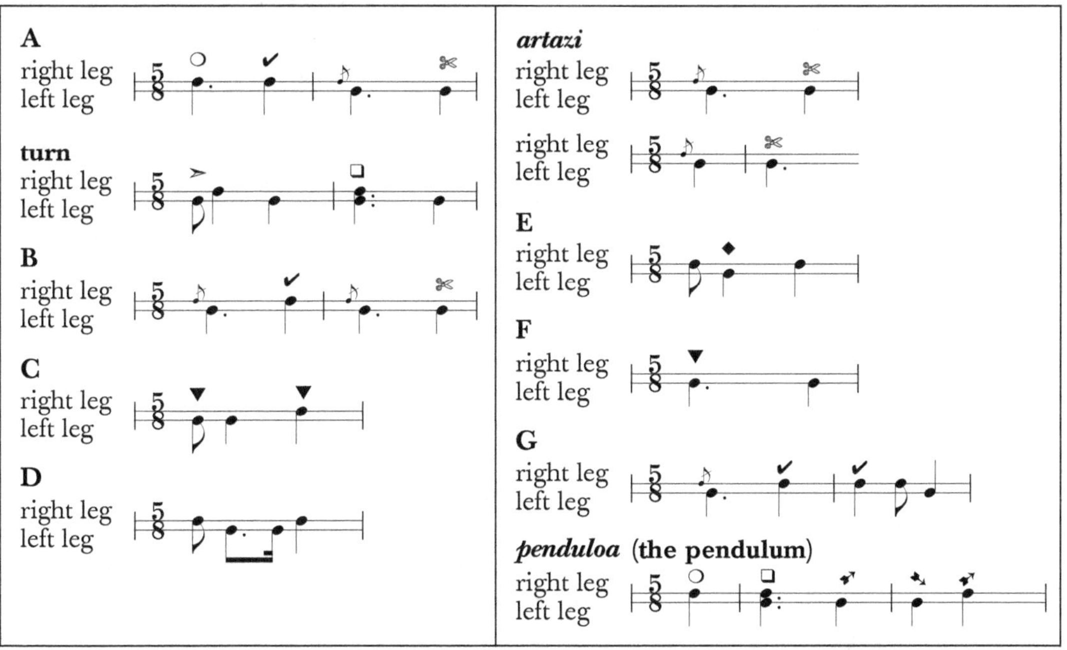

These are the main patterns of movement, a kind collection of choreographic-movement phonemes. Combining them and adding a few single steps, it is possible to "build" bigger patterns or sequences that are repeated at different moments of the dances, and in the end, to complete whole dances. From the point of view of the transcriptions, there is one exception: the *aurreskua.* The first three phrases of the *aurreskua* are played in 2/4, but the sequence of steps, the dance, is just the same as the beginning of the 5/8 section. This combination of steps is repeated later in the same *aurreskua* and at other moments of the *atzeskua* and *kunplitzekoa*, a sequence of eight bars (E, 2 steps, C, 2 steps, A, turn) that some dancers call *pausoak* (steps).

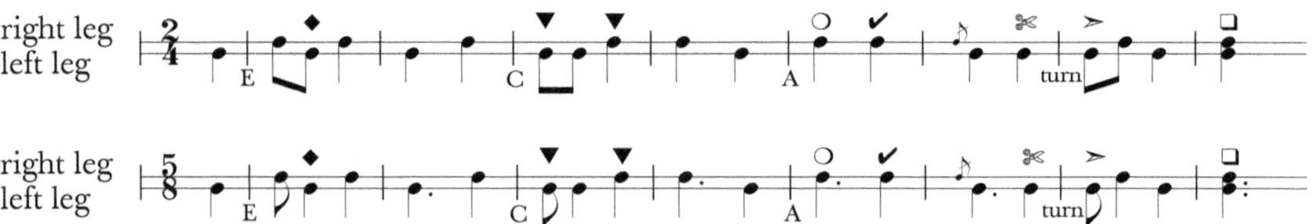

This equivalence between the two rhythms shows how different our analytical academic understanding of the dance music, its rhythm, and its notation is from that of the local traditional dancers and musicians, something discussed in depth in chapter 5.

The steps for *eskasak* are fixed. It is a group dance, and there is no room for improvisation, but in the *aurreskua, atzeskua,* and *kunplitzekoa,* the soloist dancer, apart from his own personal style variations and ornaments, is allowed to build certain variants using the above-mentioned movement phonemes. For example, the eight-bar-sequence of *pausoak* (steps) admits the following four variations. The first four bars are fixed, while for the second half, the dancer can choose among A+turn, B+turn, A+C, B+C:

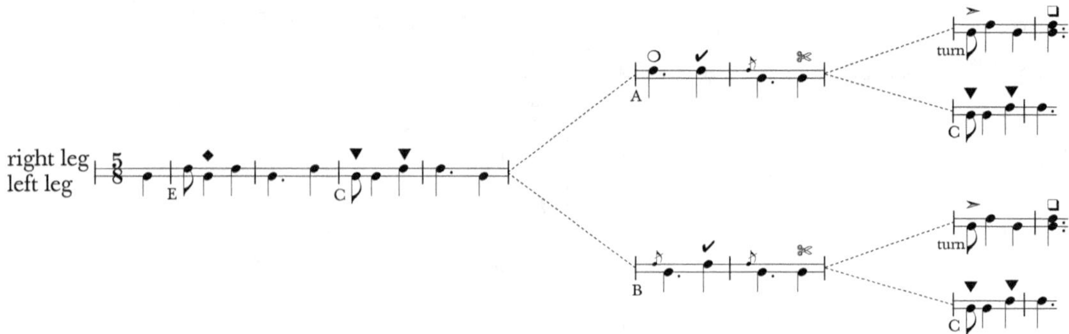

Although I could not ask Aldekoa about it, finishing with a turn is meant to be a more conclusive end. Because of that, the turn at the end of this sequence is compulsory when there is a conclusive cadence in the music, at the end of a section or at the end of the dance, although I found these criteria certainly to be flexible. Perhaps this is related to the fact that the sequence of the *deia*, or call used to begin and finish some dances or dance sections, is just A+turn:

right leg 5/8 A turn
left leg

The Ezpata-dantza *(6/8–3/4) Rhythm:* Zortzinangoa, Banangoa, Binangoa, Launangoa, *and* Banango Zaharra

It is often said that whoever knows one of these dances knows them all, because the basic pattern of movements is the same (except for the *banango zaharra*, which shows certain particularities). What changes is the choreography of the dances, the figures and movements described by the group of dancers, as can be seen in the video. There are two basic step sequences, both very similar. This is the first one—what I term sequence H:

right leg 6/8 3/4
left leg

The other sequence (I) is identical, except for the three movements performed after the *artazia* (✂), a single step and two *grabilletak*:

right leg 6/8 3/4
left leg

The structure of each repetition of the whole dance would thus be H+H+I+I. These sequences of steps are maintained (as far as possible) when the dancers move from one place to other during the performance of the dances, executing the choreography of the dances.

The *banango zaharra* uses the same movements as the other dances (*banangoa, binangoa, launangoa*, and *zortzinangoa*) although their distribution varies according to the peculiar structure of the dance. There is one exception: a different and peculiar movement in the *banango zaharra* known as the *grabilleta* and performed with the left leg. This is the only moment in the dances of Berriz where such a movement is danced with the left leg.

Sword and Stick Games: Ezpata joko txikia, *the* Jokoa *(the Game) of* Ezpata joko nagusia *and* Makil jokoa

These dances are named "games." The most important feature of the dances is the choreographic use of the sticks and swords. As regards the common steps, there is a pattern worth mentioning, a kind of polka step performed by the dancers in the *ezpata joko txikia* and at the end of the *makil jokoa* while crossing their swords or sticks:

right leg 2/4
left leg

The sequence of the *deia* A+turn is performed at different moments in the *ezpata joko nagusia* and *makil jokoa*, but this time in 2/4:

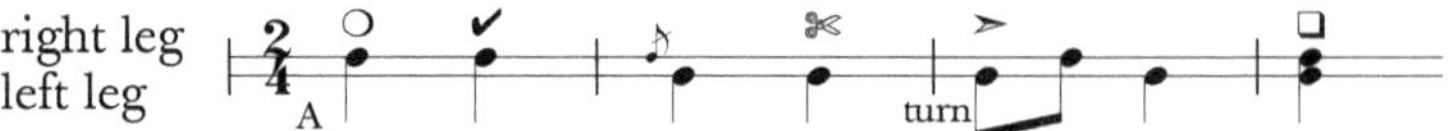

Trikitia: Jota *or* Fandangoa *and* Arin-arina *or* Porrusalda

These two dances form a kind of independent suite, so that in certain areas, the two dances receive the name of *lehenengoa* (the first) for the *jota*, and *bigarrena* (the second) for the *arin-arina* danced after it. Both share similar steps, a similar language of movement, although different rhythms and tempo. As Iztueta observed, the *Bizkai-dantza* (Bizkaian dance, the old name for *arin-arina*) is a dance that people from Bizkaia dance like the *fandangoa* to the music of the 2/4 country dances.[4]

I have transcribed the *jota* or *fandangoa* in 3/4, following the custom of contemporary Basque *txistulariak*, among them Alejandro Aldekoa. I will call it mode A:

Sometimes the *jota* is written in 3/8, trying to reflect the fast tempo of the dance. I will call this mode B:

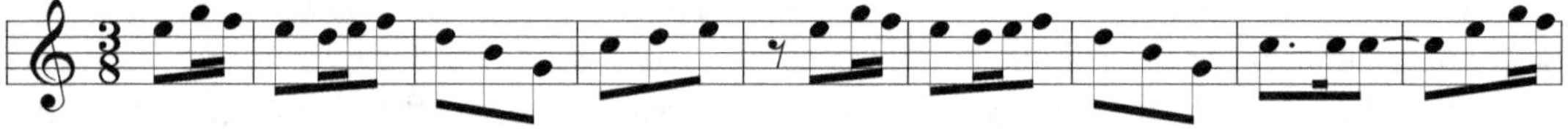

In a few papers, the dance is written in 3/4, but with a rhythmic division that better reflects the real structure of the dance and its choreography, This I will call mode C:

The scores of the *jota* and the *arin-arina* do not include the transcription of the steps. Rather, they show only the melody of the pipe and the rhythmic accompaniment of the tabor. This has been done for various reasons. For one thing, the *jota* and *arin-arina* are not considered proper ritual dances. For another, the music is ordered following a ternary structure (ABC), while the steps are two (AB). The *jota* that Aldekoa played has three sections, the first one is sixteen bars long and termed *puntapioa*, the second is sixteen bars long and called *hara-honakoa*, and the third is twenty bars long and known as *balseoa* or

4. Juan Ignacio de Iztueta, *Gipuzkoako dantza gogoangarrien kondaira edo historia* (1824; Donostia: Euskal Editoreen Elkartea, 1990), 180.

kanteue (literally, the sung one, the section where verses were sung). The *balseoa* used to be danced by couples like a waltz, holding one another. Nowadays, most people in Berriz dance only two steps, so that there is no correspondence between the music in three sections and the two steps.

Also, as Aldekoa pointed out, the *jota* and the *arin-arina* are dances open to improvisation, with a rich variety of patterns depending on the skills of the dancers, even though today in Berriz, most people dance using only the above-mentioned two steps, as can be observed in the video.

The most common *jota* pattern for dancing would be, transcribed in mode A:

This main pattern has the following two very common variations:

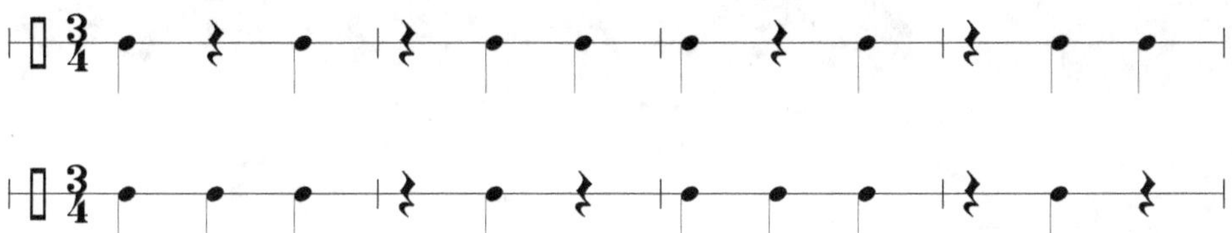

The pattern marked by the dancers is emphasized by the tabor. Notated with the drum rolls transcribed as mordents, it would be:

Transcribing the drum rolls as real notes (as is common practice among Basque taborers), it would be:

Some of the dancers in the video show a trend to mark any of these three patterns, but not very clearly, as can be seen in the DVD (as I was able to observe during my dancing practices) making transcription almost impossible. As Aldekoa said, for his dancers, it was much more difficult to dance a *jota* (with a minimum quality) than the rest of the ritual dances, and that must be true, because most of the dancers in the video mark the rhythm of the *jota* in a quite peculiar manner. Transcribed in the mode A, it would be something close to:

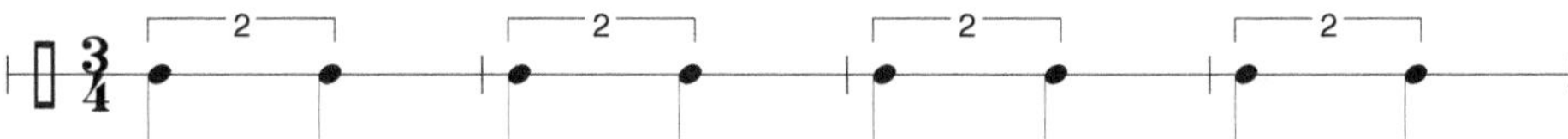

That is, they mark the *jota* as if it were the binary rhythm of the *arin-arina*, instead of the proper rhythm of the *jota*. What they dance is a kind of polyrhythm pattern, but performed unintentionally, a pattern that is not natural or correct from the emic point of view or part of the choreographic tradition.

Figure 41. The first San Lorenzo group dancing *txontxongilloa* (1952). Photo by Iñaki Uribe.

Miscellaneous: Agintariena, Txontxongilloa, Andra soiñua, Biribilketa

The step patterns of the *agintariena*, *txontxongilloa*, *andra soiñua*, and *biribilketa* are quite simple, and the most relevant feature of them is the choreography of the group of dancers—in other words, the movements of the whole group. These dances are not easy to classify into a group or class of dances, which is why they are included under the "miscellaneous" heading. The *agintariena* is a walk that culminates in the waving of the flag. The main feature of the *txotxongilloa* is the lifting of the first dancer. The *andra soiñua* is not a proper dance, but instead is the music used to accompany the walk of the women when they are led to the chain of dancers. During the *biribilketa*, the chain of dancers performs different figures while their feet mark the rhythm of the dance:

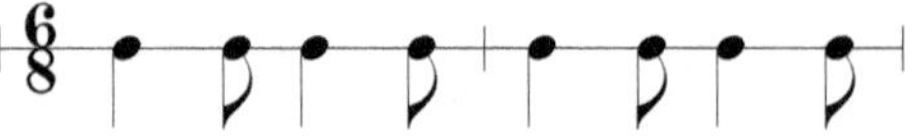

01 *Agintariena*

pipe
tabor
right leg
left leg

(1)

1.

2.

dancers kneel down
and the *banderaria*
throws the *txapela*

pipe
tabor
flag to the right
flag to the left

(1) Alejandro played among others the following variations:

02 *Zortzinangoa*

03 *Ezpata joko txikia*

04 *Banangoa*

05 *Binangoa*

06 *Ezpata joko nagusia*

Jokoa (the game)
pipe
tabor
swords up
swords down
right leg
left leg
attack/defence
attack/defence
1.
2.

1.
2.
attack/defence
attack/defence

07 *Launangoa*

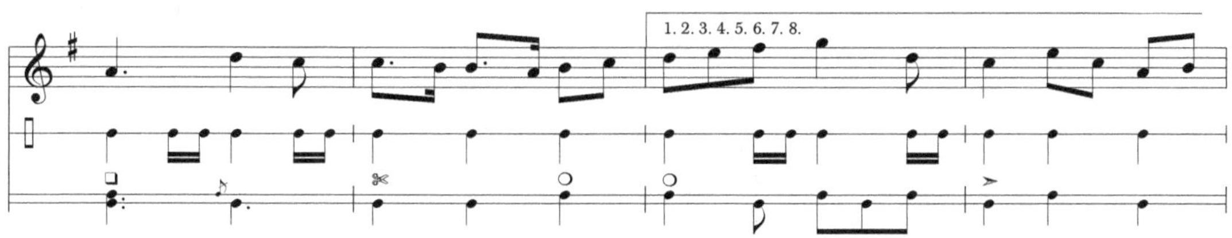

08 *Makil jokoa*

right leg
left leg

Jokoa (the game)
pipe
tabor
sticks
right leg
left leg

1.
2.

09 *Txontxongilloa*

10 *Aurreskua*

3
3

11 *Atzeskua*

penduloa (the pendulum)
3
left
behind

12 and 14 *Andra soiñua*

pipe

tabor

(1)

At any point in the melody, when the chain was ready, Alejandro finished playing something similar to the following *deia* (coda), connecting with the beginning of the next dance, the *banango zaharra*:

(1) Alejandro always played that bar in 3/4 instead of the original 4/4:

13 and 15 *Banango zaharra*

16 *Kunplitzekoa*

When the chain was ready, Alejandro finished playing something similar to the following *deia* (coda) at the end of any of the two sections of the dance:

17 *Jota*

pipe

tabor

CODA

D.C.

Frequently, Alejandro finished the piece introducing this coda at the marked point and began to play the rhythm of the following dance, the *arin-arina*:

18 *Arin-arina*

Regularly, after playing the dance two or three times,
Alejandro finished the piece introducing this coda at the marked point:

✳ *ossia*

19 *Biribilketa*

pipe

tabor

(1)

D.C.

(1) Alejandro played that bar in 3/8 instead of the usual 6/8:

Appendix 2: Transcriptions

Contents

1. Conversion Table

(♩=150)

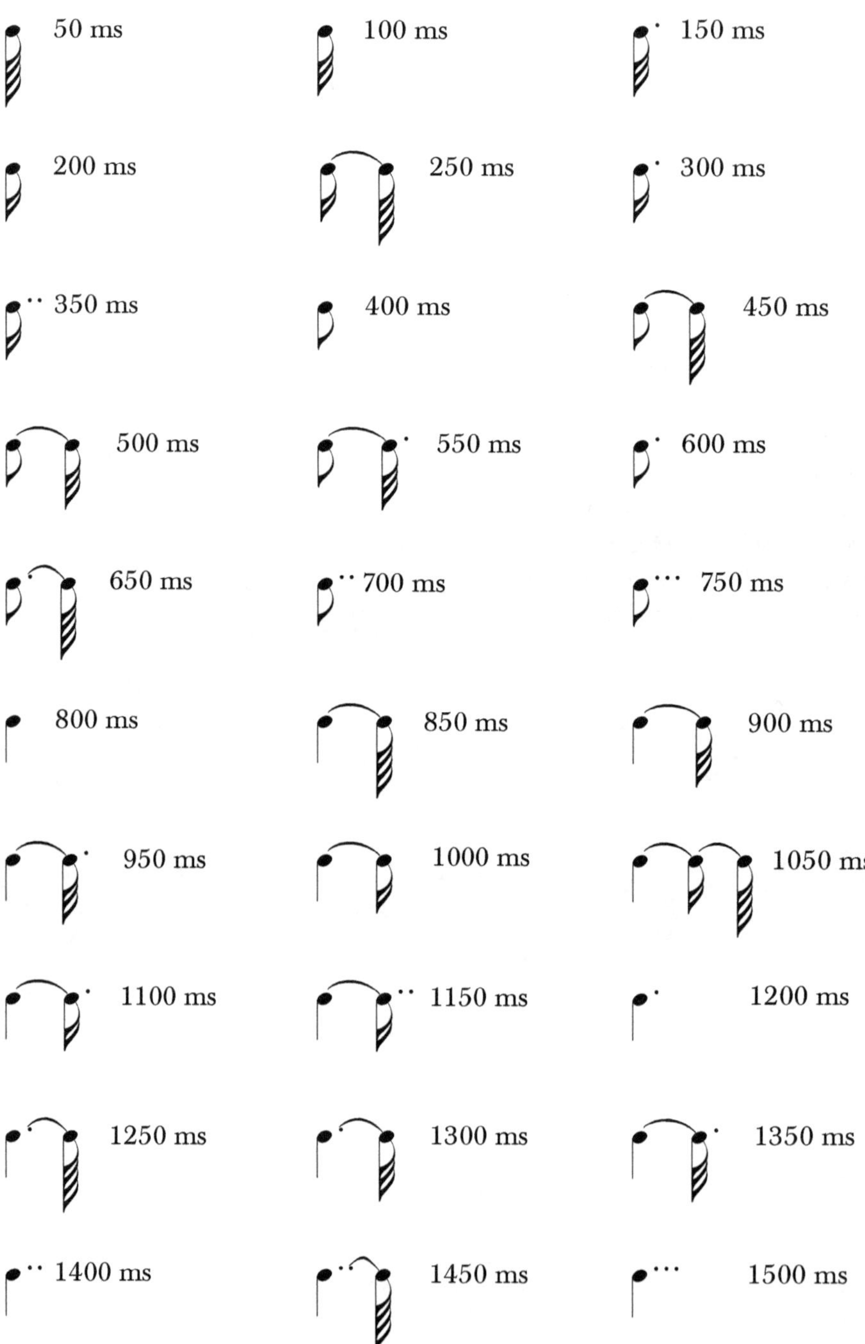

2. *Eskasak* played by Serafín: Descriptive

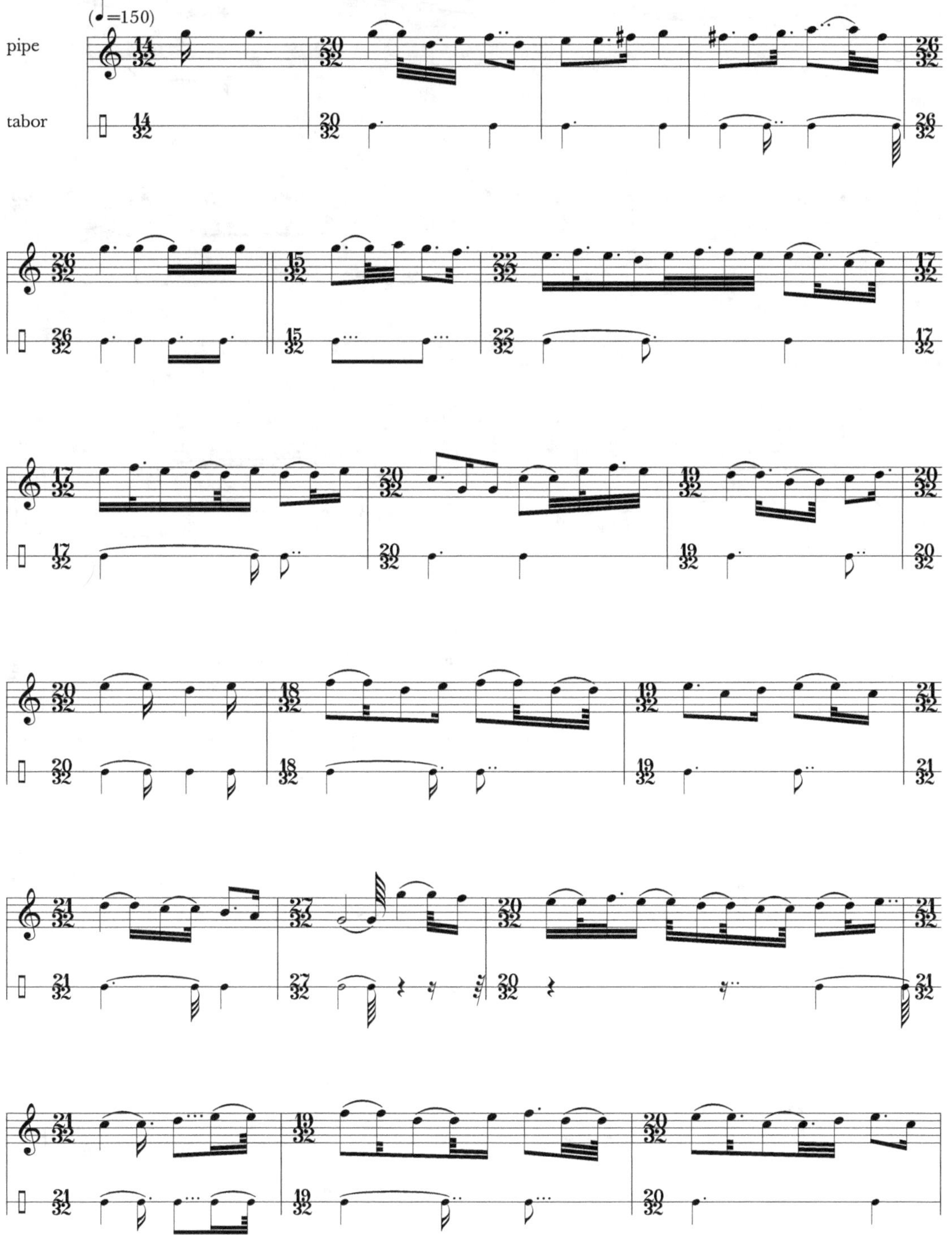

18
32
22
32
19
32
27
32
16
32
20
32
21
32
17
32

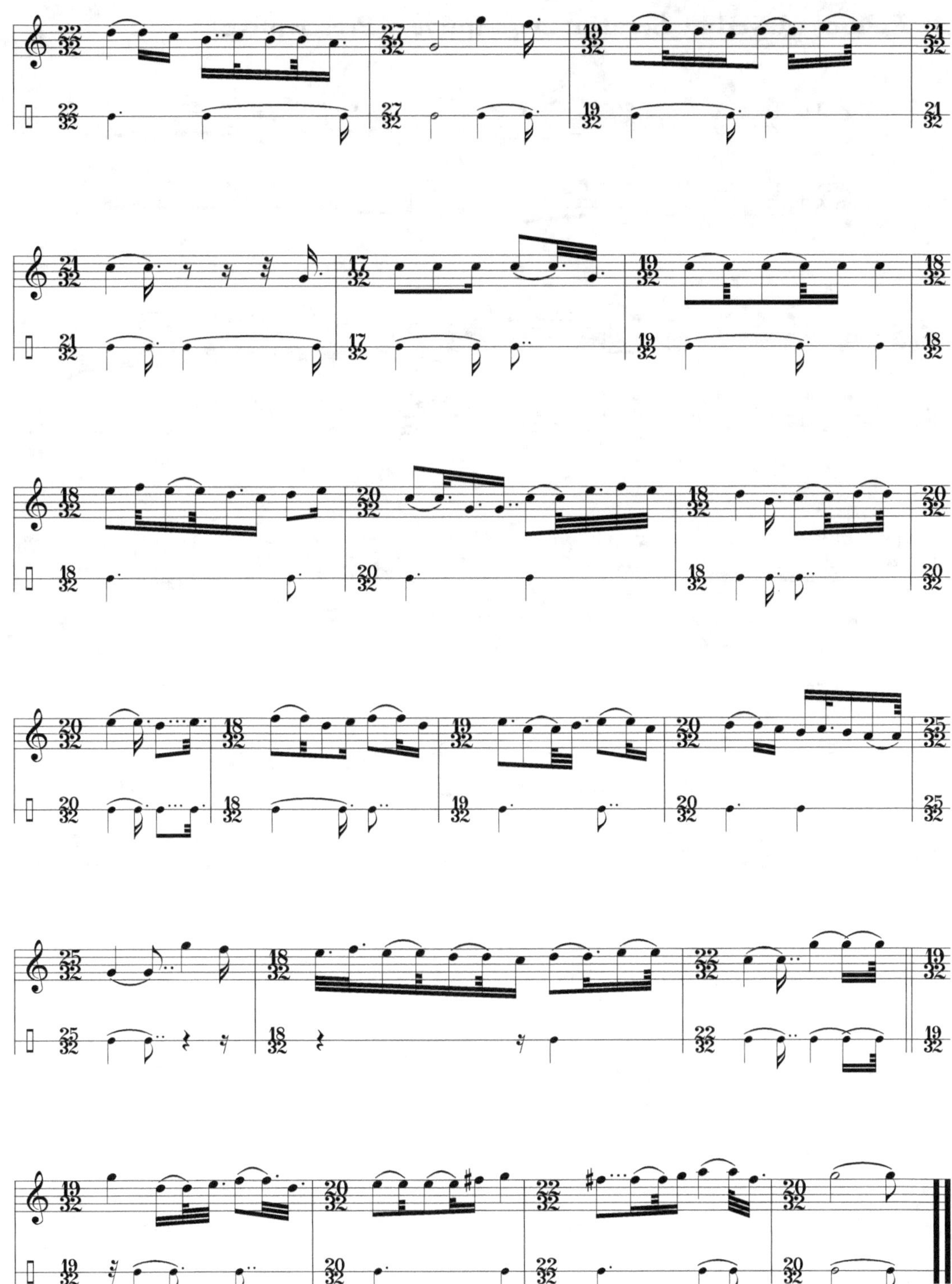

3. *Eskasak* played by Serafín: Descriptive + Prescriptive

4. *Eskasak* played by Alejandro: Descriptive

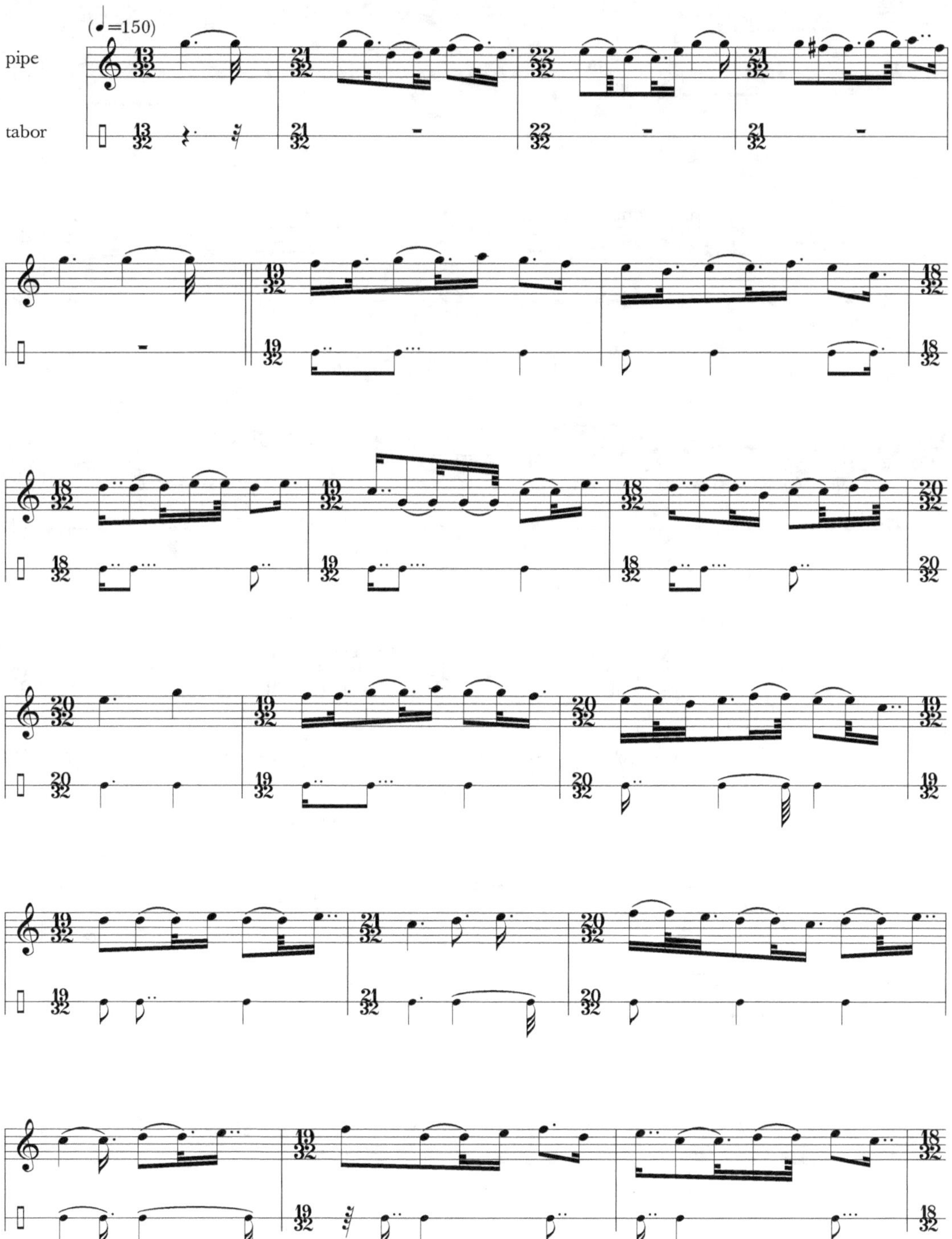

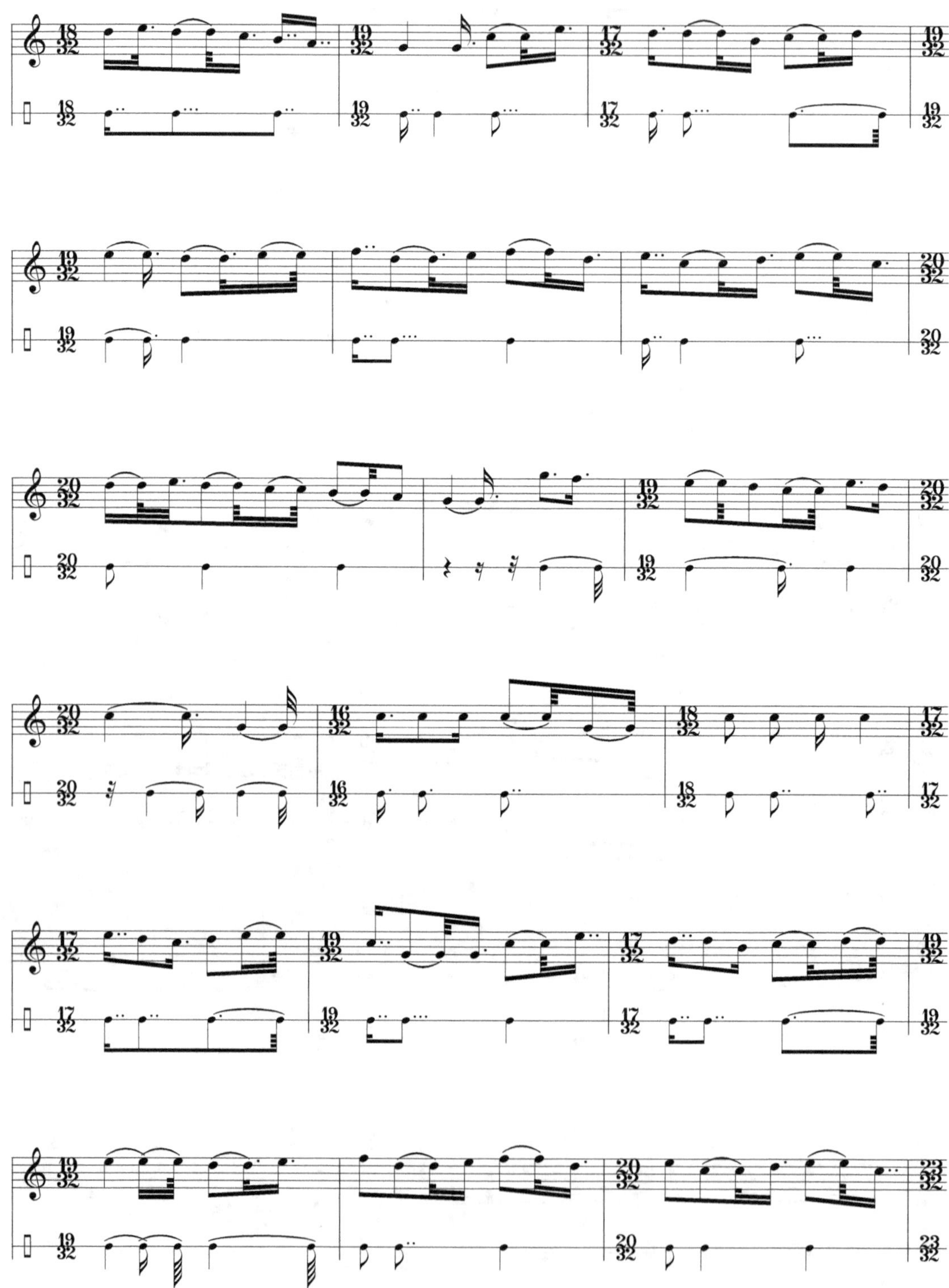

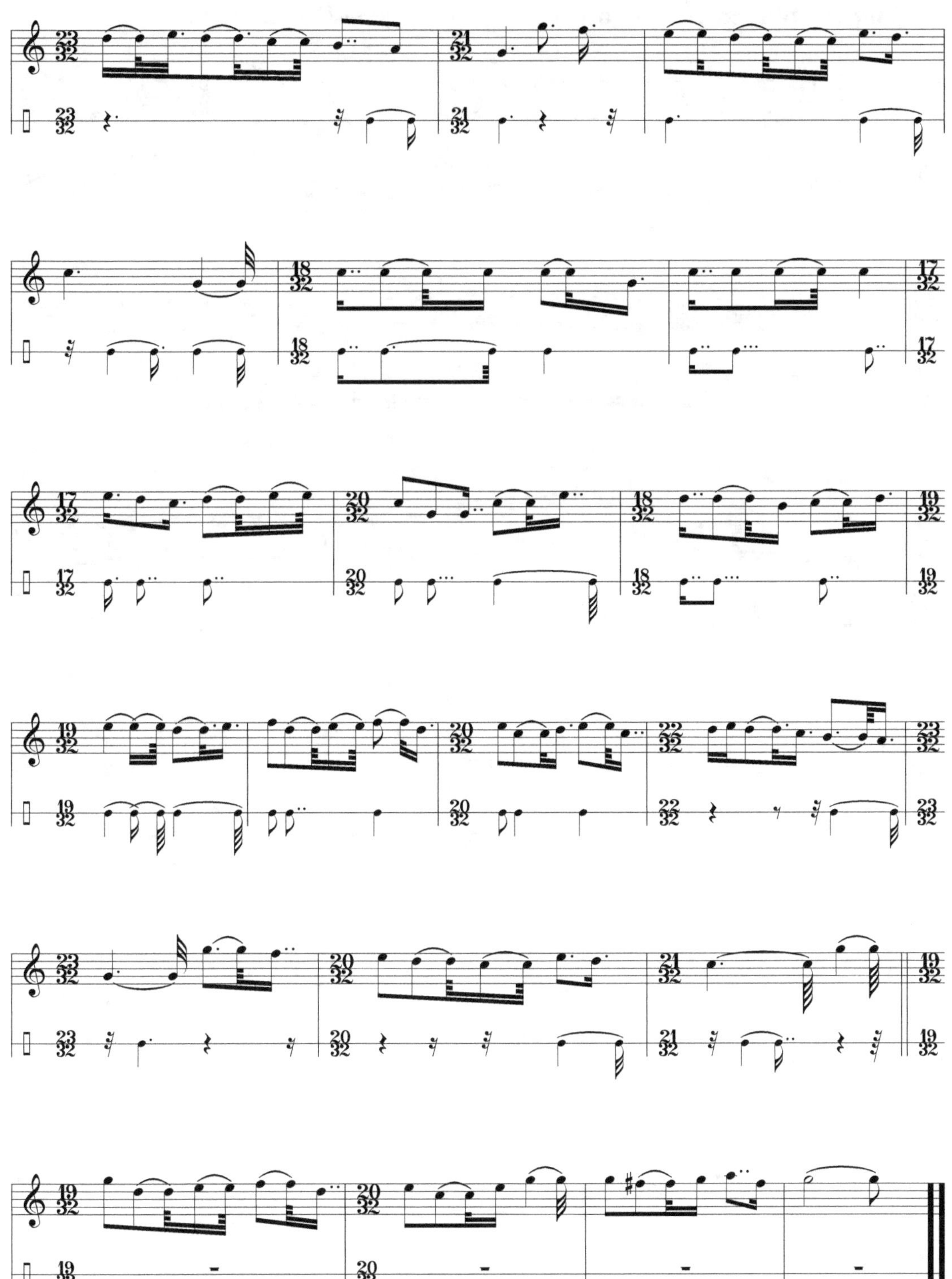

5. *Eskasak* played by Alejandro: Descriptive + Prescriptive

6. *Banangoa* played by Serafín: Descriptive

7. *Banangoa* played by Serafín: Descriptive + Prescriptive

8. *Banangoa* played by Alejandro: Descriptive

9. *Banangoa* played by Alejandro: Descriptive + Prescriptive

Appendix 3: Statistics

Eskasak

	Serafín		Alejandro		Total	
	Mean	Std. Dev	Mean	Std. Dev	Mean	Std. Dev
a1	1112.07	102.25	1124.89	86.66	1118.48	94.17
a2	765.21	94.22	788.07	86.31	776.64	90.27
b1	1268.53	219.91	1177.82	163.53	1223.17	197.39
b2	882,47	165.24	846.60	123.40	883.89	155.78
a	1877.28	165.24	1912.96	158.22	1895.12	161.302
b	2151.00	263.86	1977.63	110.62	2064.31	218.66
a+b	4017.00	387.56	3887.37	256.85	3952.18	332.16
a1–a2 %	69.18	9.21	70.08	5.85	69.63	7.65
b1–b2 %	74.22	15.19	72.24	7.16	73.23	11.80
a–b %	115.35	10.58	103.87	5.35	109.61	10.13
a1–a %	59.26	2.99	58.86	1.98	59.06	2.52
a2–a %	40.73	2.99	41.13	1.98	40.93	2.52
b1–b %	57.80	4.81	58.15	2.43	57.97	3.78
b2–b %	42.20	4.81	41.84	2.43	42.02	3.78

Banangoa

	Serafín		**Alejandro**		**Total**	
	Mean	Std. Dev	Mean	Std. Dev	Mean	Std. Dev
a1	1246.40	40.41	1160.30	27.75	1203.35	55.58
a2	1166.72	51.53	1090.18	56.52	1128.45	65.72
b1	686.20	64.64	655.00	28.69	670.60	51.24
b2	731.80	72.92	649.20	35.54	690.50	70.09
b3	765.40	61.53	700.20	22.51	732.80	56.14
a	2415.40	79.71	2246.10	62.28	2330.75	111.31
b	2183.40	174.15	2004.40	37.49	2093.90	153.18
a+b	4598.80	234.00	4250.50	76.38	4424.65	246.65
a–b%	111.06	6.66	112.08	3.53	111.57	5.21
a1–a%	51.61	1.08	51.68	1.46	51.64	1.25
a2–a%	48.38	1.08	48.31	1.46	48.35	1.25
b1–b%	31.43	1.76	32.68	1.33	32.05	1.65
b2–b%	33.49	1.29	32.37	1.35	32.93	1.41
b3–b%	35.07	1.45	34.94	1.28	35.01	1.33

Appendix 4: Graphs

Contents

Notes

Eskasak

To make the analysis of the rhythmic characteristics of the *eskasak* easier, the following division has been used, with **a** being even bars, and **b** odd bars:

Banangoa

To make the analysis of the rhythmic characteristics of the *banangoa* easier, the following division has been used, with **a** being even bars in 3/4, and **b** odd bars in 6/8:

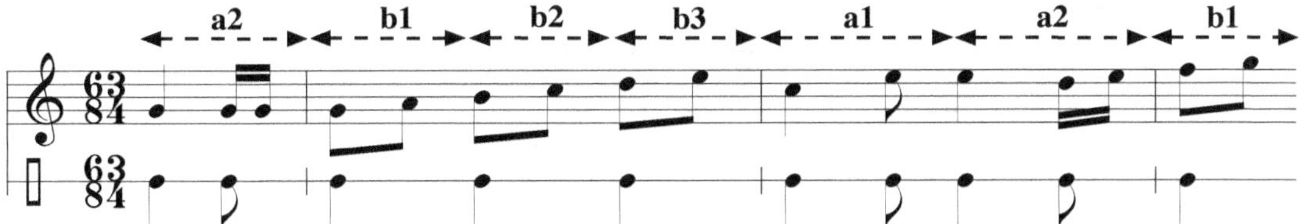

1. *Eskasak* played by Serafín: **a** and **b** bars, in ms

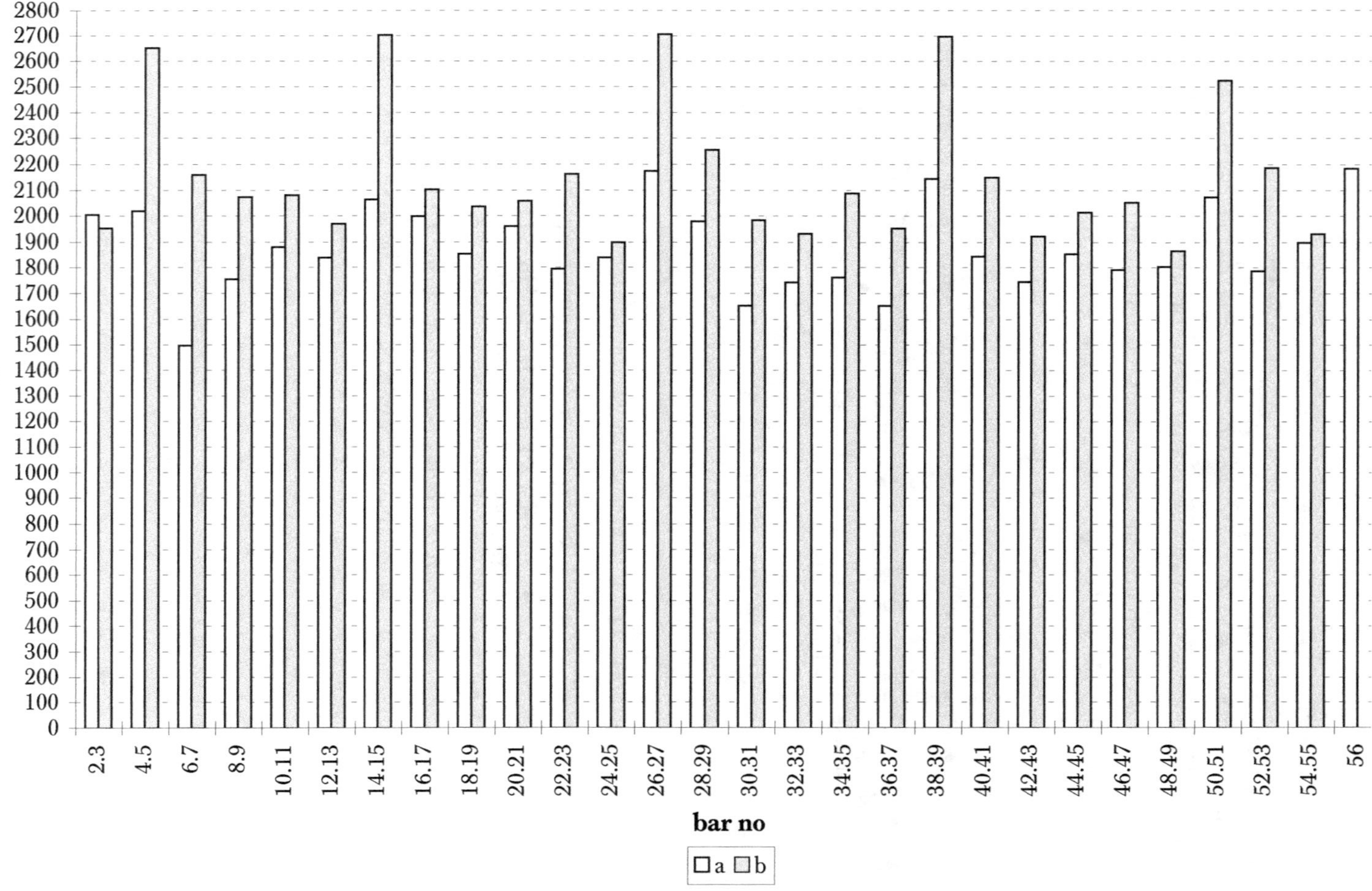

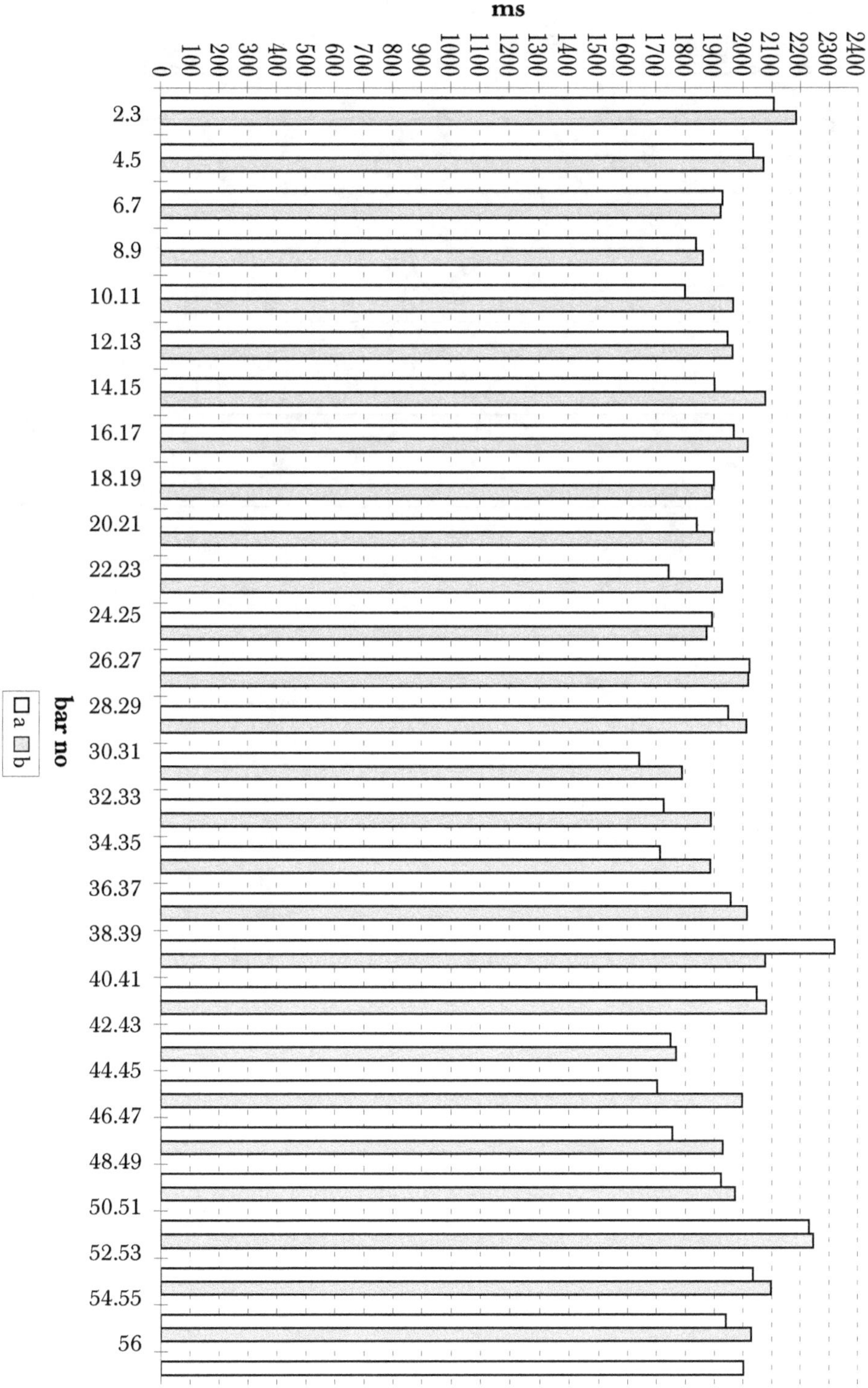

2. *Eskasak* played by Alejandro: **a** and **b** bars, in ms

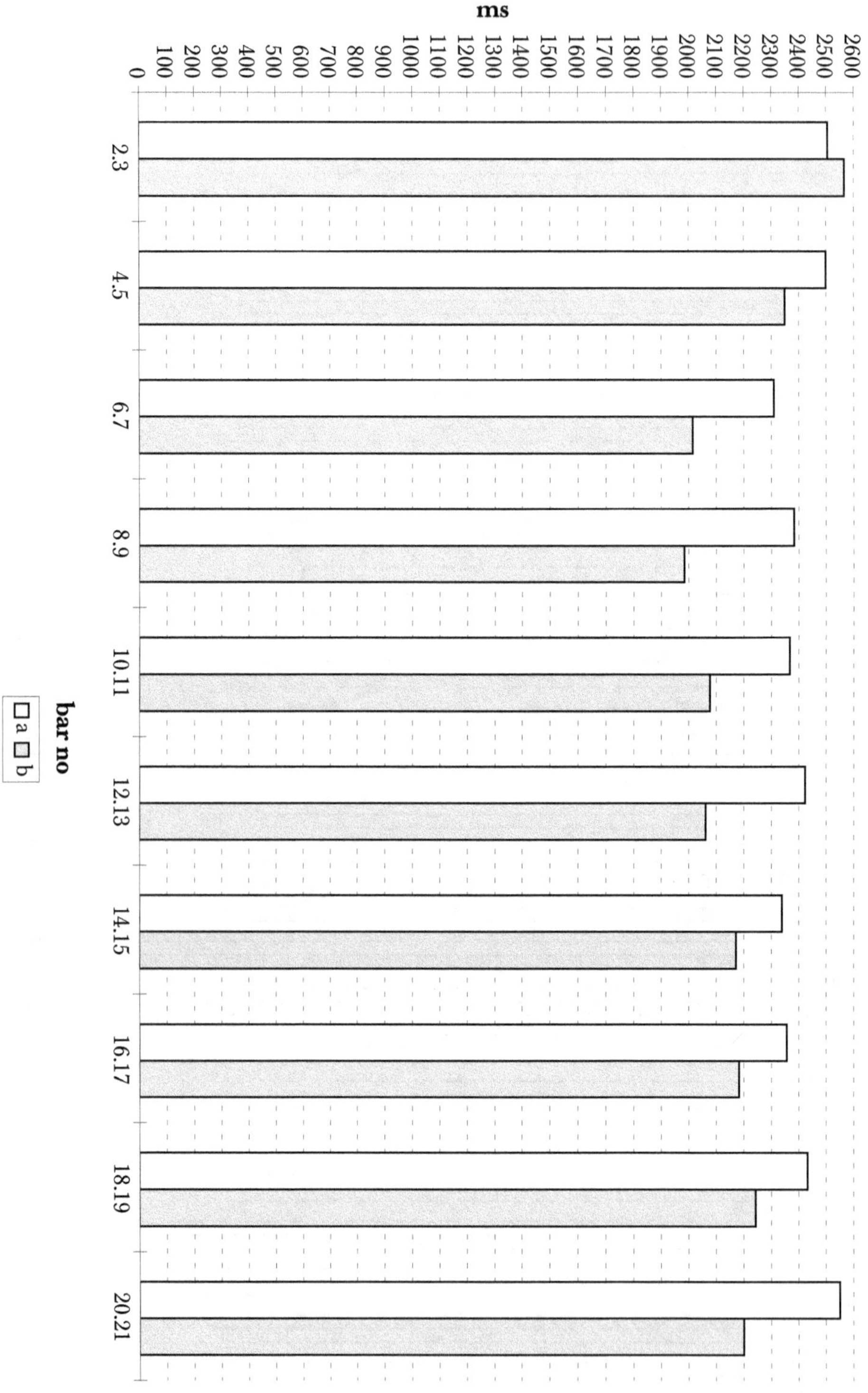

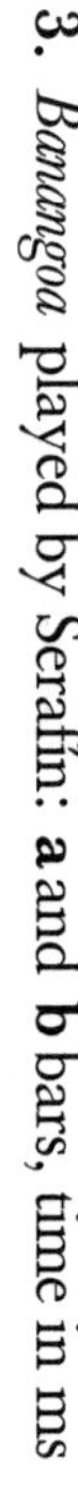

3. *Banangoa* played by Serafín: **a** and **b** bars, time in ms

4. *Banangoa* played by Alejandro: **a** and **b** bars, time in ms

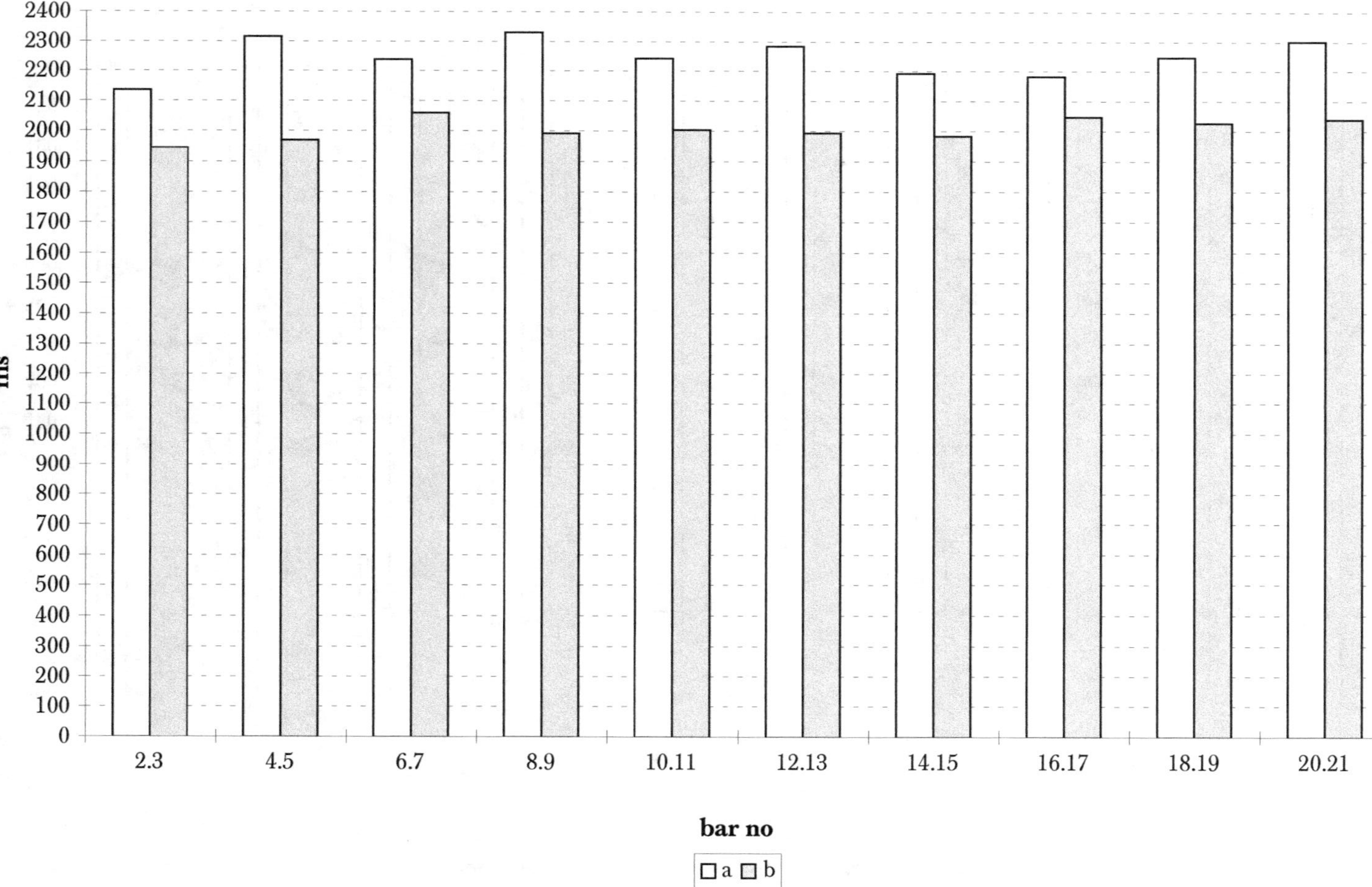

5. *Banangoa* played by Serafin: **b1–b2–b3**, time in ms

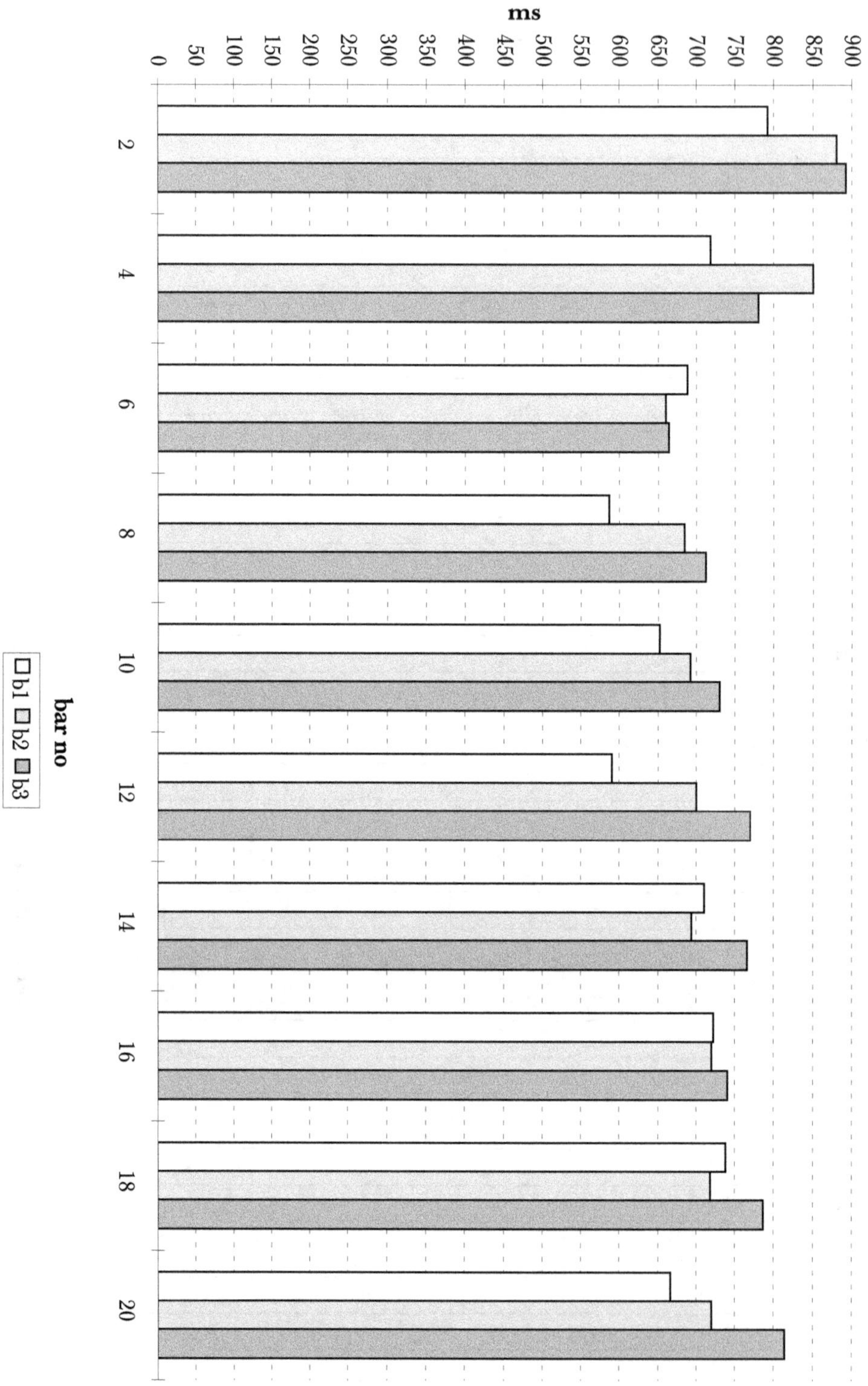

6. *Banangoa* played by Alejandro: **b1–b2–b3**, time in ms

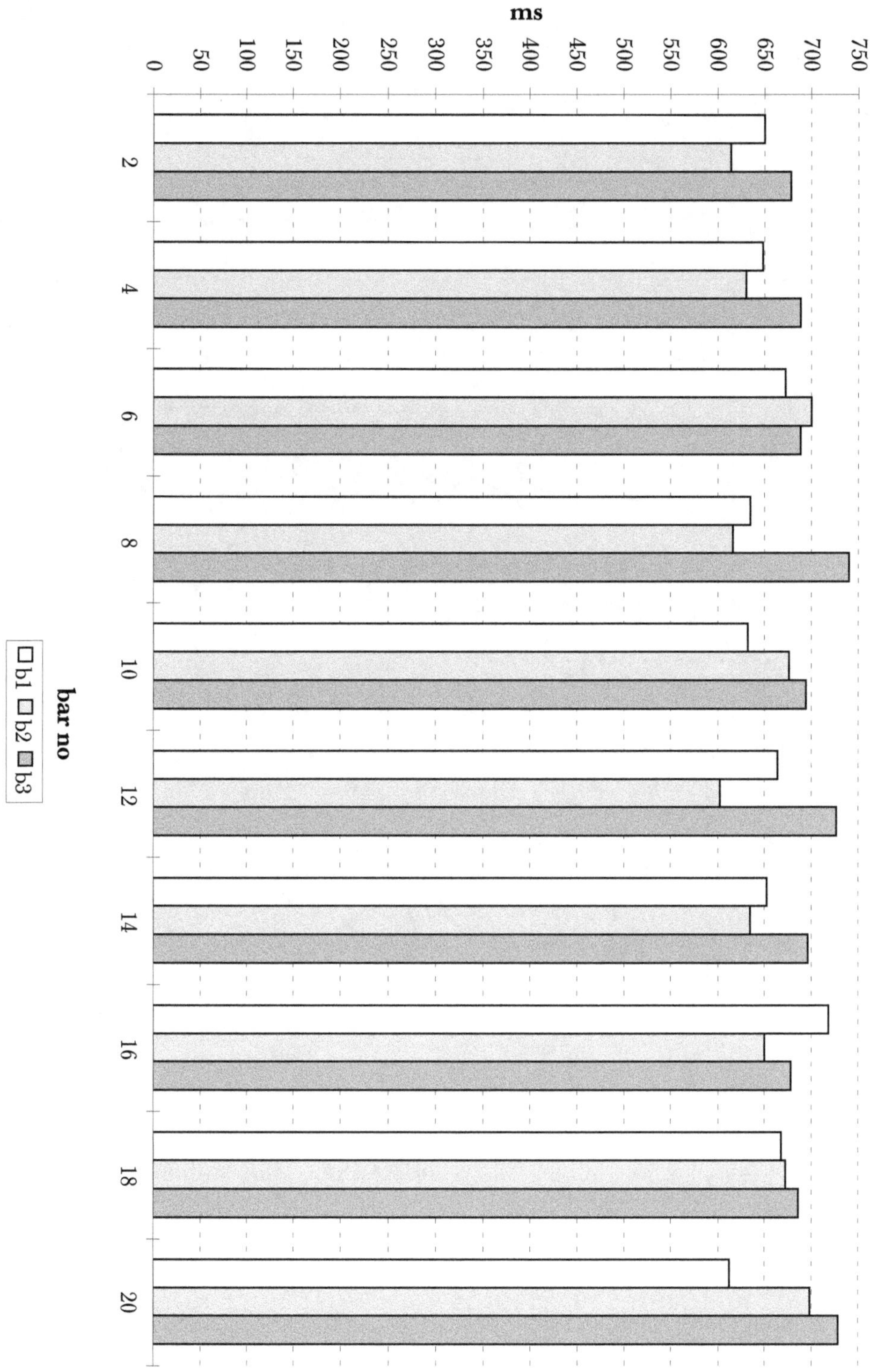

Glossary

abarketak (espadrilles). The name for one of the dances from the *soka dantza.* Now out of use in Berriz.

agarreure (holding each other). Another name for *loture.*

agintariena (of the authorities). Also called *banderariena.* First dance of the *dantzari-dantza* ritual dance suite.

alboka. Double-piped hornpipe played in the Basque Country, similar to the pibcorn from Wales and the stockhorn from Scotland. It has single reeds, a horn bell at the lower end to project the sound, and a horn at the upper end also to serve as a wind cap.

albonada. Term used by Alejandro Aldekoa, who differentiated between *albonada* and *alborada.* As Aldekoa explained, during the *albonada,* the official *txistularia* is sent by the mayor to say hello to the citizens and neighbors visiting and playing in front of each house.

alborada. Dawn song.

andra soiñua (women's melody). Third and fifth dances (including the choreography and the music) of the *soka dantza.*

arin-arina (fast-fast). *Solture* or *trikitia* dance rhythm in 2/4. Usually it is played after the *jota* or *fandangoa.* Its most common rhythmic pattern would be:

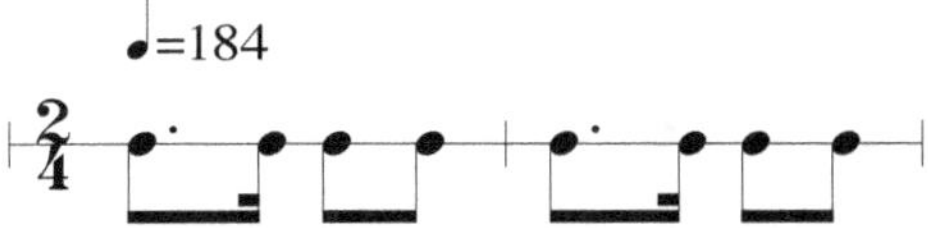

artazia (scissors). Another name for *puntapioa.*

atabala. Snare drum wider and shorter than the tabor used with the *txistua.* It is played by one person with two sticks.

atabaleroa. Player of *atabala.*

atzeskua (the hand in the rear, or the last hand). The dancer who is at the end of the chain or rope of dancers (*soka*) performs this dance after the *aurreskua.* It is the second dance (including the choreography and the music) of the *erregelak* or *soka dantza* suite.

atzeskularia/k. Dancer/s of *atzeskua*.

aurreskua (the hand in front, or the first hand). The first dance (including the choreography and the music) of the *erregelak* or *soka dantza* suite performed by the first dancer.

aurreskularia/k. Dancer/s of *aurreskua*.

auzoa. Neighborhood grouping within a town or urban setting marked by a sense of community. In some areas such as Berriz, it even used to have an official representative, known as the mayor of the *auzoa*.

balseoa (dancing like a waltz). Another name for *loture*.

banangoa (one-by-one dance). Also called *banakoa*. Fourth dance (including the choreography and the music) in the *dantzari-dantza*. Usually transcribed in 6/8+3/4. It is where the dancers perform one by one.

banango zaharra (the old *banangoa*). Formerly, it was danced in the *dantzari-dantza* instead of the "normal" *banangoa*. Today, it is the fourth and sixth dance of the *soka dantza* suite, and it is danced in honor of the women who are selected to join the *aurreskularia* and the *atzeskularia*.

banderaria (standard bearer). The dancer in charge of carrying and waving the flag in *agintariena*, the first dance of the *dantzari-dantza*.

banderiena (of the flag). Another name for *agintariena*.

baserria. The word *baserria* in Euskara is made up of *basoa* ("woods" or "forest") and *herria* ("village" or "town"). Originally, it denominated a group of houses or farmhouses (hamlet, settlement) situated in a rural, dispersed area. Today, the term *baserria*, along with its Spanish translation *caserio*, is used to refer to an isolated, rural house. In English, it could be translated as a "rural home." Sometimes the term also includes the land and other property around the *baserria*, implying that this land is used for farming purposes. In this case, it could be translated into English as "farm." The term *baserria* is also used to refer to a typical Basque-style house, differentiating it from the *masia* in Catalonia or the *barraca* in Valencia, for example.

baserritarrak. Inhabitants of the *baserria*. Could be translated as "farmers."

batzokia. A Basque Nationalist Party (EAJ-PNV) center or club.

bertsoak. Improvised verses.

bertsolaria/k. Improvised verse singer/s. They improvise verses with complicated rhymes, using different airs that give them the basic metric structure and the points of rhyme at the end of each musical phrase or sentence.

bertsolaritza. The art of singing *bertsoak*.

bidekoa (of the road/route/way). Another name for *pasakallea* or *biribilketa*.

bikotxa (the twin). The name given by Alejandro Aldekoa to the simplest tabor pattern of the *biribilketa*:

binangoa (two-by-two dance). Also called *binakoa.* Fifth dance (including the choreography and the music) of the *dantzari-dantza* ritual dance suite. Usually transcribed in 6/8+3/4. It is where the dancers perform two by two.

biribilketa. A genre of musical piece written in 6/8. Also called *pasakallea* and *bidekoa.* Its most common rhythmic pattern would be:

Bizkaia. Basque name for Biscay or Vizcaya in Spanish.

danbolina. Small drum played with the *txistua.* In English, tabor.

danbolinteroa. Player of *danbolina.* In English, taborer.

dantzaria/k. Dancer/s.

dantzari-dantza (dancer's dance). Ritual dance suite from the County of Durango consisting of nine dances: *agintariena, zortzinangoa, ezpata joko txikia, banangoa, binangoa, ezpata joko nagusia, launangoa, makil jokoa,* and *txontxongilloa.*

deia (call). A kind of coda used in certain dances to call the dancers to attention and mark the beginning and the end of each part of the dance.

desafioa (challenge). Formerly, it was the first and last dance of the *soka dantza.*

donien-aretxa, donienatxa (oak of the saints). Maypole. Also called *txopue.*

dultzaina. A kind of shawm used in the Basque Country.

erdalduna. A speaker of a language that is not Euskara (the Basque language). Foreign, foreigner.

erdara. A language that is not Euskara It is applied especially to French in the northern part of the Basque Country and to Spanish in the south of the Basque Country.

erregelak (the rules). Another name for *soka dantza.* Sometimes it is used to name only the first two dances, the *aurreskua* and *atzeskua.*

erromeria/k. Open-air dance/s.

eskasak. First part of the *makil jokoa* and *ezpata joko nagusia* dances.

Euskadi. The Basque Country.

euskalduna. Basque. Literally, a Basque speaker.

Euskal Herria. The Basque Country.

Euskara or Euskera. The Basque language. The orthography of the language recognizes both spellings.

ezpata-dantza (sword-dance). **1**. The name given by many people in the Basque Country to the *dantzari-dantza.* **2**. A type of melody and rhythm pattern based in the 6/8–3/4 combination found in the *banangoa, banango zaharra, binangoa,* and *launangoa* dances from Berriz. Its most common pattern would be:

ezpatadantzaria/k (sword dancer/s). **1**. Name given to the dancers of *ezpata-dantza* or *dantzari-dantza.* **2**. Basque male dancer/s.

ezpata joko nagusia (main game of the swords). Sixth dance of the *dantzari-dantza* ritual dance suite.

ezpata joko txikia (small game of the swords). Third dance of the *dantzari-dantza* ritual dance suite.

fandangoa. A dance rhythm in triple time. In Berriz, it is also known as *jota.*

flabiol. Catalan eight-holed flute played normally one-handed with a drum played by the other hand, like the tabor pipes.

flabiolaire. A *flabiol* player.

grabilleta. A step characteristic of the dances of Berriz that consists of making circles in the air with the foot.

hara-honakoa (from one part to the other). The second step or section of the *jota.*

hilandera/k (spinner/s). Female dancer/s.

ikastola. Basque school.

ikurriña. Basque flag.

jokoa. Game.

jota. A dance rhythm in triple time, quite fast. Usually it is played before the *arin-arin.* Its most common rhythmic pattern would be:

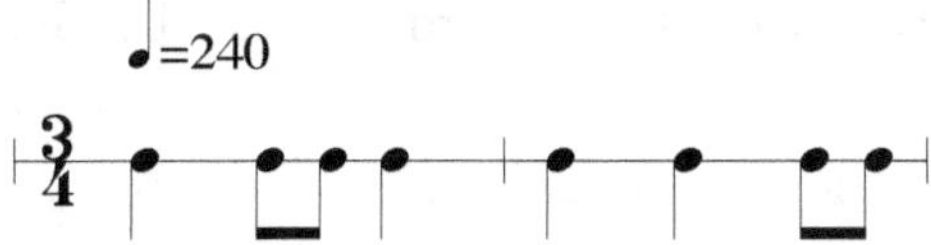

kanteue (the sung). The third step or section of the *jota*, where the verses are sung and the dancers dance holding each other (*agarreure*, *balseoa*, or *loture*).

kontrapasa. A kind of melody in 4/4 and slow tempo.

kunplitzekoa (to compliment). Another name for the seventh dance of the *soka-dantza.*

launangoa (four-by-four dance). Also called *launakoa.* Seventh dance (including the choreography and the music) of the *dantzari-dantza* ritual dance suite. Usually transcribed in 6/8+3/4. It is where the dancers perform four at a time.

loture. Tied, dancing tied, together, holding your partner. A slow dance. Also called *agarreure* or *balseoa.*

makil jokoa (game of sticks). Eighth dance of the *dantzari-dantza* ritual dance suite.

martxa. Another name for *biribilketa.*

minuetoa. A kind of melody developed in the repertoire of the *txistularia* with the same name as the classic minuet, but with a different structure and rhythm.

musikea. Music.

musikoa. Musician.

Nafarroa. Basque name for Navarre.

neskazaharra/k (literally, old girl/s). Single, unmarried woman/women.

ostikoa. Kick.

panderoa. Basque tambourine (*tambour de Basque* in French).

pasakallea (*passacaglia* in Italian). A sort of musical piece written in 6/8. Also called *biribilketa* and *bidekoa.*

pausoak (the steps). Used to name one of the step patterns of the *aurreskua* and *atzeskua.*

penduloa (the pendulum). Characteristic step performed in the *atzeskua.*

Patxiku. Nickname of the Amezua family, pipe and tabor players in Berriz for at least five generations.

plaza mutilla (literally, town-square boy). An unmarried man, older than seventeen, eligible to perform the ritual dances of Berriz.

pontxie (the punch). The break between the *dantzari-dantza* and the *soka dantza*, when the dancers drink the punch.

porrusalda (literally, leek soup). Another name for the *arin-arina.*

puntapioa. **1**. The first step or section of the *jota.* **2**. A step characteristic to the dances of Berriz that consists of raising the left leg into the air. Also known as *artazi.*

puntoa/k, punteoa/k (point/s, punctuation/s). Refers to the rhythm marked by the movements of the dancer.

sapak (the mane). The set of sixteen bells worn by the dancers of Berriz.

seiak. 1. Another name for *eskasak*. **2**. One of the step patterns used in the *aurreskua*, *atzeskua*, and *eskasak*. **3**. Another name for the seventh dance of the *soka dantza*, also known as *zortzikoa* or *kunplitzekoa*.

seiko (of six). One of the steps of the dances from Berriz.

sienprebibea (sempervivum or ever-living). *Helichrysum stoechas*, a small yellow flower worn by the dancers of Berriz.

silbotea. Three-holed pipe, longer than the *txistua*, played with both hands, without tabor, and tuned a fifth lower than the *txistua*.

soka (rope or chain). Line of dancers or chain formed to dance the *erregelak* or *soka dantza*.

soka dantza (rope dance). Also known as *erregelak* or *aurreskua*. Ritual dance suite of the County of Durango formed at present by the following dances: (1) *aurreskua*; (2) *atzeskua*; (3) *andra soiñua*; (4) *banango zaharra*; (5) *andra soiñua*; (6) *banango zaharra*; (7) *zortzikoa*, *seiak*, or *kunplitzekoa*; (8) *jota* or *fandangoa*; (9) *arin-arina* or *porrusalda*; (10) *biribilketa*, *martxa*, or *bidekoa*. Note that in the accompanying DVD, suite parts 7–10 are called the *kunplitzekoa*, *jota*, *arin-arina*, and *biribilketa*; it is important to remember however that there are important variations and all included dance names are listed here.

solture (free or untied). Swift dance.

tarrañuelak. Stick clappers held in one hand used to accompany other instruments such as the accordion.

trikitia/trikitrixa/trikitixa. Formerly (and still today in Berriz) synonymous with *solture*, but at present in the Basque Country, the term *trikitrixa* (and its variants) is used mainly to name the two-row diatonic accordion.

trikitilaria. Diatonic accordion player.

txalaparta. A kind of very basic and primitive xylophone consisting in one or two big wooden bars, usually played by two musicians.

txapela. Basque hat or beret.

txistua/k. Basque three-holed pipe/s.

txistularia/k. Basque pipe and tabor player/s.

txontxongilloa. Ninth and last dance of the *dantzari-dantza* ritual dance suite. A 2/4 dance in which, after some figures, one of the dancers is hoisted up by four of the members of the team and the others bow to him with their swords.

txopue. Another name for *donien-aretxa*.

zortziko (of eight). **1**. See *zortzinangoa.* **2**. Referring to the number of verses, dancers, etc. **3**. The seventh dance of the *soka dantza,* also known as *seiak* or *kunplitzekoa.* **4**. A type of very well-known melody and rhythm pattern used by the Basque pipe and tabor players, usually transcribed in 5/8. Its most common patterns would be:

zortzinangoa or **zortzikoa** (eight-by-eight dance). Second dance of the *dantzari-dantza* ritual dance suite.

Contents of the DVD

Bibliography

Books and Articles

Alford, Violet. "Ceremonial Dances of the Spanish Basques." *Musical Quarterly* 18, no. 3 (July 1932): 471–82.

Anderson, Benedict. *Imagined Communities: Reflections on the Origin and Spread of Nationalism.* Revised edition. London: Verso, 1991.

Ansorena Miner, Jose Inazio [pseud. Iker Bidegorri]. "Iztueta eta Albéniz-en musika bilduma." *Txistulari* 163, no. 3 (1995): 10–27.

——. *Txistu Gozoa: Txistu Ikasbidea-Método de Txistu. Lehenengo maila. Primer Curso.* 1985; Donostia: Erviti, 1995.

——. *Txistu Ikaskizunak.* Donostia: Euskadiko Kutxa, 1978.

——. "El zortziko: La frase de ocho compases y el cinco por ocho." *Txistulari* 141, no. 1 (1990): 7–10.

Ansorena Miranda, Jose Luis. *Txistua eta Txistulariak: El Txistu y los Txistularis.* San Sebastián: Fundación Social y Cultural Kutxa, 1996.

Apezetxea, Patxi. *Hernani eta txistua: Bere txistulariak / Sus txistularis.* Donostia: Kutxa Fundazioa, 1992.

Arana, José Antonio. "Folklore de Vizcaya." *Enciclopedia Histórico Geográfica de Vizcaya.* Vol. 4, 305–40. San Sebastian: Haranburu, 1984.

——. *Musica Vasca.* 1976; Bilbao: Caja de Ahorros Vizcaína, 1987.

Arana Fuldain, Modesto. "Erregelak." Transcription. *Txistulari* 74, no. 2 (1973): 2040–42.

Arbeau, Thoinot [pseud. Jehan Tabourot]. *Orchésographie.* 1589; Langres: Dominique Guéniot, 1988.

Armistead, Samuel G., and Joseba Zulaika, eds. *Voicing the Moment: Improvised Oral Poetry and Basque Tradition.* Reno: Center for Basque Studies, University of Nevada, Reno, 2005.

Armstrong, Lucile. "Hitzaurrea / Prefacio." Preface to Juan Antonio Urbeltz, *Dantzak.* Bilbao: Jakin, 1978.

Aulestia, Gorka. *Improvisational Poetry from the Basque Country.* Translated by Lisa Corcostegui and Linda White. Foreword by William A. Douglass. Reno: University of Nevada, Reno, 1995.

Azkue, R. Mª. *Cancionero Popular Vasco.* 1922–1925; Bilbao: Euskaltzaindia, 1990.

Baily, John. "Anthropological and Psychological Approaches to the Study of Music Theory and Musical Cognition." *Yearbook for Traditional Music* 20 (1988): 114–24.

——. "Learning to Perform as a Research Technique in Ethnomusicology." In *"Lux Oriente" Begegnungen der Kulturen in der Musikforschung,* edited by Klaus Wolfgang Niemöller, Uwe Pätzold, and Chung Kyo-chui. Kassel: Gustav Bosse. Cologne: Gustav Bosse Verlag Kassel, 1995.

——. "Music Structure and Human Movement." In *Musical Structure and Cognition,* edited by Peter Howell, Ian Cross, and Robert West. London: Academic Press, 1985.

——. "Some Cognitive Aspects of Motor Planning in Musical Performance." *Psychologica Belgica* 31, no. 2 (1991): 147–162.

Baily, John, and Veronica Doubleday. "Patterns of Musical Enculturation in Afghanistan." In *Music and Child Development: Proceedings of the 1987 Denver Conference,* edited by Frank Wilson and Franz Roehmann. St. Louis: MMB Music, 1990.

Barandiaran, Gaizka. "Berriz, nido del folklore vasco." *Programa de fiestas.* Berriz: Berrizko Udala, 1964.

Barceló, Fermin. *Alejandro Aldekoa Berrizko txistulari zahar-berria.* Berriz: Berrizko Udala, 1993.

——. "Aproximación a las fuentes para el estudio de la música popular en una comunidad local: Berriz." Ph.D. dissertation, University of Deusto, 1993.

Bedialauneta, Julian de. "Resurgimiento consolador: Los 'nidos' de txistularis—Los cuadros de ezpatadantza." *Txistulari* 3 (1928): 3.

Berguices, Angel. "Dos siglos de música culta y tradicional en el Duranguesado (1800–1986)." Unpublished manuscript, 1986.

——. "Trikitrixa (farrea) y acordeón en Busturialdea: Historia y hombres." Unpublished manuscript, 1990.

Billig, Michael. *Banal Nationalism.* London: Routledge, 1995.

Borneman, John, and Abdellah Hammoudi, eds. *Being There: The Fieldwork Encounter and the Making of Truth.* Berkeley: University of California Press, 2009.

Brennan, Helen. "Reinventing Tradition: The Boundaries of Irish Dance." *History Ireland* 2, no. 2 (Summer 1994): 22–24.

——. *The Story of Irish Dance.* Dingle, County Kerry: Brandon, 1999.

Clark, Robert P. *The Basques: The Franco Years and Beyond.* Reno: University of Nevada Press, 1979.

Corcostegui, Lisa. "To the Beat of a Different Drum: Basque Dance and Identity in the Homeland and in the Diaspora." Ph.D. dissertation, University of Nevada, Reno, 2005.

Donostia, Aita José Antonio de. *Cancionero Vasco.* San Sebastián: Eusko Ikaskuntza, 1994.

Durkheim, Émile. *The Elementary Forms of Religious Life.* Translated with an introduction by Karen E. Fields. 1912; New York: Free Press, 1995.

Egaña, Domingo Ignacio de. *El guipuzcoano instruido en las Reales Cédulas, Despachos y Ordenes, que há venerado su Madre la Provincia.* San Sebastián: Imp[a] Lorenzo Riesgo, 1780.

Enríquez, José Carlos. *Sexo, género, cultura y clase.* Bilbao: Beitia, 1995.

Etxebarria, José Luís. *Danzas de Vizcaya: Bizkai'ko Dantzak.* Bilbao: La Editorial Vizcaína, 1969.

Gallop, Rodney. *A Book of the Basques.* 1930; Reno: University of Nevada Press, 1970.

García, Felipe Andrés. *Berriz: Estudio Histórico-Artístico.* Bilbao: Diputación Foral de Bizkaia, 1997.

Garzia, Joxerra, Jon Sarasua, and Andoni Egaña. *The Art of Bertsolaritza: Improvised Basque Verse Singing.* Donostia: Bertsozale Elkartea; Andoain: Bertsolari Liburuak, 2001.

Geertz, Clifford. *Local Knowledge.* 1983; London: Fontana Press, 1993.

Gregory, R. L. "On How Little Information Controls So Much Behaviour." In *Towards a Theoretical Biology*, vol. 1, edited by C. H. Waddington. Chicago: Aldine Publishing Company, 1969.

Guis, Maurice, Thierry Lefrançois, and René Venture. *Le galoubet-tambouirin: Instrument traditionnel de Provence.* Aix-en-Provence: Edisud, 1993.

Harris, Marvin. *Culture, People, Nature: An Introduction to General Anthropology.* New York: Harper and Row, 1975.

Heros, Martín de los. *Historia de Valmaseda.* Bilbao: Excma. Diputación de Vizcaya, 1926.

Humboldt, Wilhelm von. *Reiseskizzen aus Biscaya.* Berlin: G. Reimer, 1841–52. Spanish translation consulted: *Los Vascos.* San Sebastián: Roger Editor, 1999.

Irigoien, Iñaki. "Bizkaiko Dantzak." *Dantzariak* 1 (1978): 20–29.

Iztueta, Juan Inazio. *Euscaldun anciña anciñaco ta are lendabicico etorquien dantza on iritci pozcarri gaitzic gabecoen soñu gogoangarriac beren itz neurtu edo versoaquin.* 1826; Facsimile edition in *Txistulari* 163, no. 3 (1995): 61–78.

———. *Gipuzkoako dantza gogoangarrien kondaira edo historia.* 1824; Donostia: Euskal Editoreen Elkartea, 1990.

Jimeno, Jose María. *Navarra, Gipuzkoa y el Euskera. Siglo XVIII.* Pamplona: Pamiela, 1999.

Kartomi, Margaret J. *On Concepts and Classifications of Musical Instruments.* Chicago: University of Chicago Press, 1990.

Lange, Roderyk. *The Nature of Dance: An Anthropological Perspective.* London: Macdonald & Evans, 1975.

Larramendi, Manuel de. *Corografía: O descripción general de la Muy Noble y Muy Leal Provincia de Guipúzcoa.* 1882; San Sebastián: Sociedad Guipuzcoana de Ediciones y Publicaciones, 1969.

Madariaga Orbea, Juan José. *Anthology of Apologists and Detractors of the Basque Language,* trans. Frederick H. Fornoff, María Cristina Saavedra, Amaia Gabantxo, and Cameron J. Watson. Reno: Center for Basque Studies, University of Nevada, Reno, 2006.

——. "Municipio y vida municipal vasca de los siglos XVI al XVII." *Hispania* 39 (1979): 505–57.

Malinowski, Bronislaw. *Argonauts of the Western Pacific.* 1922; New York: E. P. Dutton, 1961.

Mas, Carles. "La danza antigua y la pedagogía musical." *Txistulari* 157, no. 1 (1994): 13–29.

Mendizabal, Juan Mari. "Erregelak (Bertsotan)." Transcriptions. *Txistulari* 75–76, nos. 3–4 (1973): 2069–72.

Merriam, Alan. *The Anthropology of Music.* Evanston, IL: Northwestern University Press, 1964.

Mersenne, Marin. *Harmonie Universelle: The Books on Instruments.* Translated by Roger E. Chapman. 1635; The Hague: Martinus Nijhoff, 1964.

Monreal Zia, Gregorio. *The Old Law of Bizkaia (1452): Introductory Study and Critical Edition.* Translated by William A. Douglass and Linda White, preface by William A. Douglass. Reno: Center for Basque Studies, University of Nevada, Reno, 2005.

Montagu, Jeremy. "Significación del conjunto flauta y tamboril: ¿Dónde comenzó? ¿Ha sido siempre tal y como la conocemos ahora?" *Txistulari* 172, no. 4 (1997): 69–74.

______. "The Pipe and Tabor Is Alive and Well and Living in Euskadi." *FoMRHI Quarterly* 89 (1997): 17–19.

Myers, Helen. "Ethnomusicology." In *Ethnomusicology, Volume 1, An Introduction,* edited by Helen Myers, 1–18. The New Grove Handbooks in Musicology. London: Macmillan, 1992.

Nettl, Bruno. *Theory and Method in Ethnomusicology.* London: The Free Press of Glencoe, 1964.

———. *The Study of Ethnomusicology: Twenty-Nine Issues and Concepts.* Urbana: University of Illinois Press, 1983.

The New Grove Dictionary of Music and Musicians. London: Macmillan, 1980–.

Olazaran, Father Hilario [pseud. Alejandro Olazaran Salanueva]. "Koreografia." *Txistulari* 2 (1933): 14–19.

———. *El Txistu, lo que es y cómo se toca.* 1927; Donostia: Txistulari, 1994.

———. *Txistu, método y repertorio de flauta baska.* Bilbao: Ordorika, 1933.

Palacios, Francisco Antonio de. *Viva Jesús: Respuesta safisfactoria del Colegio de Misioneros de N. P. S. Francisco de la Noble Villa de Zarauz, con ocasión de una proposición sobre bailes equivocadamente atribuida á dos Misioneros del Sobre Dicho Colegio en la Misión que últimamente predicaron en la mencionada Noble Villa. Y de paso una disertación sobre lo lícito ó no de los bailes regulares de las Plazas, y Saraos.* Pamplona: Josef Longás, 1791.

Royce, Anya Peterson. *The Anthropology of Dance.* Bloomington: Indiana University Press, 1977.

Sánchez, Carlos. *Del danbolin al silbo: Txistu, tamboril y danza vasca en la época de la ilustración.* Pamplona: Euskal Herriko Txistulari Elkartea, 1999.

———. "En torno al zortziko." *Txistulari* 146, no. 3 (1991): 44–53.

Santa Teresa, Fray Bartolome. *Euscal Errijetaco Olgueeta ta dantzeen Neurrizko Gatz-ozpinduba.* Edited by Patxi Altuna. 1816; Bilbao: Universidad de Deusto, 1987.

"Se crean en Donostia la Academia de Txistu y Danzas." *Txistulari* 3 (1928): 11.

Seeger, Charles. *Studies in Musicology 1935–1975.* Berkeley: University of California Press, 1977.

Turner, Victor. *The Ritual Process: Structure and Anti-Structure.* Foreword by Roger D. Abrahams. 1969; New York: Aldine de Gruyter, 1995.

Urbeltz, Juan Antonio. *Dantzak.* Bilbao: Jakin, 1978.

Urquiza, Vicente de. *Antigüedades de Berriz.* Bilbao: Caja de Ahorros Vizcaína, 1988.

Watson, Cameron. "Folklore and Basque Nationalism: Language, Myth, Reality." *Nations and Nationalism* 2, no. 1 (1996): 17–34.

Williams, Martin. "Ancient Mythology and Revolutionary Ideology in Ireland, 1878–1916." *The Historical Journal* 26, no. 2 (June 1983): 307–28.

Zulaika, Joseba. *Basque Violence: Metaphor and Sacrament.* Reno: University of Nevada Press, 1988.

———. *Del Cromañon al Carnaval.* Donostia: Erein, 1996.

Periodicals

Txistulari. Journal issued by *Euskal Herriko Txistularien Elkartea* (the Asociation of *Txistulariak* of the Basque Country).

Dantzariak. Journal issued by *Euskal Dantzarien Biltzarra* (the Basque Dancers Asociation).

FoMRHI Quarterly. Journal issued by Fellowship of Makers and Researchers of Historical Instruments.

Revista Internacional de Estudios Vascos. Journal issued by Eusko Ikaskuntza-Sociedad de Estudios Vascos (the Basque Studies Society).

Index

Page references followed by *t* indicate tables. Page numbers followed by n indicate footnotes. Page numbers in italics indicate photographs or illustrations.

B

F

R

S

U

V

W

X

Y

Z

www.ingramcontent.com/pod-product-compliance
Lightning Source LLC
LaVergne TN
LVHW080309110826
845155LV00023B/99

* 9 7 8 1 8 7 7 8 0 2 9 3 5 *